W9-BGA-823

MORALITY
AFTER
AUSCHWITZ

MORALITY AFTER AUSCHWITZ

The Radical Challenge of the Nazi Ethic

PETER J. HAAS

Fortress Press   Philadelphia

COPYRIGHT © 1988 BY FORTRESS PRESS

First paperback edition 1992

All rights reserved. No part of this publication may be reproduced, stored in a retrieval system, or transmitted in any form or by any means, electronic, mechanical, photocopying, recording, or otherwise, without the prior permission of the publisher, Fortress Press.

Cover design: Jim Gerhard

Library of Congress Cataloging-in-Publication Data
Haas, Peter J. (Peter Jerome)
    Morality after Auschwitz.

    1. Holocaust, Jewish (1939–1945)—Moral and ethical
aspects.   2. Ethics—Germany—History—20th century.
I. Title.
D804.3.H33   1988   940.53'15'03924   87–45891
ISBN 0–8006–0857–7 (cloth)
ISBN 0–8006–2581–1 (paper)

The paper used in this publication meets the minimum requirements of American National Standard for Information Sciences—Permanence of Paper for Printed Library Materials, ANSI Z329.48–1984.

Manufactured in the U.S.A.   AF 1-2581
96   95   94   93   92   1   2   3   4   5   6   7   8   9   10

To my parents
Eric Haas
Marga (Schlamm) Haas z"1
survivors

Contents

Preface

This book grows out of a number of years' experience in teaching the Holocaust to a largely non-Jewish university student body. It reflects my struggles to find a way of conveying the content and the meaning of the Holocaust in fourteen short weeks to students with often little or no background. In good part this book is a result of my students' questions and concerns. I owe all my students a measure of gratitude.

There are a few people I want to mention by name. Special acknowledgment must go to my former teaching assistant Jeffrey Tucker, who encouraged me to write this book and, when I agreed, pestered me until I finished. I must also acknowledge here in a small way my immense debt to Beverly Asbury, chaplain at Vanderbilt University, from whose friendship, concern, and spirit I have gained much. If in any way this book helps build bridges of better understanding, he deserves a large measure of the credit. Finally, I could not have seen this project through to publication without the help, advice, and encouragement of my department chair, Professor Daniel Patte. I treasure his support in ways I will never be able fully to express.

Finally, this book is dedicated to my parents, Eric and Marga, themselves survivors of the monstrosity with which I have tried to come to terms in these pages. This is my attempt to grapple with what they experienced and learned to live with but could never describe.

July 9, 1987
12 Tammuz 5747

INTRODUCTION

This book studies the Holocaust as a problem in ethical theory. It asks how it was that a whole society could participate in an ethic of mass torture and genocide for well over a decade without any significant or sustained opposition from political, legal, medical, or religious leaders. By framing the question in terms of ethics, I mean to exclude certain types of explanations that have already been proposed, and to open up a possible new field of investigation concerning how societies come to adopt certain kinds of behavioral norms. This, then, is a study of how societies create and adopt ethical systems.

The study began as a negative reaction to the common description of the Holocaust as evil incarnate. That description leads to the notion that people performed evil as a matter of routine and, in Hannah Arendt's memorable term, that the Holocaust demonstrates the "banality of evil." I find this response inadequate for a number of reasons. Although I agree with Arendt that making the Holocaust utterly foreign allows us to dismiss its lessons too easily, at the same time, making the Holocaust banal strips it of its power to instruct. It seems to me that if the Holocaust does have any lesson to teach, it is precisely because its perpetrators were not banal or unthinking people. I do not find the actions of Eichmann or of the tens of thousands of Germans and others like him banal. Quite the reverse, it appears that Nazi doctors, lawyers, theologians, teachers, camp commandants, and railway personnel did their jobs with a dedication, determination, and professionalism that indicate that they found value in what they were doing. To claim that all this was banal dismisses the very commitment to the Holocaust's ideals that its ethic generated in people. Further, the claim deeply contradicts the idea that all societies have an ethic that guides people's lives. The claim of banality in essence says that the perpetrators of the Holocaust acted out of no real convictions at all.

Finally, I reject the description of the Holocaust as utter evil because such an isolation of evil for its own sake seems philosophically untrue. One of the characteristics of the modern world is the unseating of the classical vision of the cosmos as containing ideal types, including objective, built-in cosmological standards of good and evil. For us, good and evil no longer are ideal and isolable standards but are conceptualizations intimately bound up with human perception, imagination, and discourse. No one can be said systematically to operate out of purely good or purely evil motives. To continue to describe the Holocaust and its actors in terms of pure guilt or innocence, then, eliminates the possibility of taking these modern insights into account. Rather, the Holocaust becomes a sort of medieval morality play in which angels and devils do battle. Although emotionally satisfying, such characterizations of the Holocaust seem to me to oversimplify the nature of evil and so block any deeper understanding of what occurred in Europe.

What then is our alternative? I propose in the following to accept what seems on the surface to be true, namely, that the perpetrators of the Holocaust (including all its silent witnesses) knew what was going on, found it to be at least ethically tolerable, and consciously acted accordingly. This way of looking at matters also seems to be in perfect accord with the often-noted fact that the perpetrators themselves were not amoral or banal people. One moment found them shoving young children into gas chambers, the next moment found them rational, intelligent, and sensitive members of society. What I have come to see is that if for many the Holocaust seems to reflect ultimate evil, for the perpetrators and witnesses it represented nothing of the kind. For them it was a difficult but justifiable way of dealing with their situation. What is reflected in these people, I am arguing, is not the banality of evil but the human ability to redefine evil. Europeans committed what we judge to be heinous crimes under Nazi rule not because they were deficient in moral sensibility, and not because they were quintessentially evil and brutal people, but because they were in fact ethically sensitive. They were fully aware of what they were doing and displayed principled acquiescence. The difference is that for them such deeds were simply no longer understood to be evil. Under the influence of what I shall be calling the Nazi ethic, vast numbers of people simply came to understand evil in different terms and, in perfectly predictable and comprehensible fashion, acted upon their understanding.

Once the problem of the Holocaust is described in this way, the question shifts from how it is that people can do what they presumably know to be evil to the more interesting question of how evil is understood in the first place and by what mechanisms it is redefined so that people can be led in good conscience to commit Holocausts. That is, our focus moves away from individual psychology to the social, cultural, and linguistic context in which people come to understand good and evil to begin with. We ask not why people do evil—a prejudicial question—but how people come to understand the ethical obligations to which they dedicate themselves.

The Holocaust is an unusually good source of data for a study of this sort because it represents such a clear reversal of what the ethical system of the West had demanded of people up to that point. That is, it offers a striking example of how new ethical systems come to take hold of people's minds. Further, since the Holocaust developed over some twelve years, and at one point encompassed most of Europe, it is clear that we are dealing with a successful and sustained transformation of an ethic, not with a transient or sectarian community. We have before us in the Holocaust an excellent opportunity to watch a successful ethical system be formed and empowered. Finally, the processes of ethical thought leading to Auschwitz are documented in astounding detail. The thoughts and deeds of a whole society—from grand theoreticians to policy coordinators to bureaucratic managers to onlookers to victims—are known in stunning detail. For all these reasons, the Holocaust promises to offer a unique example of how the values that make up a system of ethics emerge, become credible, and so can drive complex modern societies to dehumanize, torture, and kill vast segments of their own populations as a matter of ethical routine.

PRESUPPOSITIONS

A number of presuppositions govern the study and need to be spelled out at the start. My primary claim will be that what the Nazis perpetrated can in fact be described as an ethic. By the word "ethic" in this context, I mean a complete and coherent system of convictions, values, and ideas that provides a grid within which some sorts of actions can be classified as evil, and so to be avoided, while other sorts of actions can be classified as good, and so to be tolerated or even pursued. By stating matters in this way, I hope to avoid some of the inadequacies mentioned early. It clearly is not the case that Germans suddenly became unable to tell right from wrong; to the contrary, Nazi society had a strict, almost puritanical code of moral standards. In fact, I would want to argue that all people must have some kind of ethic to function. To say Nazi collaborators had no ethic simply will not do. Nor do I think that it is adequate to say that perpetrators knew that what they were doing was evil but chose to do what they did anyway. That would run counter to the notion that ethical systems channel behavior. I shall assume, therefore, that an ethic did in fact operate in the Holocaust and that notions of right and wrong did in fact exist in that ethic in a coherent and systematic way. This claim is the governing hypothesis of the study. The task, then, is to describe the system of values that drove the Holocaust—its ethic—in a way that is true to the Holocaust experience and yet represents accurately the nature of ethical systems as we understand them.

In order to pursue this investigation, we need a working hypothesis about the nature of ethics and ethical systems. I am not assuming at this point that a system must display a specific content in order to be an ethic. I am suggesting simply that it must meet certain formal criteria, namely, that it must provide a standard against which its adherents can declare certain goals to be good or bad and so judge particular types of actions to be right or wrong. My hypothesis is that any formal system that enables evaluations of this sort is an ethic, no matter what its particular judgments or content might be. That is why I am able to call the Nazi standard of right and wrong an ethic—without thereby claiming that it was proper or moral. I merely claim that it was regarded by its adherents as a proper system for judging the rightness and wrongness of behavior. An ethic, to achieve popular subscription, however, cannot merely throw up random standards. The power of an ethic, and the reason it can be regarded by people as correct, ultimately resides in the fact that it provides a system for judging every action in a coherent, non-self-contradictory, and intuitively correct way. If an ethic projects itself as able to do this, I claim, it will be capable under the right conditions of winning broad public acceptance and so of becoming the governing norm of a civilization.

The claim that an ethic must be coherent and non-self-contradictory means that the ethic must allow people who think in its terms to understand clearly the distinction it posits between good and evil. In fact, drawing on structuralism, I wish to assert that the concepts of good and evil are never merely different from each other but are mirror images, each reflecting the logical structure of the other. I should stress that I see such a binary opposition operating only at the foundational conceptual level of an ethic. I understand that on a conscious level, in confrontation with reality, actual moral judgments are usually much more ambiguous and nuanced. I merely claim now that on the subconscious level of basic category formation, the conceptions of good and evil take on diametrically opposite contents. My claim that such a binary opposition lies at the base of all ethical thinking has two ramifications that will be important for the study to follow. The first is that each member of such a pair helps define the other on a conscious level. Thus in any ethic we come to understand how good operates by observing evil and vice versa. The second is that if ethical thinking is pushed to its logical limits, good and evil will end up being mutually exclusive. A phenomenon that has some characteristics of good will have to be deemed totally good, and a phenomenon that has some characteristics of evil will have to be deemed totally evil. We shall see the result of this deep structure of ethical thinking at work again and again in the Holocaust. If the greatest good of the German Volk is to create a homeland, then the greatest evil of the enemy is its drive to destroy homelands; if an attribute of my superiority is my language, then the fact that others speak different languages is a sign of their inferiority; and so forth. Pushed to its logical limit, this formal characteristic of ethical systems is taken to mean that the cosmos can be fully divided up into forces of good and forces of evil. Its ultimate development is the notion that whoever is not for me is against me—a perfect division of the world into binary oppositions. That this is so is, I claim, a necessary consequence of the deep structure of every ethic.

By "intuitively correct"—the other predicate describing what an ethic attempts to be—I do not mean that the ethic must conform to certain innate feelings or standards such as one's conscience. That would merely repeat in a different way the thesis I rejected above that an ethic must have a specific content. Rather, I mean that an ethical system, besides being logically coherent, must in some way be perceived as advancing individual or group values or interests: a collection of beliefs and values that apparently work against a community's survival or welfare will ultimately be rejected by that community as improper. On the other hand, an ethical system that is logically coherent and that also appears to advance the foundational interests of the community has at least a chance of gaining widespread acceptance and so becoming normative. As will be argued in due course, the Nazi ethic was able to gain adherents precisely on the grounds that it provided a scheme of behavior which was deemed by Germans to address appropriately the problems they imagined to be of greatest threat to themselves and their culture. Had the ethic been counterintuitive in this sense, it could not have established the hold that it did.

The two criteria I have been discussing operate on different levels. The systemic logic of an ethic is a deep-seated characteristic that, I assume, is true for all meaning systems, not just ethics. The criterion of intuitive correctness or appropriateness depends on the particular social situation in which the ethic is asked to operate. This is a matter not of the deep structures of thought but of the public way in which reality is described and cultural norms are expressed in the real world. In short, this is a function of how the particular content of an ethic is understood and applied by its practitioners. The vehicle for this is language, the system of signs and symbols we use publicly to express meaning. We begin with certain inherent predispositions to think in terms of the diametrical opposites of good and evil but then define specific instances of good and evil as we confront the world through a certain cultural and social setting. It is through ethical discourse, then, that we move from implicit values and convictions to conscious thought and analysis. If an ethic can generate and sustain a coherent and internally reinforcing evaluative discourse, and if it produces results that seem to conform to and address the needs at hand, people can be motivated to adopt and conform to whatever evaluations it generates.

METHODS OF ANALYSIS

This description of ethics suggests that there are three potential levels at which analysis could be pursued. It is important to see what these are and the role each will play in the ensuing discussion of the Holocaust.

1. The most basic level open to analysis is that at which concepts—any concepts, including concepts of good and evil—are formed in human

consciousness. Here I shall assume that concepts are basic, prelinguistic convictions that operate subconsciously to structure how we perceive the world. Among the features of such convictional patterns are paired oppositions that define basic nodes of meaning, like good and evil. Any basic conviction that there are good things will always be accompanied by a mirror-image conviction that there are evil things. And as I have said, the conviction as to the nature of good will be exactly the inverse of the conviction as to the nature of evil. I am claiming that this phenomenon is fundamental for any ethic because it is a fundamental part of how we think.

2. The level of central concern to this study is that of the public way these foundational patterns of thought are linked together in consciousness. At this level we assign the overt symbols, linguistic and other, by which we relate our basic convictions to one another in the public realm and are able to refer to them in reasoned discourse. It is at this level, in other words, that basic values and convictions are discursivized. In ethics, this level supplies the vocabulary, the analogies, metaphors, and reasonings to make and warrant ethical judgments. It is at this level also that right and wrong acts take on specific conscious identities. I refer to this level as providing the form of a particular ethic. I want clearly to distinguish my use of the word "form" here from my use of it as regards the first level of ethical formation. When talking about basic binary oppositions, I am talking about patterns that make up the foundational structure of ethical discourse per se. That is, all ethics have certain formal features in common by virtue of the fact that they are systems of thought. These formed features impose certain formal constraints on how we think morally. In the present context, however, I am referring to specific ethical systems operating in the public realm; here I use the word "form" to denote the values, metaphors, justifications, and arguments available for use by a particular ethic. An ethic has form in the sense that only certain symbols, warrants, or arguments are meaningful, and not others. It provides a linguistic grid within which specific ethical judgments are made. It is in this second sense that I shall use the word "form" in the study to follow.

3. Finally we come to the level of concrete decision making. Once we have a conviction of good and evil, and once we are able to give that conviction some formal character and definition through public discourse, we face the task of assigning to our formal system a specific content. It is at this level that the Nazi ethic strikes us as so foreign; it makes evaluational assignments in a way utterly different from what we would expect. What I wish to argue is that the assignments made at this level—at the level of content—are in large part determined by the form of discourse through which the ethic's concepts are enunciated. My theory is that the way a culture formally symbolizes and then talks about evil will determine the kinds of phenomena it will view as evil. Thus we move from basic formal patterns of how we think, to the overt symbolization of these in discourse, to the application of this discourse to the evaluation of real-life phenomena.

The assumption made in this study is that the Holocaust as a sustained way of acting in Europe was possible because a new ethic was in place that did not define the arrest and deportation of Jews as wrong and in fact defined it as ethically tolerable or even good. In this there was an assignment of ethical value on the third, most self-conscious level. But how could the assignment be made and persuasively demonstrated? The answer lies, to follow our scheme, on the second level, at the point at which basic ethical concepts are given linguistic shape. In other words, people were persuaded to tolerate the deportation of Jews, I argue, because such a deed made sense within the universe of discourse that gave public definition to concepts of good and evil in Nazi society. In fact, as Nazi propaganda shows, the deportation of Jews was portrayed as compatible with an overall good that people could see and with which they could sympathize—that of self-preservation. Once the Jews could be symbolized as posing, by their very nature, a mortal threat to German culture, there were certain ethical ramifications. These ramifications, based on formal ethical notions such as self-defense, are perfectly understandable in light of our style of ethical discourse, a discourse that has operated in unbroken continuity from the past, as we shall see in ample detail. In other words, the formal character of Western ethical discourse remained largely intact; what shifted was the particular application.

This volume shows, then, that the Nazis did not fundamentally alter basic ethical convictions. In fact, they maintained much of the secondary, discursive character of Western ethics. What they did change radically was only on the tertiary level—how these basic ethical concepts and warrants were applied, that is, what actions or phenomena in the real world were to be placed under one rubric or another. What was new was not the basic Nazi concept of evil but the fact that Jews were now made the primary locus of that evil. Given sufficient historical, intellectual, and theological warrant, Nazi propagandists could make people believe that the Nazi evaluation of reality, the Nazi use of accepted ethical categories, was correct. For the Nazi description was coherent, non-self-contradictory, and apparently appropriate to the reality Germans faced. Once the new discursivization of ethics was accomplished, there were inevitable ramifications for behavior, and people allowed to happen to the Jews what they would have allowed to happen to any other locus of evil had it been identified with sufficient force and clarity. Thus the Holocaust became ethically possible because the basic character of ethical argumentation remained unchanged. This is the reason that Germans, and others, could tolerate the utter destruction of Jews and Judaism in Germany over a period of at least twelve years while in other ways continuing to be thoughtful, intelligent, charming people. It is not that they had lost the ability to behave ethically; they simply evaluated certain activities in a different, yet still ethically coherent, way.

The Holocaust, culminating in Auschwitz, is a case study of the most graphic sort of how one ethical system can be radically remade at the discursive level and yet continue to motivate people because it retains its form and so its power. Our aim in the following is to investigate not only if that description is viable but also, if it is, how such a rediscursivization happens and is sustained.

To recapitulate, my general argument is that the Nazi ethic was able to impose itself on Europe because it maintained a formal continuity with the conventional Western system of ethical convictions and symbols that had evolved at least since the Enlightenment. The Nazi decision to murder all the Jews in Europe did not, after all, develop overnight; it was a policy that gradually emerged out of the intellectual—and, I shall argue, ethical—history of modern Europe. As we shall see, no sudden or formal break in political, legal, or moral thinking occurred along the way. The Auschwitzes and Treblinkas of 1943 had their roots in a myriad of political and moral decisions that were made years before, decisions that seemed innocent and even self-evident at the time they were made. The revolution took place gradually and on the surface. By the 1940s, Treblinka and Auschwitz were possible because they were ethically defensible. If we wish to understand the Holocaust, then, we must focus not only on its particular events but on the long chain of attitudes and policies which formed its justification in ethical discourse and which gave it its sanction. The fact is that in a matter of a few years, using the tools of modern technology, the Nazi party leaders managed to persuade people from every walk of life to allow the overt rules of the received ethic to be overridden by a different set of rules. And in time, a critical mass of the population of the West learned to make its peace with the new rules, whether as active supporters or silent onlookers.

ORGANIZATION OF THIS STUDY

The present volume develops this theory in four parts. In the first is set forth the intellectual background of the Nazi ethic which established the social, political, and historical grid within which the Nazi ethic achieved expression. On the scheme sketched out above, this involves the second level, with a focus upon the occasion at which basic convictions about good and evil are given conscious definition and placed within a meaningful system of discourse. In the first five chapters we shall see how basic moral terms in the Nazi ethic came to take on their specific fields of meaning.

Part 2 carries the task forward by tracing how the formal Nazi ethic was articulated as it moved from its sectarian and partisan context to become the regnant ethic of a continent. Here the investigation concerns the third level, that at which the ethic takes on specific content and produces specific judgments, and we see precisely how the formal demands of the Nazi ethic—the conviction that Jews constitute a race, for example—shaped perceived reality.

With the trajectory of Nazism's ethical development before us, part 3 examines how such an ethic took on institutional expression, creating cultural norms that channeled human and economic resources in the ways demanded by its definitions. It is at this juncture that we are struck by what Arendt calls the banality of evil: the dedicated work of millions of people toward bringing about the destruction of a defined enemy.

Part 4 counterbalances the rest by examining the reactions of various outsiders and dissenters: rescuers, military adversaries, and survivors. Our aim is to see whether even such dedicated critics as these are able to sustain the notion that the Holocaust is an example of utter evil rather than an ethic. We shall find that they cannot. For all of these outsiders, the search for an absolute standard by which to indict the Holocaust ends in failure. The failure demonstrates that indeed the Nazi ethic was coherent and self-sustaining on its own terms. Through the experiences and writings of these outsiders, we see once again that the Holocaust was not the incarnation of evil but instead reflected the human power to reconceive good and evil and then to shape society in the light of the new conception.

PART ONE

THE INTELLECTUAL MATRIX
OF AN ETHIC

An ethical system, a way of separating right from wrong, never occurs in a vacuum. It always operates in a particular society, as part of a certain culture, and in full consciousness of the realities its practitioners must face. To be believable and normative, an ethic must make sense to the people whose behavior it proposes to define. This is no less true of the Nazi ethic that controlled so much of Europe for over a decade. This ethic made sense to its practitioners because it presented itself, in form, as a workable system of defining right and wrong that was fully compatible with their principles, values, and experiences. It was able to draw on intellectual, political, social, and historical warrants to verify its claim to be a proper form of moral discourse. Once it had achieved theoretical acceptance among the German population, all that was left was to fill in the details.

In the following chapters, the intellectual heritage that gave the Nazi ethic its cogency and credibility will be described. This background establishes a framework within which good and evil take on particular definitions and a certain mode of discourse which makes rational discussion about these concepts possible.

1

Conceptualizing Evil:
The Jew as Symbol

The years from Hitler's coming to power in 1933 through the collapse of the Third Reich in 1945 witnessed the creation of a new German empire. This empire was based on an ethic that defined racial domination as the greatest good and that made eugenics, slave labor, and mass death morally acceptable in pursuit of that good. The ethic, together with the capabilities supplied by modern mass-production industry, motor and rail transportation, and advanced communication technologies—all coordinated through modern management techniques—turned Europe's population into participants in a great race war of the most bloodthirsty and brutal sort. Virtually all Europeans played a role, a few as resisters and rescuers, many more as supporters and active participants, the greatest number as possibly troubled but finally silent onlookers. The cultural center of Western civilization became embroiled in a sustained racial conflict of unprecedented proportions. How did such a state of affairs come to be accepted and even to be considered by some attractive? How are we to understand such an outburst of cultural violence?

What seems clear from the very outset is that the social, political, and ethical ideals that structured these events were not the invention of the Nazi rulers. In fact, the Nazis were generally uninventive and unimaginative. Rather, the content of Nazi ideology carried forward a number of political, religious, and social themes that had been a part of European thinking for centuries. The Holocaust was possible because so much of its intellectual, and therefore ethical, form was already familiar. In talking about the institution of racial warfare in the West, then, we need to think in terms not of a revolution in ethical thinking but of a shift of definition in which already understood and accepted conceptions of good and evil were given new applications. Such a transformation of ethical norms was possible because the new ethic was sufficiently cogent and persuasive to override what was up to then the operative ethic of most Europeans. The thesis I am developing and testing here is that any ethic, even one as brutal as the Nazis', can become dominant if it is internally consistent and can be made persuasive to a sufficiently large population. That it is the formal characteristic of an ethic that makes it viable, not its particular content, seems to be the overarching lesson of the Holocaust in Europe.

Take a rough example of what I propose to argue. It can reasonably be said that for the Nazi ethic, killing Jews in death camps was not regarded as murder. In essence this ethical valuation has to do with basic convictions about the taking of life, especially human life. For the West in general, killing another person outright for personal gain is wrong, presumably because Western culture understands good to be bound up with the freedom and opportunity of individual human beings, who are believed to be created in the image of God. But even Western culture can conceive of the validity of killing others for social or communal needs. Killing enemy soldiers in battle is not murder, for example, and juridical killing for crime (capital punishment) is at least an arguable possibility in Western ethics. It follows that if a group can see the existence of Jews (Gypsies, homosexuals, whatever) as a cultural and social threat, then killing them can be cast as a morally defensible act in pursuit of a higher good, without destroying the inherited and accepted meanings of such concepts as those of murder and the sacredness of human life. This shift in content is fully possible at any time as long as sufficient warrant exists—that is, if a convincing ethical discourse can be constructed around that content. This means, in our example, establishing the "fact" that Jews (Gypsies, homosexuals) are social or cultural enemies. Such an argument can be framed quite empirically, drawing on a variety of historical, sociological, and scientific "observations." Once this labor is done, a villain can be identified the killing of whom is not murder in the classic sense. What is open to discussion is who such villains are. Any group could theoretically serve, provided a sufficiently persuasive argument for seeing it as such could be advanced and appropriately warranted.

The Nazi ethic was built around the already familiar and fully accepted moral category of the just war. For this reason, a shift in the definition of the "enemy" could produce multiple and drastic ethical ramifications. By claiming that the overriding moral paradigm was war—in which the killing of the enemy was not wrong—and by asserting that the primal enemy in the war was the Jewish race, a whole series of ethical possibilities immediately became available within the system already established by Western ethical convictions. The choice of this paradigm, and of the Jews as the quintessential enemy within the paradigm, was neither arbitrary nor, for Europeans at the time, particularly surprising. The notion of warfare or struggle as a primary category of how life-forms of all sorts operate in nature rested on a number of experiences and intellectual initiatives taken in Europe over the century or two preceding the rise of Hitler. What is more, Jews could convincingly be portrayed as mortal enemies because of deep connotations already a part of the religious and intellectual heritage of the Christian West.

The choice of them as quintessential enemies had a certain compelling quality on what we have just defined as the empirical level. Further, the particular character that could plausibly be imputed to "the Jews" inversely reflected the very categories that the Nazis and other Europeans used to define their own self-identities—thus maintaining the systemic balance of good versus evil, according to our hypothesis. In short, the entire constellation of discourse and events to follow is but a reflection of a moral grid in which the ciphers of "Aryan" and "Jew" not only are juxtaposed but also define each other as binary opposites. To understand both the cogency and the persuasiveness of the Nazi ethic, then, we should begin by examining the content of its central mythic symbol, that of "the Jews."

ANTI-JUDAISM IN LATE ANTIQUITY

The Nazi obsession with the Jews and the concept of the Jews as evil did not spring out of nowhere. They rested on a long tradition in Western Europe of regarding the Jews as evil outsiders.[1] For seventeen hundred years, Jews had been the objects of scorn and contempt in Europe, a socially manufactured pariah people. The foundations of the Jews' social status were already laid down in the New Testament. Within the pages of the Gospels and later church writings, Jews are portrayed as hypocrites, evil schemers, vipers, and murderers of the Messiah. They are the epitome of those people who will have no place in the kingdom of God.

This portrayal of the Jewish religious community itself has even more ancient roots. It begins in the negative view of Jews current in imperial Roman society. Roman contempt was based on the Jews' almost unique refusal in late antiquity to acquiesce to Roman civilization, as well as their rather successful efforts at proselytizing. These negative views were later taken over by the religious leaders of nascent gentile Christianity as a means of distinguishing their religion from Judaism. Their depiction of Jews and Judaism, canonized in early church writings, became part of the religious heritage of the West.

From the very beginning of Roman intervention in the Levant, Judea stood out as different. The Judeans were the one group in the empire that for centuries persisted in resisting Roman rule. All other groups assimilated themselves to Roman political and religious hegemony, but the Jews never did. Their refusal probably drew its force from the Judean experience under the Babylonians and Persians some five centuries earlier. In 586 B.C.E., the kingdom of Judah had been conquered by the Babylonians and the Temple in Jerusalem had been destroyed. With the subsequent exile of Judah's leading families, its national integrity was destroyed. Yet a sense of national identity persisted during the two or three generations of Babylonian rule. When Cyrus, the emperor of Persia, offered Judeans a chance to return to Jerusalem and to reestablish self-rule under their priests in their destroyed cultic site, significant numbers of descendants accepted the offer.

Jerusalem was gradually rebuilt, and the worship of God at the Temple resumed. As the Book of Ezekiel depicts matters in a powerful parable, the Judean community was reconstituted in Jerusalem out of dead and dry bones. It was this renewed and distinctive community, governed by its own legal tradition, that entered into the Roman world. Having had the experience once of being conquered and yet maintaining its distinctiveness, the surviving community seemed determined again to resist assimilation. Despite all the attempts of Rome, the forces for assimilation had no lasting success. The Judeans held on to their identity and their particular worship of God. They remained an identifiable mass of unassimilable people within the Roman Empire.[2]

The Romans took the Judean refusal to accept their culture as an insult, laying it down to Judean insolence and misanthropy. Tacitus, writing in the first century C.E., says,

> The Jews . . . reveal a stubborn attachment to one another, an active commiseration, which contrasts with their implacable hatred of the rest of mankind. They sit apart at meals, they sleep apart, and though, as a nation, they are singularly prone to debauchery, they abstain from intercourse with foreign women.[3]

From Tacitus's point of view as a Roman patrician not particularly familiar with the ways of the East, these remarks have a fairly solid grounding. The Jews were, after all, hostile to all the known Roman gods. How else describe this attitude except as impious? In fact, since the Jews worshiped no known god and could point to no images or icons of their god, they might even be seen as atheistic, that is, without a god. Since the Judean province was in a constant state of disquiet and rebellion, it followed that the Jews hated others. Their refusal to join with others in the beneficial worldwide culture created by the Roman Empire could be explained only as sheer stubbornness. Their desire to stick together smacked of hostility and snobbishness. All of this became especially frightening to Roman aristocrats and leaders in the first century because of the widespread success of Jewish missionary activity. It is estimated that some ten percent of the Roman population at this time were, if not fully Jewish, at least Judaizers.[4] This explains the vehemence of Roman anti-Jewish writings, as exemplified, for example, by Seneca: "Practices of this villainous nation have so greatly prevailed that they are accepted throughout the universe; the vanquished have given laws to the victors."[5]

ANTI-JUDAISM IN THE EARLY CHURCH

The negative Roman attitudes toward Jews and Judaism were commonplace when Christianity, Judaism's rival, began its meteoric growth in the empire. The alliance of Christianity with Roman culture added new theological dimensions to the already traditional Roman antipathy toward Jews.

The church's theological deprecation of Judaism grew out of three needs. The first was to shield itself from the harsh Roman criticism of Judaism in general. To succeed in Roman society, Christianity could not be seen as a type of Judaism. Second, Christianity under the influence of Paul became a gentile religion, and thus was anxious to establish its identity as something other than the Jews' particular religion—to universalize Christianity despite its Judaic roots. Third, there was the theological need for the church to accept the Old Testament as its own while rejecting the community that still regarded it as its Scripture; that is, Christianity needed to establish itself as the legitimate successor to Judaism. Judaism was thus portrayed as the old faith that God had rejected and which was left to suffer while the New Israel, the church, emerged triumphant. Those Jews who stubbornly insisted on remaining Jews were deemed to be blind to God's message, killers of the prophets, and murderers of Jesus. For these reasons it was thought that they fully deserved their status as a destroyed and dispersed people suffering the divine wrath. Combined with the general Roman disdain of Judaism, the church's theological devaluation of Jews became the basis of a powerful myth that could explain as well as justify the social and spiritual oppression of Jews and Judaism. The result was an ideology of Jew hatred that was woven into the fabric of late Roman culture when Christianity became the state religion.

This attitude not only was part of a general cultural bias but received explicit expression and encouragement in the canonical writings of early Christianity. Jewish leaders were portrayed as a "brood of vipers" (Matt. 3:7) and as "hypocrites" (Matthew 23). Jews were killers of Jesus (Mark 15:6–15) and even called for his blood to be upon them and their descendants (Matt. 27:25). The view of Jews as the ontological rejecters, torturers, and killers of Jesus led by duplicitous leaders achieved the status of a self-evident truth in later Christian literature. Gregory of Nyssa, an early church leader, reflects the adoption of these views in his description of the Jews:

> Murderers of the Lord, assassins of the prophets, [who] resist grace, repudiate the faith of their fathers. Companions of the devil, race of vipers, informers, calumniators, darkeners of the mind, pharisaic leaven, Sanhedrin of demons, accursed, detested, lapidators, enemies of all that is beautiful.[6]

When church leaders could speak in such terms, it is no surprise that the mass of semi-Christianized peasants of Europe held the Jewish residents in their midst in suspicion and contempt. In David Rausch's powerful phrase, the church, wittingly or not, had created a "legacy of hatred."[7] Within the context of this legacy, the marginal position of the Jews in Europe during the Christian Middle Ages becomes completely understandable.

ANTI-JUDAISM IN THE MIDDLE AGES

In the Middle Ages there were two different degrees of Jew hatred: that of the official church position and that of the popular superstitions and beliefs of the masses. As long as the church remained the dominant power in the West, Jews were tolerated and treated with a modicum of respect, albeit as outsiders. Not only did the church generally preach against violence but it had a theological interest in Judaism's survival as a people that would finally be forced to witness the final days and the second coming. But as the church's power waned and the popular religion of the European masses achieved greater expression, Jewish life in Europe entered one of its bloodiest and most brutal periods. The Jews became the objects of all sorts of popular superstitions and prejudices. Since this period serves most directly as a model for Nazi atrocities, its thought and character must be traced in some detail.

The deterioration of Jewish status and security in Europe began in about the eleventh century, coincident with a number of social, political, and economic trends taking shape around that time.[8] Changes began on the economic front. Up to this period, Jews had been welcomed in Europe as merchants and traders providing an economic basis for a largely rural and feudal Europe. But as cities developed and more and more Christian Europeans began to establish businesses, Jews became competitors. Beginning in Italy in the eleventh century and gradually over time throughout Europe, Jewish merchants and businessmen were systematically driven out of business, usually by local competitors with family ties to the ruling elites. This economic trend had political implications as well, since once Jews no longer offered anything of importance to the government, they lost monarchical protection. As the Middle Ages progressed, Jewish communities that had existed and prospered for centuries were slowly driven into poverty and at times completely expelled from their homes.

Economic and political events were joined by a third force, the attempt by the church to extend its authority over against rising secular governments at the same time that it tried to purge itself of internal heresies. There was a rising church militancy that saw Christian armies moving toward the Near East during the crusades and later against Spain to win that area back from the Moors in the thirteenth and fourteenth centuries. At about the same time, the intellectual revival of the Renaissance was taking hold, resulting in an increased challenge to the church's intellectual hegemony. To combat these trends, the church organized a concerted effort to identify heretical centers and to bring their leaders to justice. Although Judaism itself was not regarded as a heresy, many church leaders were convinced that contact with Judaism encouraged the emergence of heretical lines of thought. Thus, by the thirteenth century, the church began to feel the necessity for instituting its own anti-Jewish program. In the Fourth Lateran Council (1215), Pope Innocent II encouraged the passage of a number of anti-Jewish measures. Among the decrees issued by the council was a requirement that all Jews wear a special badge to distinguish them from Christians, thus discouraging unnecessary social intercourse.[9] Other measures followed. In addition, a number of public disputations were arranged, for example, in which a local rabbi was to engage in a debate with a Christian theologian over the truth of biblical prophecies concerning the coming of Jesus as Messiah. The point was to show in an open forum that the birth, life, and ministry of Jesus fulfilled prophecies in the Jews' own literature. When all this failed to shake the Jews' allegiance to their tradition, Jewish books, especially the Talmud, were destroyed. One of the most notorious actions took place in Paris in the 1240s, in which twenty-four cartloads of books from all over Europe were reportedly burned publicly. When Judaism survived despite the destruction of its sacred texts, Jews were expelled entirely.[10] The earliest expulsion was from England in 1290; France followed in 1306, and various German territories expelled Jews at one time or another over the next century. (In fact, as late as the eighteenth century, Jews needed special residence permits to live in many parts of Germany.) The most notorious of the expulsions was from Spain in 1492, shortly after the country had been retrieved for Christendom from the Moors. Jewish Spaniards were forced to convert to Catholicism. Those who did convert eventually became subject to the Inquisition on the suspicion that they were Judaizing in secret. Those who did not convert were forced to leave the country. By 1500, Jews had been subject to massacres, inquisitional trials, and expulsion all across western Europe.

The upsurge of anti-Jewish violence by the church in Europe during these centuries was accompanied by a whole catalogue of popular superstitions and caricatures of Judaism.[11] The church had always held that Judaism was inferior to Christianity as a religion. Since Christianity was obviously held to encompass all good, its theological antithesis, Judaism, became in the popular mind the seat of all evil. Some mythic portrayals took on religious characteristics: that Jews gleefully desecrated the eucharistic host, for example, or that Jewish ritual required the drinking of Christian blood. Other portrayals were rooted in social concerns. The black plague of the fourteenth century, for instance, seems to have occasioned the emergence of a number of anti-Jewish claims that had no particular theological basis. Jews, it was claimed, poisoned wells or secretly killed unsuspecting Christians. In the terrible uncertainties and overwhelming grief of those decades, the Jews emerged in the popular mind as the very incarnation of disease and death. An entire ideology had developed that explained in grisly detail why communities had to expel the Jewish vermin from their midst.

ANTI-JUDAISM IN THE REFORMATION

With the beginning of the Reformation, the church's actions to stem the influence of Jews and thereby to cut the Reformers from their supposed intellectual roots reached new extremes. Expulsions were apparently no longer feasible. But it was possible to segregate Jews. Jews could be restricted to certain parts of town and their opportunities for contact with Christians regulated. In 1516 the first ghetto was established, in Venice. The church was now committed to treating the Jews in Europe as unwelcome and dangerous outsiders, people who had to be kept segregated.

Luther and the Reformers bear their own share of guilt for encouraging and solidifying European Jew hatred. Luther at first was respectful of Jews and Judaism, apparently expecting the Jews to flock to his "reasonable" articulation of Christianity. When this failed to occur, he became rabidly anti-Jewish—in fact, embarrassingly so. He wrote in "Concerning the Jews and Their Lie,"

> Let me give my honest advice. First their synagogues or churches should be set on fire, and whatever does not burn up should be covered or spread over with dirt so that no one may ever be able to see a cinder or stone of it. And this ought to be done for the honor of God and of Christianity in order that God may see that we are Christians, and that we have not wittingly tolerated or approved of such public lying, cursing, and blaspheming of His Son and His Christians. . . .
>
> Secondly, their homes should likewise be broken down and destroyed. For they perpetrate the same things there that they do in their synagogues. For this reason they ought to be put under one roof or in a stable, like gypsies, in order that they may realize that they are not masters in our land, as they boast, but miserable captives, as they complain of us incessantly before God with bitter wailing.
>
> Thirdly, they should be deprived of their prayerbooks and Talmuds in which such idolatry, lies, cursing, and blasphemy are taught.
>
> Fourthly, the rabbis must be forbidden under threat of death to teach any more. . . .
>
> Fifthly, passport and travelling privileges should be absolutely forbidden to the Jews. . . . For they have no business in the rural districts since they are not nobles, nor officials, nor merchants, nor the like. Let them stay at home.
>
> Sixthly, they ought to be stopped from usury. All their cash and valuables of silver and gold ought to be taken from them and put aside for safekeeping. For this reason, as said before, everything that they possess they stole and robbed from us through their usury, for they have no other means of support. This money should be used in the case (and in no other) where a Jew has honestly become a Christian. . . .
>
> Seventhly, let the young and strong Jews and Jewesses be given the flail, the ax, the hoe, the spade, the distaff, and spindle, and let them earn their bread by the sweat of their noses as is enjoined upon Adam's children.[12]

By the end of the Middle Ages, then, Jews were distrusted and vilified by the church, by the Reformers, and by the common people—each group for its own reasons. The Jews had become Europe's most versatile and patent symbol of evil.

The point here has been to describe the general associations that developed about the linguistic symbols of Jews and Judaism as the culture of Christian

Europe took form and substance. The various associations, whether derived from late antiquity, from the political and theological struggles of the church, from the Reformers, or from the superstitions of common peasants and burghers, are important because they created a complex and stable constellation of symbols of evil centered on Jewry. What is relevant to our purpose is that by the sixteenth century it was absolutely normal in Europe to think about evil and the Jews together and in utterly mythic terms. As we shall now see, these views were taken out of theological discourse and placed into scientific discourse of nineteenth- and twentieth-century theories of race.

2

The Dynamics of Evil: Nineteenth-Century Theories of Racial Conflict

The concept of "the Jew" took on a new layer of meaning in the nineteenth century with the development of the notion of race. This development was of incalculable importance for the emergence of the Nazi ethic because it provided a new, nontheological vocabulary and system of symbols through which Jew hatred could be expressed. It provided, in other words, a way for Jew hatred to be understood in a new and scientifically compelling way. That became important because by the nineteenth century the older style of Jew hatred, based on medieval theology, was no longer culturally persuasive. This is not to say that there were no people still under its sway. But the older theological mode of discourse was not politically or socially powerful in the context of the post-Enlightenment nation-state. Nevertheless, by rendering the same negative connotations in racial theory and social Darwinism, one could reject medieval, theologically based anti-Judaism and yet retain the Jews and Judaism as a potent symbol of evil. The creation of a vocabulary of racial struggle had the advantage of maintaining a traditional characterization of evil while packaging it in contemporary terms.

NINETEENTH-CENTURY THEORIES OF
RACE

On the medieval view, Judaism and Jewry were the locus of an evil that transcended individual Jews or particular Jewish beliefs. It was the Jewish peoplehood itself that bore the seeds of evil, at least in part because of the curse the gospel reports the Jews brought upon themselves at the time of the crucifixion of Jesus (Matt. 27:25). That all people were entangled in original sin was taken for granted. The Jews as a transcendent community played a special role in this typology because in addition to suffering the sinfulness that is part of the human lot, they systematically, generation after generation, replayed their forebears' satanic role in rejecting and mocking the saving Messiah. The ancient biblical struggle between good and evil was understood by medieval theologians to be played out again and again between the church and Judaism. Any individual Jew, no matter how upright or likable, was associated with the sin of the starkest type simply by being a willing part of the community. Jewry and Judaism functioned in church symbol and rhetoric as the primal symbols of evil.[1]

This deeply theological contempt for Jews and Judaism underwent a radical transformation in the eighteenth century as a result of the Enlightenment. The Enlightenment represents the ascendancy of scientific, empirical, secular thinking in the West. The older theological and doctrinal views of the world retreated into "religion," as the public and political discourse of Europe found its new focus in humanism. The new center of attention was the individual human being, who was an autonomous political and moral agent. The highest good was not the sustenance of the church as the body of Christ but the provision of freedom and opportunity to each individual so that he or she could develop his or her talents to the fullest degree possible. Truth was a matter no longer of doctrinal cogency but of what the free minds of intelligent people could accept on the basis of reasoning and empirical evidence.[2] The medieval theological typologies of good and evil lost their ability to move cultures. Good and evil were now located in individual moral choices.

At the same time that the individual was taking his or her place at center stage, a countermovement was developing in Western thought. Undoubtedly, the confrontation with non-European civilizations, with the "inferior races and cultures" of the world, provoked European imperialists to retain or resurrect typological models. Europeans saw themselves as clearly superior to the "savages" being encountered in Africa and elsewhere. The Enlightenment destroyed the possibility of explaining European domination on theological grounds, but as it turned out, more secular ways of saying the same thing were at hand. If membership in the church could no longer serve as a self-evident justification for conquering and ruling "pagans," then membership in a certain culture or race could. Thus European colonialists turned for a justification of their rulership not to a sense of theological chosenness but to the scientifically verifiable "fact" of superior culture and intelligence.[3] By the middle of the nineteenth century, the analysis of good and evil, and so of right and wrong, had shifted away from individuals and back to cultures. But in acknowledgment of the power of Enlightenment thinking, the justification of this shift rested not in theology but in scientific studies of human intellectual and civil achievements. In all this, racial theories played a central role. Racial theories allowed Europeans to continue to espouse Jew hatred but to do so in a modern, that is, nontheological, way.

Can there be a general definition of the term "race" as it relates to different human beings? In fact, framing a definition has promised to be all but impossible. Every group that develops a theory of human taxonomy does so in its own particular terms.[4] The ancient Greeks, for example, made a kind of "racial" distinction between themselves, a people who had language, and others who had only gibberish (who could utter only "ba-ba-ba," and hence who were designated by the term "barbarians," which has since gathered its own negative connotations). In Hebrew Scripture, those people who joined together to create Israel later regarded themselves as genealogically different from their social and political neighbors, the Canaanites. In America, where people share a common language and a more or less common religion, distinctions are made on skin tone. In each case, the defining society chooses as a reference point for its taxonomy that aspect of human form or culture most relevant to its own situation. This means that distinctions that are self-evident in one culture may be completely invisible in another. The result is that groups linked together as a single "race" in one culture may turn out to be perceived as utterly distinct in another. Thus Americans lump together Scandinavians and Italians in a single racial taxon as whites, even though each of the joined groups sees itself as unrelated to the other. Similarly, Westerners associate the Japanese and Koreans as Orientals, even though these people regard themselves as radically different from each other. Since every group makes distinctions on the basis of what is obvious to it, a unified notion of how to determine race is unattainable.

Nonetheless, since the nineteenth century dawned there have been a number of more sophisticated attempts to define race and racial groups scientifically. Rather than dealing with accidental or arbitrary folk taxonomies, such as those based on skin color, religion, or language, scientists have tried to base racial taxonomies on body structure or genetic makeup. Far from establishing an objective basis for racial distinctions, however, these endeavors merely move the debate to another plane of discourse. As it turns out, one still has to choose arbitrarily which single criterion out of many possible ones to take seriously. The choice turns out to be just as crucial as before because each available criterion yields an entirely different racial map of humanity. The scientific criteria finally turn out to be no more objective than folk taxonomies.[5] A few examples of "scientific" classifications will illustrate what I mean. The inherited ability to taste PTC can be associated with a certain type of lactose deficiency. This trait might serve as a taxonomic indicator of a genetic race. But this taxonomy proves to be awkward, because it makes for some nonintuitive linkages: West Africans and South American Indians, for example. Another scheme proposes to link racial distinctions to genetic traits such as sickle-cell anemia, but this makes for even stranger bedfellows: West Africans and Greeks, on the one hand; the English and the Japanese, on the other. Using blood type B as a criterion brings West Africans, Greeks, and Japanese together. The list of examples could go on and on. Many of these results seem intuitively wrong, but no objective basis for choosing one scheme or criterion over another emerges. Our best scientific evidence today is that race in a scientific sense does not exist but is always a matter of more or less arbitrary definition.

Scientists in the nineteenth century, however, were sure that the concept of race described an ontological reality that could be identified genetically. They were convinced that real racial distinctions existed and could be discovered. Their research work was designed not to prove the existence of the distinctions, which was taken for granted, but to work out their cultural and ethical implications.

Part of the impetus for this kind of work came from the European imperialist experience.[6] Europeans of the nineteenth century found themselves ruling over a variety of "primitive" peoples from America to Africa to Asia. This raised the question of why the Europeans alone were civilized and able to rule others. Two explanatory theories were available, both anchored in but moving beyond the theological speculations inherited from the Middle Ages. One theory, monogenesis, held on to the biblical story that all people are descended from a single ancestor, Adam. The implication was that all people are intrinsically the same. But then why are human cultures in fact radically different? The answer was that there are differences in climate, geography, and local resources—an explanation most often associated with Montesquieu, its most articulate spokesman in the Enlightenment. Europeans, on this view, were no better than, say, the Zulus but only better placed in terms of environment. The second theory, however, claimed that variations in cultural level in fact reflect different basic realities. According to this view, species of people are not all equal in ability or capacity for culture. Sometimes labeled "polygenesis," the second theory argued that there were in fact several creations of people, with the story of Adam and Eve an account of only one of them. The point was that the Oriental and Negroid peoples encountered in Asia and Africa were not of the same seed as Europeans but of other, inferior, roots. Their cultural inferiority was simply a reflection of the primordial fact of their separate creation.

One of the most prominent early exponents of the polygenetic theory was Count J. A. de Gobineau, and his articulation of the theory was exemplary. Gobineau was a French nobleman who felt a need to justify not so much European lordship over Africa as the lordship of the French aristocracy over the French peasantry. For Gobineau the vast difference in cultural level between these two social strata must be based on more than mere chance; for him it represented the divine order of things. Writing in the post-Enlightenment world, however, he needed a "scientific," not a "theological," explanation. His reflections on the nature of the different stations of people in France led to an articulation of racial theory that became a classic of nineteenth-century European racial thinking.[7] He wrote in 1856,

> This is what the whole course of history teaches us. Every race has its own mode of thinking: every race, capable of developing a civilization, develops one particular to itself, and which it cannot engraft upon any other, except by amalgamation of blood, and then in but modified degree. The European

cannot win the Asiatic to his mode of thinking; he cannot civilize the Australian, or the Negro; he can transmit but a portion of his intelligence to half-breed offspring of the inferior race; the progeny of that half-breed and the nobler branch of his ancestry, is but one degree nearer, but not equal to that branch in capacity: the proportions of blood are strictly preserved.[8]

This statement makes a number of points. The language clearly gives the impression that the non-European groups mentioned here are genetically different from Europeans. Obviously, the differences between French peasants and French aristocrats are not based on differences in climate or locale. Too, peasants are not only different but also inferior. Further, their inferiority will be expressed in every aspect of their culture. When the different races interbreed, the offspring of their mating will be a hybrid of a higher level than the inferior parent but of a lower level than the superior parent. This means that every racial intermarriage must inevitably lead to offspring inferior to what might have been, that is, to offspring with a lower ability to be civilized. If enough hybridizing marriages occur, the standards of a culture, which are largely maintained by its aristocracy, will inevitably decline.

SOCIAL DARWINISM

To this theory must be added the speculation of Darwin and the Social Darwinists. Darwin did not set out to create a racist philosophy, but the implications of his researches and deductions were eventually adopted by racial theorists because they seemed to offer a scientific warrant for their own ideas. Racial theorists were especially attracted to Darwin's observation that in nature species are constantly engaged in a struggle for survival. In this brutal world, Darwin asserted, those best adapted to their environment are the ones that triumph over their enemies and survive. Individuals and species that prove to be inferior in the primordial struggle are either banished to undesirable geographical niches or become extinct. The universal law of nature, Darwin concluded, is the survival of the fittest. The Darwinian scientific and empirical model was soon taken over by racial thinkers and applied to human social contexts. The various human species, the racial thinkers posited, are engaged in an instinctive struggle for dominance, just as the animals in the natural world are engaged in eternal struggle for dominance. Studies of history and culture showed these researchers what they already suspected, namely, that human history is the story of the struggle for dominance among different cultural, and therefore racial, groups. In each case, they concluded, the racially and culturally superior groups emerge as dominant while inferior groups are either destroyed or made into slaves. It is this mechanism that explains why the ancient Babylonians, for example, defeated the Sumerians, the Greeks conquered the eastern empires, the Romans dominated the Greeks, and now the Europeans have gained control over the cultures of Africa and Asia. The same deep pattern of history is at work in case after case.

It was also apparent to these researchers, however, that great civilizations occasionally fell because of their own internal decay, the Roman Empire being the obvious example. The problem then became one of accounting for the recurrent defeat of superior peoples by their inferior subjects. The answer that emerged echoes the theme articulated by Gobineau: the conquered, inferior people inbred with the conquerers and so vitiated their strength and governing genius. The greatest danger to a culture once it has achieved its due dominance, then, lies in its interbreeding with its wards and so losing its genetic power.

The lesson was easily applied to Europe. The European study of culture had already shown beyond a shadow of a doubt that Europeans were superior in intellectual and cultural capacity and so had a "natural" right to dominate other, "lesser," human species. Europeans, it was thought, should consequently be able to enjoy the fruits of their conquests with no fear of effective challenge, except for a single possibility of defeat: this lay in the inferior races' ability to interbreed with Europeans so as to mongrelize them, creating a debilitated generation of halfbreeds. If the halfbreeds were defeated by other human species, the civilization Europeans had built up for themselves could be lost. Here Social Darwinism of a certain kind and the fears of Gobineau converge. For both, the world is a great stage upon which racial warfare is incessantly waged. The ultimate value is dominance and survival. The greatest danger comes from those who would sap the destined race of its innate capacities for dominance.

HOUSTON STEWART CHAMBERLAIN

By playing off theories of progress such as those associated with Hegel and by invoking the theories of scientists like Darwin, the general theory of racial warfare took on a sense of philosophical and scientific cogency.[9] What it lacked was a convincing study of how its views applied in real history. That omission was finally supplied by the most unlikely of racists: Houston Stewart Chamberlain (1855–1927).[10] Chamberlain was British by birth, French by upbringing, and Aryan by choice. Despite his varied background—or because of it—he was passionately concerned with the dynamics of race and racial conflict, and he provided a final warrant for racial theories by showing them at work in the processes of history. Attentive to the study of cultural and language groups undertaken by anthropologists and archaeologists investigating the ancient Near East, he became convinced that deep racial antagonisms between the Aryan and the Semitic "races" could be traced to the very beginning of human history. Students of the ancient Near East had already defined various language groups such as the Indo-European and the Semitic. Using language as evidence, they had also begun to trace the movement of peoples, on the assumption that each language denotes a particular racial group. Chamberlain took the results of these historical reconstructions and out of them created a history of racial conflict based on the recurrent conflicts between Aryans (who spoke Indo-European) and Semites (who spoke Semitic dialects). He concluded that even in ancient times one could notice the cultural superiority of the Aryan groups. They were always the dominant group, always able to subjugate the local Semites: thus the Hittites were able to halt the expansion of Egypt, the Persians could conquer the Babylonians, and the Greeks could win control over the entire ancient Near East. Furthermore, the Aryans had consistently built the greatest cultures (Hittite, Persian, Greek, Roman, German), had the most-developed languages, and had stunning physiques—all indications of their genetic superiority. Semites, on the other hand, were inferior and in fact largely mongrelized, being a mixture of Africans, Egyptians, Phoenicians, Canaanites, and Hittites. They could produce only weak, subservient, bastardized cultures. Philological and historical studies spanning a large portion of human history hence were believed to bear out three central notions: that races were in eternal conflict, that in particular the Aryan (now German) and the Semitic (now Jewish) breeds were ancient antagonists, and that the Aryans were intrinsically superior. Theories of race, Social Darwinism, and the scientific study of philology and language had now combined to create a single coherent picture.

This theory, while fairly coherent on one level, did leave some points to be resolved. After all, the great foundational thinkers of Christianity were all apparently Semitic: King David, the Hebrew prophets such as Isaiah, Jeremiah, and Ezekiel, and of course, Jesus and Paul. Two possible strategies were available for dealing with the problem. One was to claim that in fact these people were not Semitic at all but were Aryan "transplants." In this way the general theory not only could remain intact but would in fact be strengthened since the great religious ideas of Israel would now be further evidence for the cultural superiority of the Aryans. Although this view of matters flew in the face of the biblical evidence, it at least allowed the theoretician to remain Christian. The other strategy was to take the biblical data seriously and to conclude accordingly that since Judaism and its daughter religion Christianity were both Semitic religions, they were not appropriate belief systems for true Aryans. Some Nazi racial purists, driven to this view, in fact renounced Christianity. They claimed that the Judeo-Christian virtues of humility, mercy, and the like were recipes for defeat. For them, the true Aryan religion stressing the virtues of victory and domination was to be found in the pre-Christian beliefs of the ancient Teutonic war bands. It will become apparent later that in some ways the ideology of the S.S. (*Schutzstaffel*) can be understood as a kind of re-creation of that supposed authentic pre-Christian and Aryan religious and moral system.

The general theory articulated by Chamberlain popularized another element as well. His reconstruction of history rested on the assumption that there are such things as *pure* races. According to him, history teaches that cultures lose their power when their racial purity is debased by interbreeding. That is why even Aryan governments and civilizations occasionally suffer defeat. It is only when new, racially pure Aryan populations arise that Aryan superiority can again be achieved. In short, Aryans are assured of dominance and survival only as long as they maintain their essential Aryan racial character.

This kind of thinking gratified Germany's self-image in the later nineteenth century. For here we had a Volk, or a nation, that saw itself as distinct from the other peoples of Europe. It had its own history, culture, language, and destiny. But it alone among the nations of Europe had not been able to achieve a powerful political presence. When it did finally manage a kind of unified political expression under Bismarck, it was immediately attacked by the other peoples: the Russian Slavs, the French "Romance" people, the Anglo-Saxons. The lack of political power was especially anomalous to the Germans because, at the cultural level, they saw themselves as the heirs to the Roman Empire and hence as the main carriers of European civilization. Their ancestors, after all, made up the Holy Roman Empire, which preserved and carried into Europe the law, culture, and religion of Rome. Why, then, they had to ask, was this Germany constantly suffering defeat? Racial theories provided a ready answer. It was because other, inferior, racial groups were struggling to destroy and eliminate the German Volk in the great cosmic battle of the races. If German civilization, and all of the best of European culture that it embodies, were to survive, the Germans needed to take the struggle as seriously as their enemies did. Racial theories also explained the dynamics of the struggle. German weakness was a result of dispersion and inbreeding. To achieve its rightful victory, Germany had to prepare itself for the struggle by regaining its racial purity. The mongrelization of the Germans would have to be not just ended but reversed.

RACIAL THEORIES IN PRE-NAZI
GERMANY

For Chamberlain, the Semites constituted the primary racial antagonists of Aryans, continually trying to block their full cultural and political dominance. The earliest of the clashes between these two groups occurred in the ancient Near East, between the Hittites and the Assyrians. Later the Persians, an Indo-European-speaking group (and therefore Aryan) conquered the Babylonians and dominated Israel. They, in turn, were dominated by the Greeks, who brought a considerably higher level of civilization to the Orient and a higher form of religion, Christianity. The subsequent history of Aryan Christians and Semitic Jews in Europe made it abundantly clear, however, that although Aryan civilization and religion were vastly superior to their Semitic-Jewish counterparts, the Jews continued to exist and, of course, continued their attempts to overturn Aryan dominance. Gobineau showed to his own satisfaction that the instrument of Aryan defeat was racial down-breeding. If one looked around, one could see that in fact Jewish-Aryan intermarriages were rampant. The Jews were sapping Aryan strength, and had been so successful that Germany's efforts to carve out a place for itself in Europe had been unable to succeed. In light of this reconstruction of history, the title of Wilhelm Marr's pamphlet in which the term "anti-Semitism" first appears takes on significance: *The Victory of Judaism over Germanism* (1879). Here, in popular form, the struggle to the death between the German Volk and the Jewish race is described.

The logical entailments of these theories for Germans after World War I are now easy to see. Germany was the modern representation of Aryan culture. By rights it should therefore be dominant in Europe. Instead, it found itself defeated and humiliated. The reason had to be that it had lost the intrinsic strength of its Aryan blood heritage. This could have happened only through inbreeding with other racial groups, especially the Semitic, the eternal enemy of the Aryan. In effect, the Semitic race was doing now what history shows it to have done persistently in the past, namely, sap the strength of its Aryan overlords until they could be defeated. The Jews, with their refusal to accept German culture and with their own religion (Judaism), language (Hebrew, Yiddish), culture (their special diet and calendar), and physique (dark-haired, long-nosed), were clearly the source of the problem and the group most closely to be watched. In fact, the battle was now reaching a crucial stage. Massive Jewish intermarriage had mongrelized the German population to the point where German Aryans were almost helpless as the Jews proceeded to co-opt the very institutions of the state for their purpose, as the subsequent prominence of Jews in Weimar culture demonstrated. In these circumstances, nothing was as frightening as the continued presence of Jews in Germany. The utter care with which the Nazi party sifted out Jews in Germany has to be understood against the background provided by racial theories and German history.

It is, of course, entirely true that racial theories do not have to lead to the self-righteous indignation with which the Nazis persecuted the Jews. But an important ingredient in Nazi thinking was the symbol of the Jew as quintessentially evil. That conviction, laid out in chapter 1, "elevated" the struggle between Aryan and Jew from the racial or national plane to the moral plane. The exorcism of Jews from Aryan society could be conceived as not only a racial or historical need but an ethical imperative. Classical racist theories portrayed other "races" as not only different but inferior. Racial anti-Judaism, drawing on the inherited symbolization of Judaism, projected Jews and Judaism as not only inferior but in fact positively evil. That way of perceiving matters allowed Nazi ideology to generate an ethic that could override existing ethical norms. The arena for carrying out this transformation was national politics.

3

The Arena for Fighting Evil:
The Polity of Fascism

We have now examined two of the intellectual components that were used to establish a plausible content for the Nazi ethic. The mechanism by which a racial and anti-Jewish system of convictions was catapulted into the political arena so as to become the governing ideology of a modern state was fascism. Through this "up-to-date" theory, the new ethic was translated into politically usable terms. This opened a way for the ethic to be established within the current social reality as the governing norm of a state bureaucracy.

The rise of fascism in Germany can be understood from two perspectives. On the one hand, it can be seen as an internal development of German political history. It was, so to speak, an outgrowth of the particular pattern of German culture, especially of the traditions of the Reich, of yearnings for the Kaiser, of disgust with Weimar, and of the unfinished social business left over from the Bismarckian era. On the other hand, Nazism in Germany can also be seen as part of a larger pattern in Europe. Rightist reactionary regimes were emerging all across the continent— from Russia to Spain to Italy. In fact, a good deal of the thought and rhetoric of German Nazism is influenced by the thought and rhetoric of European fascism in general.[1]

Fascism, especially in the German form of Nazism with which we are concerned here, might be seen as the confluence of three streams of thought in the early twentieth century: the socialist critique of European economic development; the rise of nationalist sentiments; and racism. When these became a single amalgam, they created a powerful and persuasive view of the world that could draw on any number of intellectual fields to validate its political claims. It offered a single, coherent explanation for the character of the modern world and offered a single, coherent, and easily understandable recipe for the existing situation's correction.[2] To understand fully this amalgam and the power it could hold over people's moral thinking, we must look at its three major intellectual components.

THE ECONOMIC ROOTS OF FASCISM

The roots of the economic component of fascism were in the economic dislocations engendered in European society by the Industrial Revolution. The rise of early laissez-faire capitalism left in its wake a vast wash of underpaid, starving, and oppressed workers. Early socialist thinkers, especially after Marx, traced social problems to the ineffectiveness and moral laziness of the newly powerful and wealthy middle class,[3] which had no sense of how to create culture or lead nations. Instead the new petty capitalists were concerned only with increasing their own wealth and satisfying their own bourgeois desires. They tolerated political and economic oppression because they were too lazy or self-centered to give up their own immediate pleasure to help others. Early socialist thinkers were full of contempt for any political and economic movement that reinforced the bourgeoisie in its perceived mediocrity and morally blind use of power. They fought against laissez-faire capitalism as well as against liberal democracy, because they saw both as allowing power to accrue only to the middle and upper classes. What was needed, many of these social critics decided, was for power to be focused not on certain classes but on the welfare of the whole social fabric. Since those already in power could not be expected to relinquish control voluntarily, workers would have to take matters into their own hands. All that was needed was a mechanism by which the disenfranchised could seize control and ensure the just and proper distribution of resources.

NATIONALISM

These economic theories join with a second stream of thought, namely, nationalism ("Nazi" is an acronym for *Nazi*onal So*zi*alismus). Protofascist nationalism stressed the importance of each country as an ethnic and cultural collectivity. For true justice to be done, it said, the collectivity of the social group has to prevail over the interests of particular classes or individuals. Society as a whole has to function as a single organism in which each member is guaranteed his or her fair share. Any attempt on the part of an individual or a class to gain special privilege must be resisted in the name of the greater benefit for all.

All this is in reaction against a major theme of the Enlightenment, the ultimate worth of each individual. According to the Enlightenment conception, each person has inalienable rights that he or she must be free to exercise, the state existing only to aid in the free exercise of individual rights. The Enlightenment view gradually broke down in the nineteenth century for diverse reasons. First of all, Darwin was understood to show that nature is based on an incessant struggle in which only the fittest survive. From here the jump was often made to the conviction that only the fittest *ought* to survive and that there are no inalienable rights but only the ability to overcome enemies. Second, the rise of psychology showed that people are not autonomous rational beings but are really victims of innumerable unconscious, social forces. Finally, the Romantic movement stressed the importance of feeling and emotion over reason. All these cultural influences combined to dethrone the rational, autonomous individual from a position at the center of the moral universe and to set in the individual's place the needs of the social collectivity. The emerging theory was that individuals have identity only as part of a larger group. No one can survive alone; all religious and moral values, the very motors of our acting selves, are derived from our culture. Even our personalities are created by the impact of outside realities. To stress the individual is simply wrong and even pernicious: the true center of human culture and meaning resides in the group—that is, in the society and culture within which individuals emerge.

RACISM

What the protofascism described here calls for is a kind of corporate control over political and economic power. But it is not clear what the limits or boundaries of the corporation might be. Who should be in the corporation and who should be ruled an outsider? To answer these questions, fascist ideologues turned to the available theories of racism, where they found workable, "scientific" definitions to suit their needs. To understand the grounds of racism's demarcation of insiders from outsiders, it is necessary to understand the fascist concepts of nation and state.

For fascists, the nation was that ethnic, cultural, and linguistic unity that bound diverse individuals together into a common people. Thus Italians were different from Austrians not just because of political boundaries but also because they partook of different languages, cultures, ethnic practices, and the like. The Italian personality was a unity that was different in overall character from the Austrian character, and each individual would express that essential difference. It is a short move from this conception of national identity to the scientific theories of race. A race, after all, is considered a genetic pool that expresses itself not only in different physical characteristics but also in different mental, and so social and cultural, characteristics. Thus, as a Chamberlain would aver, Aryans and Semites do not only look different from each other but they also speak differently, think differently, and manufacture culture differently. It is therefore easy to identify nations with races. A nation is a population that comes out of a particular racial heritage, with its ethnic, linguistic, cultural, and genetic implications.

The state, on the other hand, was for fascists a political structure. A nation, to be able to ensure its survival in a world characterized by racial warfare, had to rise to political power. It had to be able to control a piece of territory with natural resources, from which to mount an effective defense of itself. Thus each nation had to find political expression in a state. A nation without a state was doomed to extinction. A nation with a state had to protect that state from internal decay, since in the state was its only hope of effective combat.

THE FASCIST SYNTHESIS

The three streams of thought—economic socialism, nationalism, and racism—came together in the late nineteenth and early twentieth centuries to create a powerful intellectual amalgam which claimed that the welfare of the nation depended on the stability and strength of its state. As the broker of economic and political power, the state guaranteed to each of its citizens a certain minimum of resources. The state was also the mechanism through which the race defended itself against other races. Thus, the security of the state was important not only to its individual citizens but to the transcendent racial community. The interests of individual citizens, then, had to give way before the greater needs of the state as a whole and before the greater good in the name of which it operated. In a threatening and hostile world, all this amounted to a characterization of the state as in essence the military muster of the race. All its citizens were to see themselves as soldiers in one form or another, in the service of the nation and race. In this grand task, the individual was of little concern.

There emerged at this time an almost religious fervor to fascists' descriptions of the struggle in which they claimed to be engaged. One is reminded of the ancient struggles of the Sons of Light against the Sons of Darkness marching to battle at Armageddon. In an excellent example of the rhetoric of these movements, symbols are brought together that repeat themselves over and over in a thousand variations all over Europe in the wake of World War I:

> The true elites are formed at the front, a chivalry is created there, young leaders are born. That is where you find the true elite of tomorrow . . . and there between us a complete fraternity grows up, for since the war, everything has changed. When we look to our own country and see some fat, stupefied bourgeois, we do not feel this man to be a member of our race; but when we see a young revolutionary, from Germany or elsewhere, we feel that he is one of ours, for we are one with revolution and youth. We are political soldiers, the badge of the SS shows Europe where political and social truth are found; . . . we prepare the political cadres of the postwar world. Tomorrow, Europe will have elites such as it has never known. An army of young apostles, of young mystics, carried by a faith that nothing can check, will emerge one day from the great seminary of the front.[4]

This powerful image, part military, part religious, conveys the picture of the new Europe, as conceived by fascist ideologues. The older, self-centered and militarily weak political structures would have to be entirely swept away to make room for the new order. The struggle would be glorious as the true forces of justice triumphed.

These basic convictions received concrete form in the various fascist movements of the early twentieth century. The definitive characteristic of all

European fascist movements was their supernationalism, that is, their conviction that the welfare of the state transcends all other values. This meant, for example, that all the movements identified as natural political enemies any organization or force that weakened, or threatened to weaken, or could be seen as possibly weakening, the power or authority of the state's political structure in the name of some other principle. As a result, all fascists shared a deep distrust of international organizations, such as the League of Nations, that attempted to break down differences among states, or such as the Catholic church, that promoted allegiance to a principle higher than that of the state. In the early twentieth century, bolshevism became the main enemy of fascist politics, because it stressed class unity across state boundaries. It in fact called for the destruction of existing political structures on the theory that these were created by local capitalist ruling classes as a means of oppressing the workers. All in all, any number of twentieth-century ideologies that threatened to unite people across political boundaries were the target of fascist power: pacifism, socialism, international financial capitalism, Catholicism, and of course, that paradigm of statelessness, Judaism.

Fascists did not find their enemies only outside the state's boundaries. They feared especially movements *within* the state that institutionalized political cleavages and so undermined the state's unity of purpose. Labor unions were often suspect not only because of their association with "international socialism" but also because they encouraged class tensions within a society at the same time that they challenged the monopoly of power claimed by the state. Religious groups occasionally came under similar suspicion, especially groups, such as the Jehovah's Witnesses, that refused to fight for the state. Even democratic institutions could come under attack on the grounds that they allowed leftists, labor unionists, bolsheviks, and other corrosive elements of society to bring their special internationalist interests into the highest levels of power. Fascists therefore defined enemies on two fronts: they had to keep at bay those outside forces that threatened to compromise the state's power by entangling it in treaties and associations; at the same time they had to purify the political institutions within the state. In some instances, of course, the two fronts were linked. The internal enemy of bolshevik parliamentarians could be combated also by destroying the power base of international bolshevism. In fact, without defeating international bolshevism, victory against the internal bolsheviks was impossible. So fascist policy in defense of the state demanded international action. Nor were organizations alone to be combated. When no particular institution stood behind a movement, the idea itself had to be destroyed. Thus, fascists in all countries waged vicious propaganda campaigns against a host of alleged antistate ideologies: Catholicism, labor unionism, socialism, bolshevism, and Judaism.

Since fascism conceived of its mission in essentially military terms, it comes as no surprise that its leaders imbued their movements with the trappings of a military campaign. This was nothing more than an extension of their ideology, but it had some important side effects. First, of course, the use of military tactics gave the fascist militants a tool for achieving political prominence.[5] In almost all cases, the fascists' displays of military power, along with their readiness to resort to violence and terrorism to achieve their ends, gave them a public presence, and eventually an influence, that they would otherwise not have had.

Second, the use of military imagery proved to be of tremendous propaganda value. It allowed fascism to come across as powerful, dynamic, and self-assured. That imagery proved to be powerfully attractive to a population that after World War I came to see its liberal democratic governments as weak-willed and ineffective. The qualities the fascists projected through their uniforms and parades were exactly the opposite: patriotism, aggressiveness, discipline, and above all, strength. Here virile young men appeared as the aggressive and ruthless defenders of the nation, as cadres of party troops that were devoted to the high martial virtues of bravery, toughness, and discipline. For a citizenry looking for tough leadership, the martial quality of fascist movements had an obvious attraction.

Finally, the military paradigm behind fascism's ideology allowed its thinkers to draw upon the intellectual trends we have already discussed, especially that of racial warfare. If nations or racial groups were in fact engaged in a kind of Darwinian battle for survival, then the obvious categories that came to mind to describe and meet that threat would be military ones. The racial group under attack had, in effect, to muster itself to meet the aggressor. Although national armies did exist, these were easily dismissed by fascist reactionaries as useless as long as they were under the control of liberal, democratic leaders. Fascists portrayed their own uniformed groups, rising as they did from the masses, as the true and authentic muster of the race, the sole movement willing and able to defend to the death the virtues inherent in the Volk. Fascism by the sheer nature of its public discourse provided a bridge from abstract theories of racial warfare to concrete political organizations. This is particularly apparent in Germany, where the Nazi party developed a whole system of myth and ritual that identified it with the pre-Christian Teutonic war bands. People were asked to believe that the brown-shirted young men and women marching down the city streets of Germany with torches were in fact the reincarnation of the ancient warlords, the authentic Volk rising up again to defend its ancient honor.

This characterization of fascist ideology is accurate in general outline for all the fascist governments and parties that emerged in Europe at this time, although the details vary from place to place and shift somewhat over time. Fascism is not so much a hard doctrine or dogma as a general orientation. It grows out of a mode of political thinking that has long roots in the West and that took specific form around problems characteristic of the early twentieth century.

From this general orientation, shared in its essence by all European fascist movements of the time, a simple program of implementation came into focus. The first step was to create a new mystic military elite loyal above all to the values of the nation or Volk. All individualism had to be rooted out, for only on that basis could a coherent and unified people emerge, able to act in harmony as a great army. Once organized, this army of course had to take control of the state, the political expression of the nation or race. The resulting state had to be totalitarian, because no part of a culture or civilization could stand outside the shaping power of the national collectivity. The fascist ideology, after all, posits a single unified grid in which political, social, cultural, linguistic, and psychological factors are all bound together. Anything that cannot be assimilated by this uniform social construct must, by the nature of things, be destroyed. It is this all-encompassing and revolutionary nature of fascist ideology that gives it a sense of being a movement rather than a party. It means to encompass all; it is not one point of view among others. Everything must eventually enter its vortex. The state thus became part of the party, which saw itself as the embodiment of the Volk and the spokesperson of the race.

The ideology of fascism provided a vital link in the intellectual chain that led to the Holocaust. Fascism explicitly declares that the security and the strength of the state constitute a primary value. This is so because the state alone, it declares, can satisfy the basic human needs for security, transcendent meaning, and socioeconomic justice. The state, in short, is the guarantor of public morality. Moreover, the state alone has the power, will, and resources to combat the forces of injustice arrayed against the common person. By stating matters in this way, fascist leaders could plausibly claim that the interests of the state had to be placed, on purely moral grounds, ahead of the more narrow interests of individuals. The general rhetoric about combating evil and about justice takes on mythic, and therefore specific, content when discursivized in terms of nineteenth-century racism. The racist theories explain the concrete nature of the fascist struggle against evil by projecting it as the modern version of the primordial conflict of the races. That in turn allowed the precise identity of the enemy to be identified, historically verified, and located within the existing political and international spheres. The abstract rhetoric of moral combat could now be convincingly focused on specified targets, and the script was prepared for modern state governments to engage in racial warfare. When racist theories centered largely on the pernicious character of the Semites, as they tended to do in Germany, the opportunity was established for casting the Jews as the mortal and moral racial enemies against which the state would have to fight. As we shall see, the economic, political, and social collapse of Germany during the Weimar years set the stage for the Holocaust drama. All that was now necessary was for the fascist movement to take over political control in Germany. When this happened in 1933, the ethical script began its work of controlling matters.

4

Dissolution of the Old Ethic:
The Germany
Hitler Inherited

With the intellectual components of the new ethic in mind, let us turn to the concrete formation of the ethic in nineteenth- and early twentieth-century Germany. Our governing hypothesis (see chap. 1) is that an ethic of whatever content becomes powerful when it satisfies two criteria. First, the ethic must be coherent and not self-contradictory. That is, it must bear some formal relationship to what people already perceive to be meaningful ethical categories. The ethic has to make sense in the given linguistic universe. We have already seen how the Nazi ethic was able to meet the requirements of this criterion. Second, the ethic must be capable of making sense of people's perceived reality. That is, it must account for the character of the cosmos as people then experience it. An ethic that fails to do this becomes sectarian and finally counterintuitive and irrelevant. It no longer can motivate people to act according to its dictates.

The rapid political, social, and economic changes in nineteenth-century Germany left the inherited ethic out-of-date and so progressively less able to account for perceived reality. In the old ethic's place coalesced a new one trading on the intellectual currency of the time: anti-Judaism, racial theory, and fascism. As the situation in Germany continued to change and allegedly to worsen, this new ethic proved to be more and more persuasive. The terrible defeat and aftermath of World War I catapulted it into a position of extraordinary influence.

THE EMERGENCE OF MODERN GERMANY

The central fact to be kept in mind in explaining the emergence of a new ethic in Germany is that Germany itself is a new creation. Until the Bismarckian revolution in 1870 there was no single political or social entity called Germany. There was, to be sure, a German consciousness: people spoke German (or a dialect of German), they called themselves German, they shared a common myth about the history of the German Volk. Yet it was only with Bismarck that a single German political entity came into existence in the modern world. When that entity emerged, however, it proved to be far different from the Germany that people had been imagining. It was the attempt to explain the actual political and social reality and to bring this into line with what people thought *ought* to be the case that generated the questions that occupied German minds for the next several decades and that prepared the seedbed for the ethic that spawned the Holocaust.

By the beginning of the twentieth century, Germany's mythic history of itself posited three broad periods, each reflecting the innate yearnings of the German Volk for a homeland and each providing data about the nature of that homeland. The first period covered the prehistoric experience of the German tribes in Europe before the advent of Roman civilization and the Christian religion. This mythic and idealized period came to play a prominent role in the imaginations of a number of thinkers during the Nazi period. Descriptions of the period supposed a sort of idyllic pastoral setting in which the true German Volk were able to wander unhindered in their homeland forests and develop their language and culture uncontaminated by outside influences. On this view, there is a common heritage of all Germans that stretches back beyond Christianity and Western culture to an ancient primordial tribal society binding all Germans together and that establishes the fundamental relationship Germans bear to other western European groups. The historical accuracy of this conception is not at issue here. What is at issue is only that this was the mythic picture of Teutonic origins that had tremendous power in the twentieth-century German search for identity, the search we are claiming underlies the Nazi ethic.[1]

The second period is what was later labeled the First Reich, namely, the Holy Roman Empire. This "empire" was pieced together in the Middle Ages as the political successor to the Roman Empire. It was certainly not holy. It was clearly not Roman, being centered in the vast semicivilized forests of central Europe. And as matters developed, it was not really an empire either. Rather, it was a conglomerate of duchies, dukedoms, petty kingdoms, margravates, and baronies of various sorts and sizes under the titular head of an emperor. It was a first attempt, we might say with long historical hindsight, to organize politically the Teutonic tribal forests. In later times, the Holy Roman Empire would be held up by some as a model of what Germany should be: a unified political entity that was the true heir and guardian of Roman culture and civilization. In this empire, the perception was, the Germanic people achieved a solid and respectable historical presence.

The third epoch was the Germany of Kaiser Wilhelm I and his chancellor, Otto von Bismarck: the Second Reich. The political, social, and economic developments in the Germanic lands in the late nineteenth century, culminating in Bismarck's unification of Germany, were important for two reasons. First, they provided the final mythic structure through which twentieth-century Germans thought of themselves. Herein lay the culmination of German historical aspirations. Second, they created a Germany fraught with tension and disunity. This juxtaposition of ideal fulfillment and social disappointment created the cognitive dissonance that paved the way for the new Nazi ethic.

THE SECOND REICH

Two developments led to the unification of Germany and the creation of the Second Reich. The first was intellectual and rested on the notion of a unique German character that, like the character of other nations in Europe, needed political expression. A sense of national destiny demanded that political unity be achieved in a way that would allow "authentic" German language, art, culture, and law to emerge and flourish. The creation of a German nation-state that would permit this was seen as a historical necessity.[2]

The second impetus was political and was supplied in the person of Napoleon Bonaparte. In his construction of the French Empire, Napoleon had two goals. One was political: to increase the strength, glory, and security of France. The other was social. Napoleon dedicated himself to bringing the blessings of Enlightened liberal government to all Europeans. By this he meant, in broad terms, the introduction of democratic governments committed to preserving the inalienable rights of all citizens regardless of religion. In each of the lands he conquered, Napoleon set about establishing liberal democratic governments. His conquest of western German lands thus brought in its wake enormous political reforms, including the consolidation into unified "kingdoms" of the diverse fiefdoms left over from the Middle Ages.[3] Napoleon's actions of course posed a sharp threat to the aristocracies still holding power in the eastern German states and provoked political reform there as well. Thus consolidation and political reform occurred throughout the German lands, even in the states not formally conquered by Napoleon.[4]

But with consolidation came unforeseen problems. Many groups in Germany prospered under the reforms, especially entrepreneurs and the urban middle classes.[5] But there were negative reactions as well. Not all aristocratic families were ready to give up their privileges. The same economic reforms that allowed new businesses to grow spelled the end to old tradition-bound family firms. The political adjustments that gave industrial magnates and the urban middle classes a voice in government robbed medieval Germany's traditional leadership groups of their influence. The result was decades of political struggle as conservative interests such as the old aristocracies, the military, and the landed gentry battled with the newly enfranchised entrepreneurs and the bourgeoisie for political and economic control. It was on this Germany that Bismarck proposed to impose political unity.

Otto von Bismarck became chancellor of Prussia, the largest of the German states, in 1862.[6] His sole passion was to make Prussia the foremost power in Germandom. In pursuit of his goal, Bismarck manufactured a series of crises in Europe that allowed him bit by bit to overwhelm potential opponents to Prussian expansion, Austria being chief among these, and to annex to Prussia other German territories and states. By 1870 his machinations had succeeded to the extent that most of the "German" lands—excluding Austria—were politically dominated, if not formally annexed, by Prussia. To hold the resulting social and political conglomerate together, Bismarck purposely set about establishing what we would today call a civil religion of statism, that is, a system of attitudes and symbols that focused people's loyalties on the state. To this end, Bismarck drew upon the symbols of pan-German unity represented by the Holy Roman Empire. The reunified German state was called the Reich, and its head, Wilhelm I of Prussia, became the new emperor, or Kaiser. The new realm was technically a federation: there was a legislature—the Reichstag—made up of delegates from all the component states. But Prussia clearly dominated. It controlled nearly three-fifths of the territory of the federation, and its army was by far the most formidable. Its population gave it a right to 235 of the 397 delegates in the Reichstag. Bismarck's dream of a unified Germany, united under Prussia, was well along the road to fulfillment.

Yet outward political unification masked the increasing social and political tensions that had already undermined the stability of many of the German states. Three areas of major concern can easily be identified. The first was political. By forcibly imposing a single political order on the federation, Bismarck alienated both liberals (who wanted greater democracy) and conservatives (who wanted to preserve local aristocratic power and privilege). The second was social. Bismarck faced the need to weave the diverse economic and communal structures of formerly independent lands into a coherent whole. The third was diplomatic. There was the need to work out a place for the new Germany in the political matrix of Europe. As we shall see, Bismarck's efforts toward addressing the first two needs—the political and social—were entirely inadequate, and his attempts to deal with the third generated a legacy of mistrust and hatred. All his failures stem from a single cause. Brilliant as Bismarck was in political machinations, he was unable to deal with broader social issues. The new Germany he created suffered from deep structural flaws that were never adequately addressed and that continued to fester into Nazi times.[7]

Bismarck's foreign policy provides a clear example of his shortcomings. Germany after 1870 was a major political, economic, and military power in Europe. It required and deserved a place in the European order of things commensurate with its stature. But creating such a place would require delicacy. Europe throughout the early nineteenth century had maintained peace through a careful balancing of forces. This balance was, of course, completely upset by the appearance of a united and rapidly industrializing Germany. A new balance of power in Europe would have to be created. But Bismarck was not interested in a balance of power. His approach to European politics mimicked his approach to intra-German politics. He created crises whenever he could and then exploited the situation to his own benefit. Over the years he systematically stirred up suspicion and conflict in all his neighbors, mostly against one another but inevitably also against Germany itself. Europe became through Bismarck's policies an uneasy agglomeration of distrustful states, warily eyeing one another and completely unable to accept or trust the new Germany. The old order, it is true, had been effectively unraveled, but no new international order was woven to take its place. Germany's relations to other states in Europe rested on fear and suspicion. On the surface, Germany was succeeding brilliantly in making a place for itself in Europe. But in fact Germany was never fully accepted in Europe and in fact became more and more a hated outsider. Bismarck had made a European war against Germany all but inevitable.

This same pattern is evident in internal politics. The creation of an all-German federation created a number of political problems. The confederation put together by Bismarck was made up of a number of once-independent states, each with its own political traditions and ruling elites. On these the particular Prussian political system was suddenly imposed. Had Bismarck allowed political reform to develop slowly and organically, he might have been able to co-opt the loyalty of traditional local power brokers. Instead, they were forced into the political opposition while new, untried people took over power. As if further to alienate local and regional loyalties, Bismarck abolished local weights and measures, monetary systems, postal services, and the like. Again, reforms were necessary. Had they been effected diplomatically and with sensitivity to local pride, they could have been sources of a national unity. Instead they were sources of friction and tension. Open political resistance was rare, however, because there was little opportunity and because Bismarck's moves were made in the name of German unity, a value that most people could accept at least in the abstract.

Surface unity was being undermined, however, by the increased social disunity flowing from Bismarck's reforms. The economic and political consolidation of Germany set the stage for the sudden introduction of the Industrial Revolution. With a sizable national market, a new ability to move commodities cheaply by rail from one part of the domain to the other, the abolition of internal tariffs, and the creation of a single monetary system, large-scale manufacturing expanded rapidly in Bismarckian Germany. With this came the attendant problems of rapid industrialization: urbanization, the creation of a working-class proletariat, stark urban poverty, child labor, broken families, unemployment, and a rapidly growing capitalist class. What Germany desperately needed was some vision of how its diverse economic and social interests could work together for a common good. This vision Bismarck could never provide. Rather, he allowed tensions between urban and rural interests, industry and agriculture, workers and management, liberals and conservatives to develop without providing real channels of compromise. He in fact often encouraged the tensions as a means to increasing the power of the central government.

The Germany that Hitler and his generation inherited was, hence, a Germany that on the surface had achieved an ancient dream: political unification. Yet underneath was a Germany riven with dissatisfaction and unclear about its place and identity in Europe. It was a Germany in search of itself. By the early part of the twentieth century, Germany was ripe for revolution. With the First World War, the tensions within the Reich were temporarily suppressed in the name of national unity, but they reemerged, with renewed vigor, after the defeat of Germany and the terrible punishment inflicted by the Treaty of Versailles. It was in light of that defeat that Hitler and many of his generation began to nurse the thoughts that formed the basis of German policy in the thirties and forties.[8]

THE EFFECT OF WORLD WAR I

Germany went into World War I full of hope and nationalist spirit. Germany, after all, had not lost a war since 1862 and had in fact been able materially to improve its position with each war. War, we might say, had provided Germany with a way of dealing with its needs and aspirations in a fruitful way. The opening months of World War I seemed to hold a similar promise. German troops quickly penetrated their enemies' territories. Trench lines were quickly established well into Poland in the East and into France and the Low Countries in the West. Further, Germany's internal struggles had been set aside in the *Burgfrieden,* the political accommodation reached by the nation's diverse social interests with a view to guaranteeing political solidarity and peace inside Germany for the duration of the war.[9] In all, then, the war began auspiciously. No German in 1914 had lived through a real Prussian defeat, and, it is probably fair to say, none could really conceive of defeat's happening now.

But the war progressed differently from what anybody in Europe had imagined. The massive industrialization of Europe had ushered in a new era of warfare. Railroads made it possible to muster and support extremely large numbers of troops in rather limited areas. Literally tens of thousands of troops could be engaged along a single frontal line. Industry, too, had produced massive weapons of destruction such that battlefields became lethal in a totally unprecedented way. Worst of all, the two sides turned out to be more evenly matched than the German staff had estimated. While the military establishments in other countries had begun to learn the lessons of modern warfare and to make the proper adjustment, the German general staff had become smug, bureaucratized, and self-satisfied. So the war, rather than resulting in another quick victory for Germany, degenerated into a four-year-long disappointment marked chiefly by strategic stalemate and massive casualties.

Erich Maria Remarque's *All Quiet on the Western Front* captures the deep spirit of disillusionment that gradually overcame the army. An older generation welcomed the war as opening up vast new opportunities for Prussian growth. But the young men who were sent to the front saw only friends being gassed and shot, wanton destruction of property, and gruesome and painful deaths—all in the context of seemingly nonsensical military posturing and maneuvering. These soldiers came to see the Europe outside Germany in a much different light than their parents did. For the young generation of Germans, other Europeans were brutal and murderous enemies, capable of any outrage in their insane drive to frustrate German aspirations. And of course, the German soldiers had been brutalized and traumatized. It is impossible to understand the rage and brutality that this generation exhibited in the Holocaust without recognizing the generation's formative experiences in the hideous gas attacks and trench warfare of World War I. Those experiences were part of a grid of meaning that made the Holocaust possible.

The details of the war itself need not detain us. There are, however, several effects the war had that are important for our purposes, including three in particular: the breakdown of social unity over the war's long course; the effect of the Russian Revolution on disaffected German workers; and the impact of the unexpected and sudden surrender of Germany. Each of these effects added an ingredient that would give postwar Germany, the Germany of Hitler's rise, its particular character.

The massive social tensions that were part of the Bismarckian state had reached the point of threatening the very existence of the German state by the early twentieth century. With the outbreak of World War I, these tensions were simply swept under the rug by the *Burgfrieden*. Although this accommodation was necessary for the war effort, it created an even more intractable problem for Germany after the war. Social tensions, after all, did not go away during the war; they were simply ignored. To be fair, the German politicians and leaders who forged the *Burgfrieden* in 1914 expected the war to be short. As it dragged on month after month and then year after year, it did not just leave the social tensions unaddressed, it magnified them. The Germany that emerged from World War I had not only a massive defeat to contend with but also a radically deteriorated social situation: workers were underpaid, social benefits for the urban unemployed were inadequate, rural interests were ignored.

This brings us to the second critical effect: that of the Russian Revolution of 1917. As we might expect, German workers, deeply dissatisfied with working conditions in Germany, were heavily influenced by socialist philosophies. Bismarck had largely ignored their needs, and the *Burgfrieden* had silenced them. They saw, with some reason, many parallels between their own situation and the situation of the working class in Russia: there too an authoritarian regime was dedicated to industrial expansion at the expense of workers' rights, while socialist labor organizations struggled without much success to give workers a political voice. In both countries, the urban working class was simply unable to overcome the entrenched power of the government and police, which was allied with the aristocracy and the capitalist moneyed class. The workers' dreams for economic justice seemed doomed. But then the unexpected happened: the workers in Russia not only fought the oppressive powers aligned against them, they managed to overcome them and set up a workers' government. The Russian Revolution showed that effective opposition to repressive coalitions of government and owners was possible. It opened up the hope that truly egalitarian regimes, in which the working class would have its fair share of the economic benefits of industrialization, were achievable through left-wing revolution. The more conservative elements in Germany, of course, saw the same implications but reacted quite differently. In their eyes, the successful revolution in Russia threatened the power of traditional elements in German society. It threatened the ruling power coalition that had come into being under Bismarck and his successors, as witnessed by the fact that the earliest victims of the Russian Revolution were the old aristocracy, the landowners, and the monarchists. But it was not the traditional power brokers alone who were threatened. The newly emerging urban moneyed class of industrial owners was also a target of the revolution, since their wealth and power were to be taken away to be redistributed to the working masses. Therefore, the newer industrial magnates in Germany, as well as the newly empowered political elites, were united with the aristocracy in opposition to any attempt by German leftists to repeat in Germany what was happening in Russia. The victory of the Russian Revolution, and especially of the radical bolsheviks, provoked fear and even panic in the German ruling elites at the same time that it infused the workers with new hopes that justice for themselves was attainable. The specter of bolshevism became a dominating and divisive concern in German political rhetoric after the war.

It is in the context of these widening frustrations and fears that Germany's sudden defeat must be placed. Actually, the defeat was sudden only on the surface and in the perception of the German people. In fact, the underlying developments leading to Germany's first military debacle were well under way by 1916, and by 1918 were irreversible. The problems were well known and understood by the general staff: the Schieffen plan outlining Germany's overall strategy did not work; German military manpower was inadequate; troop morale was low; German industry was unable to produce war material as quickly as it was being destroyed; shortages of critical supplies were growing. Both sides in the war had in fact worn themselves out. The introduction of the American Expeditionary Force, with its endless supply of men and material, spelled the end of German aspirations. Germany was simply not capable of sustaining a war against the United States. That was clear to anyone familiar with the details of the war.

Yet most Germans were not familiar with the details of the war. The German government, in part to bolster sagging morale, kept the German populace uninformed of the deep deterioration of the war effort. This was possible because on the surface matters were fairly reassuring. German armies continued to occupy enemy territory on both fronts well into 1918. In fact, in June 1918, the German army was able to launch a massive offensive that at first appeared to overwhelm Allied defenses. To the German population, the army seemed well in control of the situation. What was not apparent to most German citizens was that the June offensive was in fact a last desperate gamble to save the war for Germany. Five months later, Germans awoke to find that their country had surrendered and done so *unconditionally.* The struggles and privations of the previous four years were suddenly for nothing.

THE TREATY OF VERSAILLES

The surrender was provoked by a series of crises. By September 1918, the army realized all was lost and, hoping to salvage what it could, urged the government to sue for peace. Assuming the Allies would show more leniency to a democratic regime, the imperial government in Berlin formally reconstituted itself as a republic. Then, on October 30, 1918 (a mere two days after the new government was constituted), part of the High Seas Fleet mutinied. What began as an isolated incident on two ships, the *Thueringen* and the *Helgoland,* soon spread to the major port of Kiel (November 4) and finally to virtually the whole navy (November 7). The mutiny seems to have been connected not with the change in government but with the conduct of the war. There could hardly be a clearer indication of how low German military morale had fallen or of how weak the new government was. In the frantic maneuvering that took place over the next few days, Kaiser Wilhelm II was finally persuaded to resign. His resignation persuaded some of the radical left-wing groups that now was the best time to bring to fruition in Germany the revolution that had occurred in Russia two years earlier. On November 9, a band of leftist revolutionaries, spearheaded by the Spartacists under the leadership of Rosa Luxemburg and Karl Liebknecht marched into Berlin. Meanwhile the naval revolt was spreading to the army. Government leaders, afraid that Germany was about to fall to leftist socialists and unable even to control the military, saw their options quickly vanishing. To salvage what little of Germany they could, they sued for peace on any terms. The resulting armistice was signed on November 11. It is clear to us now that much of the pressure to sign came from military leaders who hoped to save what they could of the army, and from frantic politicians who hoped to neutralize the socialist revolution. These niceties were lost on the public, however. For most Germans, the surrender came to be seen as a humilating betrayal perpetrated by the new liberal government.[10] Thus the first democratic government in modern Germany began under a cloud of suspicion. When the details of the treaty it signed became known, the suspicion turned into outright disgust.

The terms of the Treaty of Versailles are important because they set the stage for all subsequent German internal and foreign-policy moves. The treaty was by any measure humilating, adding insult to the injury of losing the war. That it could be so brutal is testimony to how the war, blamed on Germany, had traumatized all of Europe. The treaty was clearly meant to be a punishment and was correctly perceived by Germans as just that. In broad detail, the treaty stipulated that Germany was to give up territory that it had annexed, territory it considered an intrinsic part of its historical domain. In addition, Germany was to be divested of all its colonial holdings, the best of which were to be divided between France and Great Britain. The economy was saddled with huge reparations (France demanded reparations for the full cost of the war!) designed, it seems, to stifle any future German industrial development. In effect, all capital generated in Germany was to be paid over to its enemies. The German military, a symbol of the nation's identity, was severely limited in size. The republic, established at Weimar (hence the name Weimar Republic), was ratified as the only acceptable government of Germany, and German military leaders were to be tried for committing "crimes of war."

The treaty, understandably, was bitterly resented by the Germans. The Weimar government, which was set up by the treaty and whose leaders signed the agreement, became instantly identified with the treaty and so became the objects of broad public scorn. Matters might have sorted themselves out more favorably had the government been able over succeeding years to deal with Germany's vast social and economic problems forcefully and successfully. Unfortunately, and maybe inevitably, matters turned out exactly the opposite. The Weimar government was a failure on virtually all fronts: political, social, and economic. In its wake numerous dissident political parties appeared, among these Anton Drexler's German Workers' party, the small group that was to attract Hitler's attention and that he would turn into the core of the Nazi party.[11]

THE WEIMAR REPUBLIC

It is disconcerting to trace voting patterns in Weimar from 1919 to 1933, the year Hitler became the last chancellor of the Weimar Republic. In 1919, there were numerous votes for both right-wing (monarchical) parties and left-wing (radical socialist) parties—both of which were ideologically opposed to the very political theory on which the Weimar Republic was based. Fortunately, the Social Democrats and their pro-Weimar allies initially enjoyed a majority of the votes. This majority, however, shrank with each election. By the early 1930s the inevitable occurred. The pro-Weimar parties actually constituted a minority within the Reichstag. Because of the diversity of the anti-Weimar parties and because of the unbridgeable chasm between the left-wingers and the right-wingers, there was, however, no actual coalition that stood ready to abolish the Reichstag. But the shocking fact remains that by the early 1930s, the majority of delegates sent to the Reichstag were ideologically committed to other forms of government.

The result was that the Weimar experience from 1919 to 1933 was a chain of disasters. In response to the peace treaty and the imposition of the Weimar government, a political backlash developed. Personal armies (*Freikorps*) roamed the streets in open defiance of the government. A wave of assassinations took place in 1918 and 1919, claiming, among others, the most prominent socialist leaders. In 1920, a serious coup (the Kapp putsch) was attempted. Then in 1922, the German economy collapsed. In 1921, the mark stood at a weak seventy-five to the American dollar. A year later, in January 1922, it sold for four hundred to the dollar. In early 1923, it had fallen to about seven thousand to the dollar, representing an annual inflation rate of ninety-three hundred percent. In January 1923, France forcibly occupied Germany's industrial heartland because of arrears in reparation payments. Not only was this a blow to German national pride but it wreaked havoc on what remained of the German economy. By midsummer of 1923, the mark had fallen to one hundred sixty thousand to the dollar; by August, one million to the dollar; and by the end of the year, an estimated one billion. The personal suffering this caused is hardly imaginable. Although the government was eventually able to bring the economy under control, the fact that such a crisis could develop at all severely undercut the government's credibility. Memories of these terrible years were surely responsible for the collapse of support in 1929 and 1930, when a new depression began to develop.

From almost any perspective it was clear by 1930 that the Weimar government was not working. In light of the government's failure, a number of trends and perceptions emerged that were to shape the subsequent German political imagination. We can identify at least five such themes running through ensuing political discussions. The first was the conviction that the current political expression of the German nation was seriously diseased.[12] This realization generated two urgent needs. The first was to identify what was wrong, and the second to devise a strategy for fixing it. On both points there was understandably vast disagreement. Voting patterns tell us that a majority of the electorate had concluded that the Weimar government was part of the problem. This meant that a whole new order of government was necessary. Various models existed for what that might be. The rightists had in mind the model of an imperial Germany, such as that of the Second Reich, which flourished under Bismarck. Here was a Germany that was— at least in popular memory—militarily successful, internationally respected, and economically healthy. It was organized, as the rightists saw matters, according to the traditional and authentically Teutonic manner of *Kaisertum,* that is, with power concentrated in a strong head of state. The leftists had in mind another model entirely. For them the problem was not in democracy but in the economic structure of capitalism. They hoped to solve Germany's problem through a socialist reconstruction of German society, possibly even on the model of Russian bolshevism. Thus while almost everyone could agree that the existing form of government was ineffectual, there was no agreement as to what was the most appropriate form of government or social structure to be put in its stead.

A second emerging theme in this period was the increasing brutality of German politics. The experience of the war was certainly one cause behind this development. The wave of assassinations that followed the war establishes a kind of pattern. People were desperate to find a solution to the ongoing anarchy in Germany, especially when faced with the prospect of a new economic collapse. When one's opponents are brutal and violent, it is all too natural to adopt brutality and violence in self-defense. As the stakes became higher, the level of violence tended to become higher as well.

Third, Germany had experienced a Europe that was vengeful and brutal. When Germany was defeated and helpless after the war, its neighbors took advantage of it in every way they could. This was to some extent the fruit of Bismarck's own actions. He had projected Germany as a violent power and had never sought to build bridges of accommodation and understanding. When the other European countries had a chance to take their vengeance, they did. But in so doing, they provided Germany with further reason to express itself in Europe through military means. The German fixation on the military as a tool for conducting foreign policy was ratified and enhanced by Europe's treatment of Germany after the war.

Fourth, there was the theme of territory. Germany had achieved honor and glory by bringing together its diverse territories and uniting them under one government. Germany's humiliation after World War I took the form, at least in part, of dismemberment. A symbol of a revitalized Germany, then, would be the reunification of the true German lands. This was a matter of not only political or economic need (although such need existed) but also self-perception, identity, and national pride.

Fifth, there was the theme of Germany's isolation among sworn enemies. In World War I, Germany had been forced to fight a two-front war, against Russia in the East and against France and Britain in the West. True, Russia had withdrawn from the war after its revolution, but for most Germans this was not comforting. Russia was now the home of bolshevism, a style of government it was clearly interested in exporting to Germany. It had in fact almost succeeded once, under the Spartacists. France, as the treaty showed, was dedicated to the utter humiliation and even destruction of Germany. So as Germany contemplated rebuilding itself and establishing security within Europe, it had to keep in mind its two prime enemies: Russia in the East and

France in the West. What united them was, clearly, their visceral hatred of "Aryans."

Thus a number of important new themes and perceptions emerged during the period in which the new Nazi ethic was incubating. What was desperately needed by Germany was a theory of why Germany was constantly suffering and a program for dealing with that problem. Any model that offered a framework for engineering Germany's salvation was sure to receive a sympathetic hearing. Such a framework Hitler developed in Munich, and it took as its central symbol the ancient and mythic Western incarnation of evil: the Jew.

5

The Social Context of the New Ethic: Jews and Judaism in the Second Reich

In the years immediately following the defeat of World War I, the inherited ethic was already in a serious state of decay (see chap. 4). All the components for a new ethic were at hand, waiting only to be assembled. What Hitler, and later his followers, did was place anti-Judaism at the center and use this as the hub into which all other intellectual trends were fitted as spokes. Once all the pieces were in place, an embryonic ethic emerged that continued to grow and find adherents. Part 2 below will trace the growth and maturation of this ethic as it developed from a sectarian vision to a political platform to government policy and finally to the basis of an empire.

Because anti-Judaism was the conceptual centerpiece of the new ethic, the specific content of Nazi anti-Judaism was the foundation for all that was to follow. This was so because the Nazis openly defined Judaism as the real enemy of the German Volk, ascribed to it a certain mode of warfare, and then consciously set about constructing their own response in light of what would be appropriate to the posited Jewish threat.

The Nazi perception was leavened by the particular character the Nazis understood Judaism to have in Germany. They believed that Jews were distinct from Aryans in all ways, but they also saw that Jews were completely and utterly entangled in German society and culture. That gave the Nazi ethic a clear-cut mission: to effect a disentanglement. The paradoxical thesis that Jews were a part of Germany and yet distinctly alien grew out of a number of "evidences" presented in the decades before the rise of the Nazi party.

THE ENLIGHTENMENT AND THE JEWS

Partly the paradoxical thesis grew out of a peculiar ambivalence felt by both Jews and Germans that goes back to the very character of Jewish reception into German society during the Enlightenment. The era of the Enlightenment—or as it is often labeled in Jewish historiography, the

Emancipation—began full of promise. The new secular states of Europe were to be governed by rational laws that recognized the inalienable rights of all people, regardless of creed. In this new age of liberty and equality, Jews were to be accorded the same civil rights as everyone else. They were to be full citizens in the modern, secular, Enlightened state.[1] The hidden expectation, of course, was that Jews themselves would be willing and able to participate on an equal basis in the social and political world of the state. From the point of view of the political and intellectual leaders of the Enlightenment, this made perfect sense. How could a country grant equality to people who refused to be a part of that country's social and political life? Yet traditional Jews, though welcoming the promise of the Emancipation in general, greeted the call for assimilation into the culture with some misgivings. They understood assimilationist expectations as calling for the destruction of traditional Jewish culture and the abandonment of the Jewish religious life style, that is, for a turning away from the covenant that called for God alone to rule the Jewish people. For traditionalist Jews such a move was unthinkable. Many Jews were thus caught in a cruel trap: in order to gain political and legal rights, they had to give up their Judaism; on the other hand, if they insisted on remaining faithful to their vision of God, they had to forgo the benefits of European civilization. Napoleon himself saw the dilemma and gave it its classic formulation: "For Jews as Frenchmen everything, for Jews as Jews nothing."[2] To Jewish ears the message was that it was permitted to be a Jew as long as that did not involve acting "Jewishly." The history of Judaism in the nineteenth century is the history of countless personal struggles to find an escape from this cruel tension.

With regard to the new pressures applied to Judaism by the Enlightenment and its political ideology, there seemed to be four options. At one extreme stood the possibility of complete and utter rejection of all that Emancipation promised, in favor of remaining loyal to God's covenant through participation in traditional Jewish communal life. Like the Amish in America today, those opting for this course maintained a separate (and holy) life by removing themselves from the modern world. At the other extreme was conversion to mainstream Christianity. That eliminated the tension too, but by granting allegiance to culture while still affirming the importance of religion. To be sure, many of the conversions to Christianity were sincere, but many others were simply a matter of social convenience, providing the convert with a "ticket to European society," in Heine's phrase.[3] Between these extremes—the extremes of Orthodox Judaism and Christianity—lay two other strategies. The first was to assimilate into European secular society without any overt break with Judaism. For many educated Jews, the loss of the credibility of Orthodox Judaism and the attractiveness of modern secular European society entailed the loss of credibility of all organized religions, a sentiment in any event consistent with Enlightenment culture. If these people could no longer be Orthodox Jews because of their Enlightened thinking, neither could they become Catholics or Lutherans. They simply slipped into the great mass of the European population that had no strong religious faith, married other such folks whether of Jewish background or not, and became indistinguishable from everyone else. Their grandchildren were surprised, even scandalized, to find in 1930 that they had Jewish roots or that there had been great rabbis in their ancestry. These three routes—Orthodox separation, conversion, and the abandonment of organized religion—all were resisted by most German Jews. The fourth response, and the second of the two strategies for avoiding the extremes of Orthodox Judaism and Christianity, sought to combine the essence of Judaism with the best features of Enlightened Europe. Such a construct would allow the individual to retain his or her psychological ties to Judaism and its God while being able fully to participate in European society. This strategy resulted in what came to be known as Reform Judaism.[4] In essence, what Reform Judaism claimed was that the central core of Judaism was its moral laws as summarized and taught in the Ten Commandments. These moral standards could in most cases be clearly distinguished from the "ceremonial laws," which were the historically contingent way in which Jewish values expressed themselves. Reform Jews found that they could give up many of the distinctively Jewish *cultural* traits—kosher dietary restrictions, special attire, the Yiddish language, and so forth—while still retaining the essential Jewish religious and ethical values. A considerable scholarly literature arose in German Judaism laying the intellectual groundwork for this enterprise. For the larger part of Germany's Jews, this model of Judaism proved by the end of the nineteenth century to be the most attractive. The reasons are easy to see. Reform Judaism allowed its adherents to function in the modern world, partaking of all its benefits and comforts, without having to suffer the turmoil of formally renouncing Judaism and betraying their heritage. On the other hand, for the Nazis this mode of Judaism was the most insidious and feared, since it allowed Jews to retain their Jewishness while "masquerading" as Aryans.

By the late nineteenth century, three of these routes—Reform, the abandonment of organized religion, and conversion—represented the choices taken by the majority of Jews in central and western European Judaism, with Orthodox Judaism being the choice of a distinct minority.[5] Most central European Jews, regardless of which of the three routes they chose, saw themselves as good, solid citizens of Germany. The tragedy was that a critical mass of other Europeans, like the Nazis, refused to see matters in this way. For them, the Jews remained essentially Jewish, and therefore outsiders, even if they adopted a veneer of modern culture. As it turned out, the Jews' sense that they were at last becoming a part of European society was a grand illusion.

The refusal to accept Jews as equal members of European civilization was due to a number of causes. Surely the agelong religious and social contempt for the Jews (see chaps. 1 and 2) was a significant factor. That legacy made people willing to believe that all Jews, qua Jews, were evil. It is also true that many segments of European society had never accepted the basic egalitarian premises of the Enlightenment to begin with—the old aristocracies, for example. These groups resented their loss of power, influence, and status, and they directed their anger against those who had gained most visibly from the Enlightenment, predominant among whom were the Jews. Finally, people found the broad humanistic values of the Enlightenment—such as the value stressing the essential equality of all people—to be counterintuitive. The Germans and the French and the Italians *were* different from one another. The universalism that was part of the very foundation of Enlightenment thought, and of Jewish Emancipation, was broadly rejected as untrue by the late nineteenth century, especially in light of the rising racial and nationalistic sentiments sweeping across Europe. At all events, by the turn of the twentieth century, the intellectual tradition that offered Jews equality and freedom in Europe had been implicitly rejected by the masses. Thus at the same time that Jews were embracing the Enlightenment and reaping its rewards, their neighbors were largely rejecting the Enlightenment and confirming their suspicion that Jews really were ontologically different.

This counter-Enlightenment strain of thought, generally labeled Romanticism, stressed the uniqueness and individuality of each culture. On a popular level, this often meant that members of any one culture came to see their culture not only as different but as actually superior to all others. In Germany, the Romantic ideology took the form of stressing Germanic and Teutonic virtues over all others'. In this context Jews were clearly outsiders. They did not share in the essence of Teutonism: Aryan blood, German Christianity, the glories of the German Christian past, the deep ethnic character of the German people that gave rise to particular German art and thought. They were, in short, unable to participate in the German Volkgeist. A passage written by the respected German historian and politician Heinrich von Treitschke gave this view a popular expression:

> I am not an adherent of the doctrine of the Christian state. The state is a secular organization and should act with justice and impartiality toward non-Christians also. But without any doubt, we Germans are a Christian nation. To spread our universal religion among the heathen, our ancestors shed their blood; to develop and perfect it, they suffered and battled as martyrs and heroes. At every step, as I progress deeper in understanding of the history of our country, it becomes more and more clear to me how deeply Christianity is entwined with every fiber of the German character. . . . Christian ideals inspire our arts and sciences. Christian spirit animates all healthy institutions of

our state and our society. Judaism, on the other hand, is the national religion of a tribe which was originally alien to us.[6]

THE DREYFUS AFFAIR

Nor was this attitude restricted to the German state. It surfaced even in France, the birthplace of the Enlightenment. The most striking example of France's retreat from Enlightenment values is in the infamous trial of Captain Alfred Dreyfus in 1894. Nothing could indicate more strikingly how shallow the acceptance of Jews in Europe had become. France, the cradle of European liberalism, exploded in a fury of anti-Semitism the viciousness of which caught virtually everyone off guard.

There are two aspects to this series of trials. The Dreyfus *case* involved a Jewish army captain accused of spying. It involved a twelve-year process of conviction, appeals, and finally a reluctant semi-vindication. The Dreyfus *affair* was a massive cultural orgy of anti-Semitism sparked by the case, a concerted protest against liberal, democratic France (symbolized by the Jew) mounted by the self-proclaimed defenders of traditional French values, including monarchists and the French Catholic church. The affair took on the ugliness and prominence it did because it extended to the highest levels of French society and government.[7]

The case began when Dreyfus was court-martialed in the fall of 1894 on charges of sending secret French military papers to the Germans. The single piece of hard evidence was a document sent to the German emissary which fell into the hands of French intelligence. On the basis of a similarity in handwriting, as well as other evidence produced in secret, Dreyfus was convicted, publicly demoted, and sentenced to prison for life.

What turned this case into an "affair" was the series of events that then unfolded. First, the French right transformed the case into a massive anti-Jewish spectacle, implicating all French Jews in Dreyfus's treason. At the same time, a number of people began to question the conduct of the trial, including the Dreyfus family itself; the writer Bernard Lazare, who had conducted his own inquiry in the accusation; and the new head of French intelligence, Georges Picquart. Picquart, who was spurred by his own suspicions, the publication of Lazare's book, and the discovery of a real German mole, Major Ferdinand Esterhazy, in the French military, called publicly for a new trial. He was immediately relieved of his post by the French government and sent to a remote post in Africa. Before leaving, he turned his file over to a senator, Auguste Scheurer-Kestner, who finally succeeded in having a new trial arranged. In this trial, Esterhazy was acquitted and Picquart was sentenced to sixty days in jail.

At this juncture, Emile Zola took up Dreyfus's case. In an open letter to the French president, Zola strongly accused the government of engaging in out-and-out anti-Semitism. This produced a swift and ugly reaction. Zola was arrested and sent to jail, the French general staff threatened to resign en masse if Dreyfus were acquitted, and anti-Jewish riots broke out throughout the country. In a tense atmosphere a new trial was finally convened. Now, however, the evidence that convicted Dreyfus was shown to have been forged. Also discovered to have been forged were papers in the file used to acquit Esterhazy and convict Picquart. The suspected forger, Major H. J. Henry, was identified and arrested but committed suicide in prison before he could be formally tried. Despite these revelations, Dreyfus's conviction was upheld, although "due to extenuating circumstances," the court reduced his sentence to ten years. In 1904, Dreyfus, having been imprisoned the ten years, was granted a presidential pardon. Two years later a special investigating committee concluded that the evidence against him was insubstantial but decreed also that a further trial to exonerate him completely was "unnecessary." On that note, the case and the affair ended.

The affair, however, had far-reaching effects.[8] With the final, half-hearted vindication of Dreyfus, liberals quickly moved to render impotent the now morally discredited right. The government of Pierre-Marie René Waldeck-Rousseau, which had pushed for the retrial, formally broke ties between the state and the Catholic church. Meanwhile, leftists in France, which had up to then identified the Jews with the capitalist bourgeoisie, came to see them as another oppressed minority and, accordingly, comrades in arms. As a result, the leftists took up the case of the Jews. The Dreyfus Affair was thus a signal defeat for the traditionalist forces that wanted to see Dreyfus hang—especially for the monarchists, the military, and the Catholic church—whereas new, liberal Enlightenment parties achieved through the affair an unprecedented victory and new political clout. The implications of this turn of events were not lost on German rightists. They had witnessed the Jews of France wage a concerted battle that resulted in the humiliating defeat and discreditation of the French religious and aristocratic establishment. For them, the danger of a Jewish victory over "indigenous nationalists" was now a historical fact.

Added to this stunning political victory of "the Jews" against the right, other evidence was mounting that convinced the right that Jewish influence had to be controlled. The evidence took the form of a bizarre document purporting to be the minutes of a secret meeting in which Jewish leaders discussed their plans to take over the world. According to these minutes, commonly entitled "Protocols of the Elders of Zion," Jewish conspirators were planning systematically to take over the various national governments of Europe under the guise of introducing liberal democracy. The takeover would provide a base for Jewish control of the world economy. Any attempt to establish a liberal democracy could thus be seen by rightist readers of the "Protocols" as a Jewish conspiracy.

The document had actually been composed by an agent in the czarist secret police, probably to influence the anti-Jewish policy of Czar Nicholas, himself an anti-Semite. This Russian version appeared in a number of editions between 1901 and 1903[9] and simply reworked an older French pamphlet written by Maurice Joly against the ambitions of Napoleon III. The forger did little more than change all references to Napoleon to references to the Jews. When it was openly published in Russia in 1905 it received almost no attention outside a few sectarian mystic circles. But to the nationalists and to anti-Semitic circles of Europe, reeling as they were from the stunning blow dealt them by the Dreyfus Affair, the pamphlet came as a godsend. At last there was an explanation of why and how they had been led to defeat. It fitted in perfectly with their own view of matters—that the real dangers in the world were liberalism and socialism, now exposed as being in reality part of a Jewish plot. This thesis was bolstered because it drew on common anti-Judaic themes from the Middle Ages. Medieval Jews, we have seen, were portrayed as ritual murderers and well-poisoners undermining Christian society. They were the anti-Christ, sinister, never to be trusted. They could draw on international connections because of their clannishness. Now the descendants of these enemies were suddenly revealed by the "Protocols" to be working in similar ways to take over all of modern Europe. A whole new myth of Jews and Judaism coalesced in the minds of German rightists, a myth that took on a life of its own by the 1920s. Nor did the myth perpetrated by the "Protocols" find an audience in Russia and Germany alone. The pamphlet went through a number of printings in the United States and was popularized in part by Henry Ford I.[10]

HITLER'S PERCEPTION OF THE JEWS

It was against this background that Hitler began his search for the enemies of Germany after the defeat of World War I. He fixated on the Jews while a starving art student in Vienna. There he encountered, possibly for the first time, the Orthodox and unassimilated Jews of eastern Europe. He asked himself, he reported, Is this a German? The answer, self-evidently, was no.

Once the Jews had been identified as non-Germans, a number of consequences followed according to rightist thinking. If the Jews were not German, then they had to be, by the nature of things, avowed enemies of Germany, for as we have seen, all racial groups are inherently enemies of one another. That the Jews engaged in racial warfare was clearly and extensively documented throughout history, from New Testament times through the Middle Ages to the present. Over the centuries, the racial war pursued by the Jews had taken on a more subtle tone. It was now political and economic. The Jews had conspired to insinuate themselves into Germany and destroy its social foundation from within. This tactic had already enjoyed success in France and would again enjoy a victory through the Russian Revolution, where Jewish association with socialism and Marxism was clear and was central to the overthrow of the Czarist regime. Now, through such mechanisms as Reform Judaism, assimilationism, and intermarriage, Jews were working their way into German society as well. In the context of this thinking, the defeat and dismemberment of Germany in 1918 took on ominous tones. The chances for an Aryan recovery were rapidly diminishing.

Once the battlefield had been located and described in these terms, certain conclusions followed. As in most classic just-war theories, the right to defend oneself could take priority over other concerns. Further, the acts of warfare that were deemed morally permissible were derived in large part from what the enemy was reputed to be doing. That is, the character of the enemy, or the character ascribed to the enemy, became the basis for evaluating what one might do in order to defend oneself. Since in this case the Jews were assumed to be stooping to the most insidious of methods, it followed that the German response would have to be just as insidious. By describing the struggle as warfare, and by imputing complete immorality to the opponents, the stage was set for suspending the dictates of conventional ethics.

It was the despair and suffering of the twenties that finally propelled people to accept the implications of this new view. When it was adopted, it was not that conventional ethical categories no longer applied. It was rather that they applied differently in a war situation. Since just-war theories were a recognized component of Western ethics, the jump to this new way of relating to Jews, Gypsies, and others required only that one concede that racial war was at hand. Once this was accepted, the rest followed relatively painlessly and naturally.

PART TWO

THE GROWTH OF AN ETHIC

The Nazi party came to power in 1933 prepared to supply Germany with a complete and functional system for explaining good and evil and defining right and wrong. That is, the Nazis had an ethic, complete with warrants, that they claimed was able to explain all relevant reality and evaluate all relevant activities. This ethic, however, was still sectarian, and so somewhat formal and abstract. It controlled a rhetoric but not yet concrete social and political institutions beyond its own narrow circle of believers. From 1933 onward, however, this formal ethic took on specific content as it engaged the real social and political world first of Germany and then of the rest of Europe. The following chapters trace the actualization of the Nazi ethic from its tentative beginnings in 1933 through the construction and management of death factories, to the culmination in Auschwitz twelve years later. These years, then, are a study of how people fitted reality into the grid of meaning created by a formal ethical discourse. In the crematoriums of Auschwitz we see clearly how completely ethical discourse does in fact create worlds.

6

The Smallest Circle:
Germany, 1933–1939

THE FIRST YEARS

Drawing on a fascist ideology that saw politics in terms of warfare and assuming that Germany's real enemies were racial and accepting that the most dangerous racial group within Germany were the Jews, the Nazis not surprisingly had among their first priorities combating "Jewish influence." It was, of course, one thing to posit a racial enemy in idealist and abstract terms and quite another to deal with such an enemy within an actual society. Once the notion that one was engaged in warfare was accepted, however, the steps necessary to fight the requisite racial war among one's own neighbors could be justified. Gradually over the next decade, the Nazi party probed the limits of justifiability as regards the new ethic it propounded.

THE FIRST STEP

The removal of Jews from German society began slowly and tentatively, gaining momentum as each new barrier was successfully hurdled. The first step was to remove Jews from the German government. This was imperative since the Nazi party in effect "annexed" the government as one of its extensions, a process labeled the *Gleichschaltung,* or "political coordination." Since the party conceived of itself as the muster of the authentic Aryan Volk, it was impossible to tolerate Jews—or other non-Aryans—as part of the leadership cadre. The first stage in the *Gleichschaltung* involved purging the civil service by retiring or in other ways removing all Jewish employees. This process proved relatively easy and apparently provoked little protest, because it affected relatively few people and was restricted to a well-defined sector of society. Yet the overall vision of the party was not merely to annex the government but to recast German society itself, to merge the Volk and the party. That would mean that Jews and other non-Aryans would have to be purged from all influential posts across the society: from financial institutions, the arts, academia, the professions, industrial complexes. This proved to be a much more difficult problem, because the neat racial categories assumed by idealist ideologies do not exist in real life. The Nazi policy of consolidation in its earliest stages was in effect a long exercise in forcing reality to fit a preconceived racial grid.

The problem of defining who was and was not Jewish proved to be a Gordian knot—one that was finally solved only by fiat.[1] The boundaries of Judaism, as of any ism, are vague and somewhat impressionistic. According to traditional rabbinic law, a Jew is one who either is born of a Jewish mother or has formally converted to Judaism. This definition seems to incorporate two different theories of Jewishness: one that is based on genealogy (born of a Jewish mother) and one that is based on faith (conversion). Because the Nazis were convinced that Jews made up a clear-cut racial group and that race was a clear-cut ontological reality, they simply assumed that the precise determination of who was Jewish would be a fairly straightforward process.[2] Certainly a person born of Jewish parents and a practitioner of the Jewish religion was a Jew. That, in fact, was the operative model. But what about a person who was of "Aryan" blood but who had formally converted to Judaism? Was such a one to be considered Jewish, despite that person's "Aryan" blood? Or, conversely, what about a person of pure Jewish parentage who did not practice Judaism or who formally adopted Christianity? Was this person to be considered a Christian or a Jew? If such a one was to be deemed a Christian, what was to happen to the theory that Judaism is a racial group? On the other hand, if such a one was still a Jew, what would be the status of children born to that person? Did not such a person in fact convey Jewish blood into the offspring despite the person's conversion to Christianity? Might not a third-generation (or tenth-generation) Christian still be Jewish? Such questions were by no means only theoretical. Tens of thousands of Germans and their offspring were in fact in such anomalous positions. There had been a marked increase over the previous century of German Jewish conversions to Christianity and of Jews marrying non-Jews and simply giving up Judaism albeit with no formal conversion. All these couples had children and grandchildren. Likewise there had been a modest number of Christian converts into Judaism. For the Nazi ideological purists, the task of purging all Jewish blood from the Aryan population was a sacred duty. Thus some order had to be made out of what was turning out to be a very complex situation. The bureaucrats clearly had their work cut out for them.

The result, not surprisingly, was a patchwork compromise and, so, doubly unfair: not only did it create an inferior category of people by law but its definition of who was included was somewhat arbitrary. In fact, a number of different definitions were tried in succession. The first definition emerged as part of the civil-service reform. It defined as non-Aryan anybody with Jewish parents or grandparents. A parent or grandparent was considered Jewish if he or she belonged to the Jewish *religion*. Note that already this definition combined both religion and blood. The parents' or grandparents' status depended on faith; the child's depended on blood affiliation. This led to a further problem in that the definition cast a much wider net than was intuitively correct. A large number of good Catholic or Lutheran Germans had at least one Jewish grandparent, for example. Suddenly, those people found themselves defined as Jews, with all that that would mean in Nazi Germany.

THE RACIAL LAWS

The stakes were raised considerably with the passage of the "Law for the Protection of German Blood and Honor," or the so-called Nuremberg Laws of September 13, 1935. These laws were designed to segregate Jews socially from the surrounding Aryans. By including stipulations that banned Jews from displaying the German flag, for example, the laws prevented Jews from participating in German national and patriotic activities—not an insignificant symbolic move in a country now driven by unbridled nationalism based on martial metaphors. More significant, the laws forbade marriages between Jews and Aryans. Given the broad definition of "Jewish" presupposed by the earlier law, this legislation had a devastating effect on a considerable number of people.

The sense that the definition of Jewishness was both too broad and too vague led to an attempt to fashion a more precise and fair definition of who was to be deemed a Jew. The new definition, promulgated as the "Reich Citizenship Law" in November 1935, established four categories of people, an important indication of how detailed and serious the consideration of this matter had become. The four categories were fully Jewish, Mischling of the first degree, Mischling of the second degree, and non-Jewish. The distinctions are complex but are worth looking at in detail because they show how closely bureaucrats were already entangled in the hopeless cause of defining racial groups in precise terminology posited on the basis of ideology. It also shows how much the implementation of Nazi policy depended on the hard work of vast numbers of civil servants at all levels of government.

The definition of a full Jew had two parts. The first stipulated that any person who had at least three Jewish grandparents was ipso facto Jewish, regardless of that person's faith. The second part dealt with people who had only two Jewish grandparents (i.e., one fully Jewish parent or two "half-Jewish" parents). In such a case, the person in question was legally defined as a full Jew if that person belonged to the Jewish religious community on September 15, 1935, or was married to a full Jew on September 15, 1935. Further, a person was deemed a full Jew if he or she were the offspring of parents who were both three-fourths or full Jews after September 15, 1935, or was the offspring of an illegitimate union of a three-fourths Jew after July 31, 1936 (i.e., nine months after September 15, 1935). The Mischling categories dealt with people who had one or two

Jewish grandparents and did not meet the criteria above. If the person in question had two Jewish grandparents but none of the other above stipulations applied, that person was declared to be a first-degree Mischling. A person with only one Jewish grandparent was a second-degree Mischling. People with no Jewish grandparents were assumed to be non-Jewish, unless they had formally converted.

The complexity of these rules indicates not only the trouble that the German bureaucracy had in dealing with the question of who was a Jew but also the determination with which they pursued an answer. Bureaucracies hate ambiguity and this particular ambiguity was solved with intricate care. The state now had a working definition of a Jew. In essence, to be cleared of all suspicion, you had to be able to produce seven certificates of baptism: yours, two for your parents, and four for your grandparents. It became one of the constant harassments of Nazi Germany to require citizens to prove their Aryan ancestry by producing these seven documents.

The new racial definitions created unprecedented problems. Overnight, as it were, there came into being whole new racial categories, the legal status of which were utterly unclear. Mischlings were certainly not Jews in the traditional sense, but now they were declared not to be really Aryan either. How, then, were they to be treated? To deal with this sizable population, two opposing policies gradually emerged within the bureaucracy. The first was simply to ignore fine distinctions and absorb these groups into the traditional binary Nazi pattern: First-degree Mischlings were to be treated as Jews; second-degree Mischlings were to be treated as Aryans. This policy had the advantage of being ideologically clean. The second, favored by the bureaucracy, was to retain the intermediate categories as reflective of reality but then to develop policies—such as eugenics—that would allow these mixed-blood categories eventually to die out. In general, the actual policy throughout the history of the Third Reich was a compromise. Second-degree Mischlings were "upgraded" to Aryan status, but first-degree Mischlings remained a separate racial taxon and so a perennial intellectual problem—a constant reminder of the world's failure to conform to the Nazi theory of clear racial divisions.

The first-degree Mischlings, some two hundred fifty thousand souls, found themselves living in a sort of twilight zone. They were too Aryan to be treated as Jews and too Jewish to be treated as Aryans. Because of their Jewishness, they were banned from the party, the civil service, and the army. Nor could they marry Aryans unless they had special permission. Since in Nazi Germany it would have been foolish for them to marry a Jew (since this would raise their status and that of their children to full Jews), they remained restricted to marrying within their own thinning ranks. It is not surprising that this group later supplied the victims for some of the Nazi experiments in mass sterilization. The only way out of this ideologically constructed trap was to have one's status legally upgraded. A whole racial court system came into being specifically to handle the problems of racial classification.

ARYANIZATION

The laws defining who was a Jew carried with them increasingly drastic repercussions. The first was the purge of the civil service that we have already mentioned. The second occurred in conjunction with the new laws promulgated in 1935. The purge of Jews in government was expanded, and those Jews forced to retire lost all pension rights. The citizenship laws, then, accomplished the final "disentanglement" of the Jews from Aryan government. The third stage was to disentangle Jews from the Aryan economy. This process came to be known as Aryanization and deserves some scrutiny because it illustrates how pervasive racial thinking had become in German society at large. Aryanization proceeded under the assumption that just as people could be classified as Jewish or non-Jewish, so too could property.[3] A firm was deemed to be Jewish if it was owned by Jews or if it had Jewish representation on its board, or at times even if its legal representation was Jewish. The law demanded that if a business was determined to be Jewish (on the basis of the racial definition outlined above), then it was to be confiscated and sold to an Aryan buyer. Large German corporations were thus forced to retire Jewish board members and managers or face the prospect of being declared Jewish. On the other hand, Jewish business people and managers were hopelessly ensnared: they could neither be employed by large corporations nor operate their own firms. They had nowhere to turn. At first, the process of selling Jewish business to Aryans was "voluntary," although certain pressures were applied such as boycotts and allocation controls. Needless to say, Jews who sold their businesses under these circumstances never received fair compensation. Later, as the party became more anxious to eliminate Jewish-owned businesses, economic and political pressures increased to the extent that many businesses were simply confiscated and assigned to new Aryan owners. Combined with the losses of pensions and the boycotts enforced against Jewish professionals (doctors, dentists, morticians, lawyers, stockbrokers, and the like), these measures led to the ever-increasing pauperization of the German Jewish community.

By 1938, the bulk of German Jewish businesses had already passed to Aryan hands. Yet many small family businesses survived and continued to operate. To hasten the completion of the Aryanization policy's goals, a law was enacted in this year that in effect took all initiative for selling Jewish business out of the hands of owners and transferred it to banks, which now became partners in the plunder. Banks, in collusion with Aryan buyers, established a price for Jewish property and presented their offer to the owner. There was still the possibility of refusal, but at this stage few saw any point. It was better to receive what little the banks and buyers proposed than to see the business confiscated. In this way the last vestiges of Jewish economic activity in Germany were slowly being erased. The effect, predictably enough, was the creation of a completely isolated and poverty-stricken class of people. Those people defined as Jews by the 1935 law now had no legal source of income by which to support themselves and their families. There was, of course, some illegal leakage of money into the Jewish economy. But to an extraordinary degree Jews who continued to live in German towns and villages had been entirely disengaged from the economy of the country in which they lived.

A final, and to some extent unplanned, step in the economic destruction of those defined as Jews was the wave of anti-Jewish riots that swept through Germany on November 9–10, 1938, an evening which has come to be known as *Krystallnacht,* the "night of broken glass." This incident is also important for the shaping of Nazi ethical discourse as Germany began to move toward war. The ostensible cause of this pogrom was the assassination of a German diplomat in France by a Jewish student. In fact, the pogroms were orchestrated by Paul Josef Goebbels, the Nazi minister of propaganda, and were abetted by the remnants of the old party paramilitary organization, the S.A., or *Sturmabteilung* (which had by now been displaced by what was once its elite bodyguard force, the S.S.). Goebbel's idea was to use the assassination of the diplomat as an occasion for taking control of the streets and thereby projecting himself as an essential power broker in the new Nazi state.[4] In particular, he hoped to use the opportunity to block the rising influence of his rivals in the S.S., the new elite "storm troops" of the party led by Himmler and Heydrich. In the end, his gambit failed: Himmler and Heydrich learned of the planned riots and quickly turned them to their own benefit. Some thirty thousand Jewish men were randomly arrested and sent to S.S. internment camps at Dachau, Buchenwald and Sachsenhausen, where they were held against the payment of ransom to the S.S. Meanwhile Himmler and Heydrich denounced the uncontrolled cruelty and brutality displayed by Goebbel's men, claiming that the S.A. tactic of physical violence threatened public support for the regime. In the end, Goebbels and his followers were discredited as brutal ruffians while the S.S. emerged as a new and respected force in Nazi Germany. The cool rationality of Himmler and Heydrich in dealing with Jews prevailed over the cruder methods of Goebbels and so made the S.S.'s single-minded pursuit of race war appear deliberate, rational, and businesslike. For the next eight years, the S.S. perpetrated barbarous outrages, at the same time appearing to be champions of law and order.

The real losers, of course, were the Jews. Virtually every remaining Jewish institution in Germany was ransacked and destroyed. Jewish stores and homes were systematically broken into and looted. So extensive and thorough was the destruction that streets throughout Germany were littered with broken glass from storefronts and synagogues. It is estimated that some seven thousand Jewish businesses were destroyed, essentially all that were left in Germany. Families were dragged out of their homes and subjected to beatings and humiliations as their personal belongings were destroyed or carried away. The American consul general filed a report on November 21: "Having demolished dwellings and hurled most of the moveable effects to the streets, the insatiably sadistic perpetrators threw many of the trembling inmates into a small stream that flows through the zoological park, commanding horrified spectators to spit at them, defile them with mud and jeer at their plight."[5]

Nor was employment the only area of life affected by one's legal racial status, especially after the passage of the Nuremberg Laws in 1935. As early as 1933 an ordinance was enacted restricting the number of Jews who could be admitted to institutions of higher education. The ordinance was passed on the pretext of solving a problem of overcrowding. It restricted Jewish matriculations to a percentage of total enrollment equivalent to the proportion of Jews in the population as a whole. By November 1938, the quotas gave way to the complete expulsion of Jews from German public schools. The year 1938 saw other regulations go into effect as well. Goebbels, for example, felt that it was inappropriate for a Jew to enjoy first-class rail travel along with Aryans. On his urging, a regulation was introduced by the transportation ministry banning Jews not only from first-class accommodations but also from sleeping cars and dining cars. This too paved the way for further decrees: in 1942, Jews in "greater Germany" were banned from waiting rooms and restaurants in railway stations.[6] These restrictions, along with the imposition of special Jewish shopping hours (between 11 A.M. and 1 P.M. and between 4 P.M. and 5 P.M. in Vienna; between 4 P.M. and 5 P.M. in Berlin) and the banishment of Jews from spas, public beaches, and even hospitals made casual contact between people defined as Jews and the rest of the population almost impossible.[7] To be classified as a Jew removed one utterly from society. The precise formulation of the law took on life-and-death importance for large numbers of people.

Matters did not end here, however. With the Jewish community in disarray and with Jewish families completely unable to support themselves any longer, the government was faced with the question of what to do with its now-indigent Jews. The policy that emerged from Berlin in the following days contained three broad economic punishments. First, the Jewish community would have to pay an indemnity of one billion marks for the death of the German diplomat in Paris. Second, the Jewish community would have to pay for all the damage caused to Aryan business during the riot, a total estimated at another quarter of a billion marks. Third, the government would promulgate a new series of economic regulations that stipulated that by the beginning of January 1939 no Jew could be employed in any way by an Aryan firm, that all Jewish businesses had to be Aryanized, that no Jewish real-estate firms or brokerage houses could operate, and that all outstanding Jewish physicians' licenses and dental licenses were to be revoked. The Jewish community was in this way dealt a double blow. It was made responsible for the payment of a huge debt at the same time that it had its last means of income shut off. The result was the final and total impoverishment of all those people who, whether they deserved the appellation or not, were defined as Jews by Nazi law. For most, their only meal of the day was earned through backbreaking work in labor battalions grudgingly organized by the German government.[8]

These actions must be understood in the context of the new ethic from which they sprang: since the Nazis, and especially the S.S. saw themselves as the protectors of German order and since the Jews were inimical to that order, clearly the Jews had provoked the riot despite what surface events seemed to suggest.

Despite the seeming arbitrariness or ad hoc nature of the economic policies, there was a rationale behind them. The goal at first was simply to encourage Jews to emigrate from Germany.[9] The theory was that if life were made difficult, Jews would eventually leave. In fact, the policies designed with this aim in mind had considerable effect.[10] At the beginning of Nazi rule, that is, in 1933, the Jewish population in Germany was approximately half a million. By 1939 it had declined to some 160 thousand persons, many of whom were too aged to leave (seventy-five percent were over forty). Germany was within sight of ridding its domain of all Jews, with the concomitant increase in national well-being which that would bring. During these years, however, a new dynamic took hold. Gradually German economic policy toward the Jews acquired a second, somewhat macabre, cast. The policy began to reflect a theory that everything the Jews owned in Germany had been illegitimately gained and that it all had to be returned. A kind of notion began to manifest itself in which German officials were convinced that Jews were still managing to steal Germany's wealth, even as they appeared at the ports with only the clothes on their backs (see chap. 14).

THE END OF THE JEWISH COMMUNITY

The arrest of Jews began even before *Krystallnacht,* although usually on an individual basis. During the *Krystallnacht* pogrom came the first indiscriminate and mass arrest of Jews. At the outbreak of war, the arrests became more systematic. With the creation of the S.S. system of concentration camps, and later of death camps, the arrest and deportation of Jews became a matter of bureaucratic routine. Jews were methodically arrested and deported to the camps. Older people and the infirm were transported to Theresienstadt. Young men still able to work were left behind to work in labor battalions until disease or starvation rendered them too weak; then they too were sent to camps. Special arrangements were even made to release Jewish inmates from hospitals, psychiatric wards, and prisons so that they could be sent to the S.S. camps. Only foreign Jews residing in Germany enjoyed any kind of immunity.[11] By 1943, the Jewish community in Germany had been entirely erased.

The elimination of "Jews" from German society created a new problem, one that illustrates the deliberateness and thoroughness with which the party pursued its racial policies while maintaining a deep dedication to fairness and due legal process in other areas of German life.[12] The problem was the need properly to dispose of property left behind by deported Jews. Beginning with the mass arrests of Jews after *Krystallnacht,* and continuing with the annexation of Austria, Czechoslovakia, and Poland, and their Jewish populations, the problem of disposing of abandoned belongings reached acute proportions. The Reich Citizenship Law of 1941 provided for the obvious solution, namely, that such property would fall to the state. Although simple on the surface, the actual administration of this law required the creation of an entire bureaucracy whose job was not only to identify and acquire title to real estate, furniture, and personal items left behind by deported Jews but also to ensure that these would be distributed equitably among Aryan claimants. At first, all such property was to fall under the auspices of the finance ministry, which alone was charged with supervising its final disposition. The ministry faced a number of complex legal problems, however. Community property, for example, could not legally be seized because technically the community, as a corporation, continued to exist. Yet the property was in fact abandoned in many communities because no Jewish trustees continued to reside in the town or village. Thus a procedure had to be worked out whereby such communal property could be legally taken over by the state for public welfare projects. Insurance policies and inheritances constituted a second sticky problem for the finance ministry. According to law, the state could claim these assets only if it could demonstrate conclusively that the benefactor as well as all beneficiaries and heirs were dead. The state was for obvious reasons hesitant to provide such documentation. The result, which affords a crucial insight into the ultimate Nazi dedication to abiding by their ethic, was that the considerable resources represented here were never appropriated by the state.

Problems emerged even in such apparently straightforward operations as the confiscation of an abandoned apartment. The process, of course, began when the Jewish residents were picked up and readied for deportation. The house or apartment keys were collected and turned over to the building janitor, who would hold the key until a representative of the finance ministry appeared. This representative arranged for the inventory and removal of all household effects and supervised their sale or conveyance to charity. Any securities he retrieved were given to the treasury department; jewelry or precious metals were given to Berlin's municipal pawn shop; works of Jewish art were transferred to the Rosenberg Institute, which was in the process of creating a museum of extinguished civilizations. This was at least how things were supposed to work. In fact, the finance ministry soon discovered that the Gestapo was helping itself to furniture and other items before handing the keys over to the janitor, thus skimming off some of the prize possessions for itself. This kind of illegal profiteering could not be tolerated, so new regulations to protect the prerogatives of the finance ministry eventually had to be drawn up and enforced. Here we see in operation something we will witness again and again: an utter dedication on the part of Nazis to preserve ethical standards while engaged in the most brutal genocide the world has ever seen.

SUMMARY

Several observations are possible drawing from our review of how the Jewish community in Germany was finally eradicated. The first concerns the tremendous attention paid to identifying and isolating Jews. This was not a matter of spontaneous hatred or blind rage but a carefully defined and deliberately administered social program. The second concerns the reliance upon a dedicated bureaucracy. The detailed definition, organization, and supervision needed to carry out anti-Jewish policies required the work of an army of bureaucrats, managers, and racial-court judges. For this the state bureaucracy was ideal: legal experts were available to draw up definitions, formulate regulations, and write field manuals; police officers were trained to handle the arrest of people; finance officials had professional expertise in managing the complex problems of deed and title transfers. The professionalism of the modern bureaucratic state allowed the implementation of programs of social segregation and genocide to appear routine, orderly, and legally correct.

The third observation concerns the gradual conception, development, and implementation of the entire project. Achieving a workable definition of "Jew," using *Krystallnacht* for political purposes, and creating procedures for handling abandoned apartments all show that the government was learning as it went along. It took until the early 1940s to perfect the bureaucratic procedures needed to administer government policies efficiently. By the time the war broke out and other countries were occupied, six years of valuable experience had been gained; policies were ready for immediate implementation in conquered lands.

The fourth observation concerns the important role that law played in the conception and execution of anti-Jewish policies. The Nazi state used the full authority of the modern state to implement its policy: laws were formally passed; regulations were drawn up by appropriate agencies, which then monitored their implementation and made adjustments as necessary; private institutions such as charities, banks, and insurance companies were allowed to participate in the process provided they adhered to published government procedures. On the surface everything was done legally and with the proper forms and signatures. This presented a major problem to the lawyers at Nuremberg. Despite the obvious unacceptability of Nazi actions against the Jews, nothing clearly illegal had taken place. All state agencies as well as private concerns operated normally with commendable ethical sensitivity and within the limits of accepted legal procedure. What we see is not a nation run totally amok but a well-regulated society operating consciously out of a particular ethic.

Finally, we should note the effectiveness of the policy. The vital and vibrant German Jewish community had been reduced to helpless pauperdom in a matter of six years. No effective resistance was encountered, nor is it clear from where any might have come. The modern bureaucratized state controls too much initiative to be successfully challenged by individuals or even by ad hoc groups of individuals. The frightening thing is how radical a government's social policy can become without also becoming impossible to implement. This is one of the most disquieting lessons of the impoverishment and imprisonment of the Jewish community in Nazi Germany.

7

Exporting the Ethic:
Austria, Czechoslovakia,
and Poland

The Nazi party began its rule in Germany with two central goals. The first was to identify Germany's internal racial enemies and to render them harmless (see chaps. 1–6). The second was to reconstitute Germany according to an idealized vision of what Germany was supposed to be like. Fulfilling the second goal was more complex than fulfilling the first, since it meant systematically dismantling the Europe established by the Treaty of Versailles. According to party leaders, Germany to fulfill its destiny had to rearm, to renounce the massive reparation debt placed upon it, and to reoccupy the German lands taken away by the treaty. On one level, all these objectives were at least somewhat reasonable. Although no one was happy with the idea of a rearmed Germany, everyone could acknowledge that the desire by a sovereign nation to mount an army of reasonable size was not in and of itself immoral or unusual. There could also be a general consensus that the war-reparation payments demanded of Germany were excessive. The demand for the return of occupied land was also understandable. So the specifics of Nazi foreign policy, as it began to be articulated in the early years of Hitler's rule, were sufficiently cogent to achieve a sympathetic hearing abroad. Like most of Nazi policy, however, what began as not unreasonable proposals soon escalated into something quite different. Europe, and we shall argue Germany as well, was being led down a slippery slope. At some point, the demands of the Nazis moved into new and sinister territory, but this was not quickly recognized, since no formal break with accepted ethical rhetoric occurred. Because the early stages of the progression seemed reasonable enough, the character of the process that was about to grip Europe did not become clear until it had developed beyond the point of no return. In this slide from normal international relations into a world of racial warfare, the annexation of Austria and then the invasion of Poland were crucial milestones.

The annexation of the Germanic lands of Austria and Sudeten Czechoslovakia are significant because they illustrate the first attempt to apply the new Nazi ethic outside the political boundaries of Nazi Germany itself. In both cases, the racial policies that had evolved over time in Germany were instituted in full and at once, as though they were completely normal and acceptable. What happened in Austria and Czechoslovakia shows that the ethical implications of Nazi theory had become self-evident and even routine to those charged with carrying them out.

THE ANNEXATION OF AUSTRIA

The first half step toward the invasion of Poland, and so World War II, was the annexation of Austria in 1938, the so-called Anschluss. Half step, because Austria represented an ambiguous situation. Never a part of modern Germany, Austria was clearly a Teutonic land. It shared with Germany a common culture and language.[1] Thus, demands to unite Germany and Austria had at least a modicum of historical plausibility that somewhat masked the revolutionary and racial nature of Nazi foreign policy.

Austria was important in another way as well. We have already sketched in outline the development of anti-Jewish legislation in Germany from 1933 to 1939. During these seven years, a full bureaucratic apparatus had come into being for identifying and isolating Jews. Austria provided the first opportunity for exporting that policy and implementing it in another country. Again the ambiguous status of Austria worked to Germany's advantage. Since the Allies had hardly protested Germany's own treatment of the Jews, they could not now protest the implementation of the same policies in the Germanic country of Austria. And once they had acquiesced to the introduction of Nazi policy in Austria, on what grounds could they suddenly protest its introduction into Czechoslovakia, Poland, or Belgium? The unique position of Austria allowed the Nazi policy against the Jews to be extended to a new arena without raising significant moral protests.

The implementation of anti-Jewish policy in Austria moved swiftly, largely because so much of the groundwork had already been laid in Germany over the previous several years: racial laws had been written, ambiguities had already been resolved in court, the bureaucracy had already been trained, the enforcement authorities had gained experience. In short, the procedure had already reached a high level of development and efficiency. The entire program could be easily and quickly grafted on to the Austrian administrative machinery. This was, of course, devastating for Austrian Jews because whereas the treatment of Jews in Germany had only gradually reached a certain level of brutality, that level of brutality was attained in Austria virtually overnight.

The introduction of Nazi rule unleashed an orgy of S.S. actions against the Jewish community of Vienna:

> For the first few weeks the behavior of the Vienna Nazis was worse than anything I had seen in Germany. There was an orgy of sadism. Day after day large

numbers of Jewish men and women could be seen scrubbing Schusschnigg signs off the sidewalk and cleaning the gutters. While they worked on their hands and knees with jeering storm troopers standing over them, crowds gathered to taunt them.[2]

A whole population seemingly had been immediately engaged by the new ethic. Within weeks, the massive concentration camp at Mauthausen was completed and began to receive its first consignment of Jews. None of these actions provoked notable public outcries in the West.

THE TAKEOVER OF CZECHOSLOVAKIA

The next step in the expansion of Nazi policy was the demand to annex the German area of Czechoslovakia, one of the new states created after World War I. This area, the Sudetenland, had a large population of German speakers who were now claiming to be ethnic Germans. The Nazi party made what was a troubling but essentially logical claim. If they could annex Austria, then why should they not be able to annex the Sudetenland, since that too was part of the German racial homeland?[3] The proposed annexation of the Sudetenland contained some new dimensions, however. First, it meant the dismemberment of a country.[4] Austria had at least been taken over whole. Second, it meant the absorption into Germany of large numbers of people who were not ethnic Germans. The lines, then, were not as clear-cut as they had been in Austria. Yet there were enough similarities to force the Western powers finally to agree to Germany's demands.[5]

The takeover of the Sudetenland in October 1938 on the heels of the annexation of Austria provoked some changes in the Nazi policy toward its "Jewish" racial enemies. Matters at any rate had been growing more serious. The original purge of Jews from the German government in 1933 had grown by 1938 to encompass their removal from all German social and political life. With the Anschluss, this policy had been successfully transplanted to Austria, where it took effect much more quickly and efficiently than it had in Germany. This period saw an escalation in the construction and use of concentration camps, for example. Barely a month after the Sudetenland was taken over, *Krystallnacht* occurred (see pp. 66–68), marking a new stage in Nazi anti-Jewish combativeness. The Jews who came under Nazi control in the Sudetenland, like those in Austria, were destined to be victims of a considerably more brutal policy than had fallen on German Jews before 1937.

Policy toward Jews took on a more desperate and fanatic tone, it appears, because of the vast numbers of new Jews brought into the Reich by these annexations. With war clearly looming, these Jews found that there was no place left to run: no country was ready to take them in. They were thus trapped in a country that was now in full-scale preparation for engaging them in a racial war.

Numbers tell the story. In 1933, there were an estimated five hundred thousand Jews living in Germany. By 1938, emigration and attrition had reduced the number to about 160 thousand. From the party's perspective, Germany was on the verge of purging itself of Jews. The Anschluss set matters back, bringing into the Reich some 180 to 190 thousand additional Jews and Mischlings. Over the next two years, in the period before the invasion of Poland, a significant number of these Jews managed to migrate or flee to neighboring countries. Again, Germany seemed to be coming close to ridding itself of all Jews. Then came the annexation of the Sudetenland of Czechoslovakia, with its 350 thousand Jews and Mischlings. The total number of Jews in German-controlled lands was suddenly again nearing half a million, just what it had been ten years earlier. By now, however, further emigration of Jews was essentially impossible. The German bureaucracy for the first time faced the prospect of a large ongoing Jewish population that it was not going to be able to reduce by encouraging migration. New measures certainly were needed, and as we have indeed seen, matters began at about this time to take a new and ominous turn. Labor battalions were formed, and deportations to camps such as Theresienstadt were soon to begin. These actions must be seen in the context of a rapidly growing Jewish population in the Reich, even as Nazi policy was becoming more fervently anti-Jewish in the face of the possibility of a real war. This was the situation then, when Poland was overrun.

POLAND

The annexation of Poland differed from the other annexations in two important ways.[6] First of all, the target population was almost entirely non-German. There could be no question of absorbing these people into the Reich. In fact, Nazi racial ideology had already determined that the Poles were an inferior race, suitable for nothing more than providing slave labor for the Aryan "master race." Thus the conquest of Poland was to take a new and unprecedented form: all Polish intellectual, political, and cultural leaders were to be summarily shot; ethnic Germans were to be moved out of central Poland and into areas contiguous to Germany proper; and ethnic Poles were to be moved out of those areas and sent into central Poland, where they would be organized into a vast slave empire.

The second difference concerns the Jews. Now some three and a half *million* Jews suddenly entered the jurisdiction of the Reich. With actual war inaugurated, the presence within the greater Reich of this mass of largely non-Westernized, traditional, Yiddish-speaking Jews was simply intolerable. Nor was there any hope that these Jews could emigrate. Nazi actions indicate the desperation felt within the Reich.

The Nazi war against the Jewish community in Poland was implemented immediately, as it had been in Austria. In Poland the process was combined with the larger policy of organizing a massive population shift in order to prepare racially the area to be annexed to the Reich (the Protektorat) and the area that was to be occupied Poland (the Generalgouvernment). A top priority was, of course, the transfer of ethnic Germans into the Protektorat area and the movement of Jews and ethnic Poles out of the German area and into the Generalgouvernment. The basic administrative procedures for accomplishing such population shifts had already been worked out to some extent in Austria and Czechoslovakia. But the policy as it was carried out in Poland had a different quality from what it had had in Austria or Czechoslovakia. This was due in part to the German disdain for Poles in general. It was one thing to arrest a German-speaking Jew in civilized Vienna. It was something else entirely to arrest a Jewish peasant in the Polish countryside. There were also none of the personal considerations that had to be taken into account with German Jews: there was no need to show honor to army veterans, there were no special or privileged classes, there was no concern with mixed marriages or with the elderly. All Poles could be treated with equal contempt. To compound matters, the administrators sent to carry out this policy were less professional than the civil servants who implemented Nazi policy in Germany and Austria. The new Polish administration was staffed not by professional managers but by party loyalists who neither understood nor cared about legal niceties. The result was that the German bureaucrats who worked in Poland displayed even fewer moral reservations about their activities than bureaucrats had shown before the war. The experience in Poland surely played a role in the quantum leap in Nazi brutality that occurred in Russia.

The S.S. also played an important role in the development of Nazi policy in Poland, because it was to it that fell the chief responsibility for pacifying and absorbing Poland. Since this organization saw itself as essentially a cadre of racial combat troops rather than bureaucrats, it comes as no surprise in retrospect that the first tentative steps were now taken toward mass murder and genocide. Under S.S. auspices, killings in Poland began on two levels: on the one hand was the systematic execution of Polish intellectuals; on the other were isolated and random attacks against Jews (the so-called *Einzelaktionen*). Attacks on Jews became so common, in fact, that civil order was soon threatened. Trucks of S.S. troops rolled through villages, horsewhipping anyone who looked Jewish or organizing ad hoc mass executions in the local synagogues. Some acts of outright sadism are recorded—of groups of Jews driven into synagogues, forced to crawl and sing, to disrobe for a session of flogging, or made to defecate and then to smear the excrement on their faces. Arrests and detailed body searches, especially of women, were commonplace, as was rape. Until the army gradually exerted some control, Poland was virtually an S.S. orgy.[7]

Even under army control, however, the destruction of Jewish life in Poland continued. As part of the official policy, Jews were systematically evicted from their homes in the Protektorat area and transported to Polish towns within the Generalgouvernment. The arrival of masses of Jews into the Generalgouvernment, however, only created new problems. The targeted reception areas were hardly prepared to receive and settle tens of thousands of immigrants. Further, the governor of the Generalgouvernment, Hans Frank, was unwilling to accommodate his impoverished and helpless charges. His towns and villages were being filled with Jewish refugees whom the S.S. and army simply brought in without so much as asking his permission. The problem was compounded by the fact that Himmler was shipping in not only Polish Jews but also Gypsies and other "inferior" racial types. Frank, fearing that his realm was becoming a racial dumping ground, demanded that the shipments stop and, incredibly, was successful in winning the right to veto future shipments of Jews into his area. This gave him a chance to evaluate the situation in his kingdom and to decide on how best to handle the masses of unwilling Jews over whom he now had authority.

Frank's first need was to organize the settlement of Jews within the Generalgouvernment as effectively as possible. Toward this end, he decided first to control the size of Jewish populations within the major cities of Poland, all of which had become bloated with dissatisfied Jewish refugees. To ease the pressure, Jews would have to be dispersed. As good an example as any of how this was to work is the ancient city of Kraków. There were in 1938 an estimated sixty thousand Jews living in Kraków.[8] Frank decided that this ancient capital should be Polonized and the majority of its Jews expelled, with only a small number of native Kraków Jews remaining in the city's ghetto to serve as a labor source. At first this migration was voluntary: the government announced that any Jew volunteering to leave would be allowed to live in any city within the Generalgouvernment area. On the basis of this offer, some twenty-three thousand Jews left. But the number of volunteers fell far short of Frank's goal. So a compulsory phase was initiated, resulting in the removal of another nine thousand people. But even with this the Jewish population of Kraków remained well above what Frank envisioned. A third phase was thus inaugurated in which people were simply rounded up and shipped out according to the first letter of their last names: A–D on December 2; E–J on December 4; and so on. In this way, Frank's goal was finally achieved. The resettlement had proved to be administratively difficult, however, and Frank was convinced that to attempt something comparable all over Poland was simply impossible. Some new, more drastic solution to the Generalgouvernment's population problem would be necessary. Frank communicated his concerns to Berlin.

In fact, other schemes were already under consideration. One idea seriously proposed in July 1940 was to resettle all the Reich's Jews in Madagascar, an island off the east coast of Africa. The scheme presupposed an agreement with the French, who administered the island as part of their colonial empire. When no peace treaty materialized with France, the idea gradually fell out of favor. Attention shifted back to Europe. At some point, the idea took shape that Jews might in fact be settled farther east, in the vast steppes of soon-to-be-conquered Russia. In the meantime, Jews would simply be ghettoized in the large cities of the Generalgouvernment. These city ghettos could serve as huge concentration camps that would at least hold the Jews apart from the rest of the population until a more permanent solution farther east was developed. How seriously the idea of settling Jews farther east was actually taken is hard to judge. It is the case, however, that massively overcrowded ghettos began at this time to be established in the major cities of Poland, ghettos like Łódź and Warsaw. In these human holding pens a new solution to the "Jewish problem" took shape.[9]

THE POLISH GHETTOS

The Jewish area of Łódź was a virtual ghetto anyway. Located in a poor and shabby part of town, the Jewish quarter covered just over four square miles. It was now officially reduced to three and four-tenths square miles and walled in. Within this prison city eventually were crammed some 144 thousand Jews from all over Europe, including three thousand from Vienna, five thousand from Prague, forty-two hundred from Berlin, two thousand from Cologne, as well as about a thousand each from Frankfurt, Hamburg, and Düsseldorf and five hundred from Luxembourg. The living conditions in this ghetto are hard to imagine. The reduced ghetto area included a mere two thousand houses, that is, one house for seventy people. The Warsaw ghetto was even worse: three times the number of people—443 thousand souls—were crushed into slightly over one square mile.[10]

The construction of the Łódź ghetto began shortly after the debacle at Kraków. Drawing on that experience, Frank's policy planners decided to form the ghettos on a planned, rational basis. The ghetto was to be constructed in the existing Jewish ghetto, the home already of an estimated sixty-two thousand Jews. In February 1940, the boundaries of the new ghetto were formally announced and all Germans and Poles in the targeted area were evicted. Moving schedules were then published for Jews in the Łódź area to move into the ghetto. This phase of the operation was completed by the first week in May. On May 10, 1940, a curfew was announced for the inhabitants of the ghetto. There was to be a general curfew from 7 P.M. to 7 A.M. Further, no one could leave the ghetto at all without permission. A wall was built to enclose the ghetto, with an entranceway guarded by the Polish criminal police.[11]

With the concentration of Jews in the ghetto, some arrangement had to be made for its administration. A council, the Judenrat, was established. It was made up of people in the ghetto and served as a sort of municipal government as well as a liaison with Frank and the S.S. It was composed of a central bureau, which consisted of a negotiations department, a correspondence department, and divisions dealing with information, the cemetery, rabbinical functions, and the like. It also had bureaus to deal with records, police, fire, postal services, housing, finance, economic development (the ghetto was seen as a source of cheap labor), agriculture, schools, public works, supply, welfare, and health. On paper, then, the ghetto seemed to be a fully equipped and administered city. In fact, however, it was a squalid and over-crowded prison camp. Jewish businesses in the ghetto were subject to seizure and Aryanization. People were forcibly recruited for labor battalions. Because the ghetto was disengaged from the Polish economy, all food in the ghetto was provided by the Polish government through the Judenrat. Food was never in sufficient quantity and was often of low quality, spoiled, and damp. Equitable distribution under these conditions was of course impossible. In February 1941, the average ration per person *for the month* was as follows: one and a half pounds of meat, an egg, twelve pounds of potatoes, thirteen pounds of bread, twelve and three-tenths pounds of flour, one pint of milk, and ten pounds of vegetables.[12] This could hardly provide a healthy diet. Combined with the incredibly crowded conditions and the obvious lack of adequate sewage or waste-disposal systems, the ghettos quickly became hotbeds of disease. Within months of their establishment, the ghettos were littered with decaying corpses: people were dying faster than cemetery crews could collect the bodies.

The problem was that the numbers were so massive that even the bureaucrats who administered the ghettos lost sight of what the numbers meant. In May 1941, for example, the Łódź ghetto consumed 1202 metric tons of flour, 82 metric tons of meat, 85 metric tons of fat, 118,586 liters of milk, 916 metric tons of potatoes, and 2324 metric tons of vegetables. These figures sound impressive. We have seen, however, that they actually provided very little food per person. As the war progressed and food shortages began to appear even in Germany, it was easy for the Nazi administrators to make slight downward adjustments in the allocations. But even a slight decrease in tonnage on this level meant a noticeable increase in malnutrition and death on the streets. Even a delay in shipments could be devastating. In the eerie world of "paper death," changing a number on a form could sentence dozens of men, women, and children to a slow and painful death.

The effects of all this gradually began to be felt in Łódź. A massive typhus epidemic broke out in the summer of 1941. That winter was an especially cold one, freezing all the pipes in the underheated ghetto (there was insufficient coal for heating). From that time on there was no usable plumbing in the ghetto. In the spring of 1942 there were the first reports of cannibalism. The death rate was approximately one and a half percent of the population *per month.* All in all, fully one-fifth of the ghetto's inhabitants died within the first two years of its existence. The ghetto achieved another record as well. In the spring of 1943, its daily food costs were twelve cents per person, one of the lowest levels recorded in any urban area in modern history. It is an interesting commentary on the depth to which ghetto life had sunk that even the German police sent to round up people for the death camps were often unable to do their jobs. They were rendered physically sick by what they encountered in the ghettos: the masses of malnourished orphans caked with excrement begging in the streets, the sick, the dying, and the piles of bloated, unburied corpses.

The situation in the ghettos had clearly become untenable, as the German authorities soon recognized. The original assumption was that the ghettos would be only temporary: as soon as the eastern front (meaning Russia) was pacified, Jews would be moved farther east, far from German territory, and out of Frank's realm. So Łódź and its sister ghettos throughout Poland were seen as only holding pens. The confused transients from Prague or Berlin would be there only a short time before moving on. But the eastern front never stabilized, the new areas of settlement projected in the Russian steppes never materialized, and the temporary stay of Jews in these inhuman ghettos stretched into months and years. The scheme for dealing with the Jewish problem was proving an embarrassing failure. Nor were there obvious alternatives. The Nazi party was hardly likely to spend energy to construct new and commodious ghettos for Polish Jews. Nor was it possible to admit defeat and allow Jews to assimilate back into Polish, let alone Austrian and German, society. Yet these festering areas of disease and death could hardly be sustained any longer in the midst of Polish cities. One possibility did open up, however. By this time, of course, the "racial war" envisioned by the Nazi ethic had become a real war. With the invasion of Russia in 1941, the next logical step in the implementation of the Nazi ethic was ready to be played out.

8

The Invasion of Russia

In Russia, the implementation of the new ethic took on a much more brutal character. For the first time, the new ethic seemed to be able to sustain a complete policy of mass murder and genocide. The situation in Russia presents us for the first time with individuals who have become so much a part of the Nazi ethic that they confront their victims face to face and yet carry out their duties. The bureaucratic layer that so often distances people from their actions was not present in Russia. We might understand a policeman who arrested a Jewish family in Austria, because he was only fulfilling the law, something he had sworn to do. He was not actually deporting, starving, or gassing the family. We can perhaps rationalize the action of an administrator in Berlin who cut a few tons of food from the Łódź ghetto, because resources were scarce everywhere and the burdens had to be shared. He, after all, did not send people to the ghetto or watch his wards slowly starve to death. But these fine rationalizations break down when we turn to Russia. There the decisions, the actions, and their consequences were immediate and concrete. Whole families were arrested, forced to dig their own mass graves, stripped naked, and shot all within a matter of hours by the same half dozen people. There for virtually the first time—the exception being isolated murders committed by S.S. members—the perpetrators looked their victims straight in the eye. That these activities could be initiated and sustained over a vast front in eastern Europe for month after month raises the central moral question of the Holocaust: How do people construct ethical constraints for their own lives?

THE INVASION OF RUSSIA

Russia was invaded by the German army in June 1941. Because of the peace pact signed between Stalin and Hitler two years earlier, the Russians were caught largely unprepared for the attack. The result was an initial retreat by the Russians, a retreat that ended only with the Battle of Stalingrad and the defeat of the German Sixth Army in the winter of 1942–43. From that point on, the German army was gradually, painfully, but relentlessly pushed back. Nevertheless, vast areas of European Russia, the heartland of eastern European Jewry, fell to the German invaders quickly and remained under their control for nearly two years.

The acquisition of Russian territory posed special problems for the Nazi party elements still struggling with the Jewish question in Poland. As Hitler himself recognized, the Jews of Russia had proved to be unusually fertile. Russia was regarded with some justification as the great "breeding ground" for European Jewry. Since the founding of the so-called Jewish Pale of Settlement by Catherine the Great in the late eighteenth century, the Jewish population of western Russia, to which Jews were restricted, had increased from one million to approximately four million, a figure that did not include the three to three and a half million émigrés the region had supplied to western Europe and the United States. Many of the Jews Hitler had encountered in his youth, and in fact a significant proportion of the Jews in Germany and Austria in the 1930s, were immigrants from eastern Europe. These Jews displayed all of the stereotypical features ascribed to Jews in Nazi mythology: they were non-Westernized, superstitious, and utterly foreign. In invading Russia, then, the German army saw itself as entering the very heartland of world Jewry.

This perception was one element leading to the escalation in Nazi ruthlessness. There were others. The ghetto system had failed to control Poland's vast Jewish population. Russia now threatened to supply another three and a half to four million Jews to the Nazi administrators. The ghetto solution clearly would not work. The Madagascar exportation scheme was dead. Some new way of dealing with the vast, teeming population had to be found.

In addition, there was what we might call the bolshevik connection. For Hitler and his right-wing allies, the greatest danger to Germany came from the left. Leftist ideology posed a problem on a number of different levels: business interests were threatened by the socialist call for economic equality and the ownership of industry by the government; monarchists dreaded socialism because of its commitment to social equality and its disdain for royalty and aristocratic privilege. Fascist political theory saw socialism as the chief threat to national unity within a state. In the mythology that developed around the end of World War I, socialists were also considered responsible for the collapse of the German imperial government and the subsequent capitulation at Versailles. So for a variety of political, nationalistic, and economic reasons, the Nazis were determined to stamp out socialism and its virulent offspring, bolshevism. Thus Russian Jews were a threat not only as Jews but also as Russians and presumed bolsheviks.

Finally, it is important to note that Nazi treatment of the Jews in Germany, Austria, and Poland had received very little international protest. In fact, neither the United States nor the Vatican, the presumed moral voices of the West, raised any serious objections. Their silence no doubt encouraged Nazi planners to reach the decision simply to eliminate Russia's Jews. For whatever reasons, at some point prior to the invasion, the decision had been made. When the German armies raced across the border on June 22, 1941, they were accompanied by specially organized, trained, and equipped killing units whose mission was to round up and shoot every Jew they could find. In typical Nazi euphemism, these were called *Einsatzgruppen,* "special units."

EINSATZGRUPPEN

The Einsatzgruppen were battalion-level units attached to the major German army groups. Einsatzgruppe A, for example, was to support Army Group North; B, Army Group Center; C, Army Group South; and D, the Eleventh Army. Their assignment was to follow directly behind the army's front-line troops and execute all Jews they could identify in the newly captured villages. The idea, apparently, was to descend on the Jewish population so quickly that there would be no time for the intended victims to hide or defend themselves. This proved especially effective for the first few months of the war, during which time Soviet defenses rapidly gave way and the front advanced quickly. Indications are that the combination of trained troops and an unprepared population produced quick results. In fact the Einsatzgruppen for a while became models of such efficiency and moved so rapidly that at times they interfered with military operations. The Einsatzgruppen would often begin their grisly work even before the last tank had rolled on. It was reported that three patrol cars of Einsatzgruppe C actually followed the lead German tank into the town of Zhitomir. In Odessa, the Einsatzgruppe was so anxious to get to work that it did not even wait for the town to be taken. As a result it was caught in the crossfire of a brief Soviet counterattack.[1]

The Einsatzgruppen never acted as full units. They were broken down into companies and at times even into platoons and fire teams, especially when several backwoods villages came into German control at the same time. The various fire teams could spread out and deal with dozens of small settlements simultaneously. The general strategy of an Einsatz-unit upon entering a village was to ask the dazed population to point out the Jews. Those pointed out, whether they were really Jews or not, were immediately gathered under guard in the town square or some other appropriate spot. They were led to a field outside town where they were forced to dig a mass grave. The victims were then stripped and told to stand at the edge of the pit. The first line of victims was machine-gunned, falling into the grave to form a first layer of dead and dying bodies. The next group was brought up, lined up along the grave and shot in turn, falling on the first layer. This continued until the entire contingent of victims was shot. In general, those who did not die from the bullets were suffocated by the mass of bodies falling on top of them. This kind of assembly-line killing could easily eliminate the Jewish community of a small village in a matter of hours, making it possible for the same squad to handle maybe two or even three villages a day. Although this relentless human slaughter went on in dozens of places simultaneously for weeks and months on end, there was never, as far as we can tell, an administrative breakdown.

A description of one such action, a minor one, is derived from the testimony of Herman Graebe at the Nuremberg trials:[2]

My foreman and I went directly to the pits. I heard rifle shots in quick succession from behind one of the earth mounds. The people who had got off the trucks—men, women and children of all ages—had to undress upon the order of an SS man, who carried a riding or dog whip. They had to put down their clothes in fixed places, sorted according to shoes, top clothing and underclothing. I saw a heap of shoes of about 800 to 1,000 pairs, great piles of under-linen and clothing.

Without screaming or weeping these people undressed, stood around in family groups, kissed each other, said farewells and waited for a sign from another SS man, who stood near the pit, also with a whip in his hand. During the fifteen minutes that I stood near the pit I heard no complaint or plea for mercy. . . .

An old woman with snow-white hair was holding a one-year-old child in her arms and singing to it and tickling it. The child was cooing with delight. The parents were looking on with tears in their eyes. The father was holding the hand of a boy about 10 years old and speaking to him softly; the boy was fighting his tears. The father pointed to the sky, stroked his head and seemed to explain something to him.

At that moment the SS man at the pit shouted something to his comrade. The latter counted off about twenty persons and instructed them to go behind the earth mound. . . . I well remember a girl, slim and with black hair, who, as she passed close to me, pointed to herself and said: "twenty-three years old."

I walked around the mound and found myself confronted by a tremendous grave. People were closely wedged together and lying on top of each other so that only their heads were visible. Nearly all had blood running over their shoulders from their heads. Some of the people were still moving. Some were lifting their arms and turning their heads to show that they were still alive. The pit was already two-thirds full. I estimated that it contained about a thousand people. I looked for the man who did the shooting. He was an SS man, who sat at the edge of the narrow end of the pit, his feet dangling into the pit. He had a tommy gun on his knees and was smoking a cigarette.

The people, completely naked, went down some steps and clambered over the heads of the people lying there to the place to which the SS man directed them. They lay down in front of the dead or wounded people; some caressed those who were still alive and spoke to them in a low voice. Then I heard a series of shots. I looked into the pit and saw that the bodies were twitching or the heads lying already motionless on top of the bodies that lay beneath them. Blood was running from their necks.

The next batch was approaching already. They went down into the pit, lined themselves up against the previous victims and were shot.

At first these groups met with tremendous success. Some of the early groups reported astounding numbers. Einsatzgruppe A reported 125 thousand Jews killed on October 15, 1941. A month later Group B could report forty-five thousand killed. On November 3, Group C reported seventy-five thousand.[3] Later, as the advance slowed and as rumors of the Einsatzgruppen began to spread, the number of victims diminished. Many Soviet citizens, Jews included, began to flee before the advancing army. How many Jews fled specifically because of the Einsatzgruppen and how many were caught in the general evacuations, we will never know. The fact remains that the Einsatzgruppen's work became more difficult as time went on.

Despite close collaboration with the army, the Einsatzgruppen were not military units. They were special units of the S.S. and police organized under the direction of Reinhardt Heydrich of the Reich Security Main Office. The fact that they were so closely coupled with army operations, however, indicates the curious dual nature that the Nazi war against Europe was starting to take on. On the one hand, the Nazi government was interested in the acquisition of land and natural resources—interests that the Army secured. Alongside this was a fierce determination to redraw the population map of Europe in conformity with Nazi racial theory. With the establishment of the Einsatzgruppen, these two pursuits became interwoven. The pursuit of Jews took place alongside, and became entangled with, army operations. In more than one case we have actual complaints from the army about the actions of the Einsatzgruppen. Not only were they occasionally underfoot but their mass killing of unarmed civilians went against the military's own code of ethics, with a resultant negative effect on army morale. Yet this side effect seems to have been largely ignored by Berlin. The point is that racial war and conventional war had now become so intermingled that they were forced to take place side by side. So thoroughly were the two linked in the minds of the Nazi leaders that even in the midst of a war zone the army was unable to control these "police" units.

THE PERSONNEL OF THE
EINSATZGRUPPEN

The men who commanded and supervised these units were more cultured and better educated than the military commanders in general. One was a physician, another a former opera singer. Several were lawyers, and one a Protestant theologian. As we shall see, these men were generally young rising stars in the bureaucracy, people who were looking for good assignments to boost their careers. In fairness, it must be said that few of them volunteered for duty with the Einsatzgruppen. Most did not know the mission of these units until they were already commissioned into them;

and in a few cases when the nature of the units became known, the commanders tried to be reassigned, although none succeeded. But once in the units and made aware of their mission, these commanders acted like good German soldiers. They may not have wanted the job and they may not have liked what they were doing, but they carried on all the same.

The men who perpetrated these mass murders were not thugs or scoundrels. If they were, it would be easy to explain their actions. The truth is much more unsettling. These were common, everyday people who were caught up in a bureaucracy that they did not create but within which they now had a job. As we shall see presently, many of these people had a difficult time in carrying out their duties. Yet it is a testimony to the power of modern bureaucracy and the persuasiveness of the Nazi ethic that despite any qualms an individual might have had, the ghastly work went on without serious moral challenge.

The Einsatzgruppen and the concentration and death camps offer the prime evidence that people are able to carry out unthinkable acts of brutality within the contexts of their everyday lives. To hear the perpetrators themselves explain their reactions and experiences is to hear how fully the Nazi ethic was allowed to override contradicting feelings and moral concerns. The diary of Rudolf Hoess, the commandant of Auschwitz, gives us insight, I believe, into the minds of Einsatzgruppen commanders:

> I myself dared not admit to such doubts. In order to make my subordinates carry on with their tasks, it was psychologically essential that I myself appear convinced of the necessity for this gruesomely harsh order.
>
> Everyone watched me. They observed the impression produced upon me by the kind of scenes that I have described above and my reactions. Every word I said on the subject was discussed. I had to exercise intense self-control in order to prevent my innermost doubts and feelings of oppression from becoming apparent.
>
> I had to appear cold and indifferent to events that must have wrung the heart of anyone possessed of human feelings. I might not even look away when afraid lest my natural emotions get the upper hand. I had to watch coldly, while the mothers with laughing or crying children went into the gas chambers.
>
> On one occasion two small children were so absorbed in some game that they quite refused to let their mother tear them away from it. Even the Jews of the Special Detachment [prison work details] were reluctant to pick the children up. The imploring eyes of the mother, who certainly knew what was happening, is something I shall never forget. . . .
>
> I had to see everything. I had to watch hour after hour, by day and by night, the removal and burning of the bodies, the extraction of the teeth, the cutting of the hair, the whole grisly interminable business. I had to stand for hours on end in the ghastly stench, while the mass graves were being opened and the bodies dragged out and burned.[4]

Although this was written about the Auschwitz death camp, it points to a psychological state that seems to have been common among Einsatzgruppen personnel. From the first few weeks of the Russian offensive, there were numerous complaints from the army about the impact the work of these death squads was having on army personnel and even on civilians who chanced to be witnesses. One ingredient in the army's complaints about the Einsatzgruppen's following the army so closely was the "negative impact" they had on the troops, an already war-hardened lot! It is an interesting indication of the party's mentality that these complaints regarding army efficiency were ignored. The expeditious killing of Jews took precedence.

As with Hoess, Einsatzgruppen and Einsatzkommando commanders were ordered to witness personally the activities of the men under their command. This was to ensure that the members of these groups carried out their duties effectively. There are reports that many of the commanders themselves suffered nightmares and other symptoms of psychological distress afterward. At least one S.S. general, Erich von dem Bach-Zelewski, eventually had to be relieved from duty because of recurring stomach problems. Bach-Zelewski was also one of the few Einsatzgruppen commanders to complain about the effect the operations were having on his own men and to wonder aloud how it could be that these Jews, who were being mowed down without resisting, could have been plotting to subdue the world.[5]

This duty surely had its effect on the enlisted men as well, the men who were doing the actual shooting. In general, they were older men, often with some combat experience but now too old for front-line duty. They were pitted instead against an unarmed population. Like their commanders, they too soon began to display negative psychological reactions to what they were doing. The use of alcohol among Einsatzgruppen personnel was unusually high, and there were an unusually high number of reports of nervous breakdowns among these men. In this regard there was an interesting conversation recorded between an S.S. general who was witnessing one operation and the head of the S.S., Heinrich Himmler, who was on an inspection tour:

> GENERAL: "Reichsfuehrer, those were only a hundred."
> HIMMLER: "What do you mean by that?"
> GENERAL: "Look at the eyes of the men in the Kommando, how deeply shaken they are! These men are finished for the rest of their lives. What kind of followers are we training here? Either neurotics or savages!"[6]

Himmler himself was apparently moved by this. Clearly this mode of killing was too damaging to the Germans. In another year the same kind of killing, albeit on a more massive scale, would be bureaucratized and depersonalized in the death camps. The seed for that idea may have been planted during this inspection tour.

If an S.S. general and Himmler could be revolted by what was going on, surely others could be as well. We saw earlier that the commanders who oversaw these operations were ordinary, even educated, people. Their life stories before joining Einsatzgruppen are those of well-educated, promising professionals, not those of mass murderers. For instance, Arthur Nebe, the commander of Einsatzgruppe B, was a lawyer and former head of the criminal police. In the new Germany, however, combat experience was important for promotion. Nebe wanted that experience, and even a decoration, to impress his boss, Heydrich. When the formation of these new volunteer units was announced, Nebe saw his chance. Like all the others, he did not learn of the units' true purpose until later. Otto Ohlendorf, commander of Einsatzgruppe D, had embarrassed his superiors by exposing some corruption. He was offered the command of one of the new units. Ohlendorf had turned down earlier orders and felt that his position was too tenuous now to refuse again. Walther Stahlecher, of Einsatzgruppe A, was a career officer in internal security. He had run afoul of Heydrich and was transferred to the foreign office. He saw an assignment in Heydrich's new units as a ticket back to internal security. Ernst Biberstein, the last commander of Einsatzkommando 6, had perhaps the most interesting background. He was by profession a Protestant theologian who had risen to prominence through the Nazi church hierarchy. He was one of the few commanders, it seems, who acted from purely ideological reasons.[7]

A number of elements, then, point to an answer to how new ethics are absorbed. Rather ordinary bureaucrats volunteered for units to gain recognition or ingratiate themselves with their bosses. They found out later that their assignment was mass murder. They were revolted and sickened by what they had to do and witness, as were the men under their command and supervision. Yet until resignations were accepted or transfer orders were received, they saw to it that the work went on and on and on with efficiency and dispatch. In fact, after the first wave was completed and the front line stabilized, the groups reversed and made a second sweep to identify survivors and those who were missed the first time. Despite all the moral qualms, these units without exception worked with cool deliberateness. Why?

The answer, I suggest, lies in the human capacity to compartmentalize negative feelings and allow them to be overridden by concerns defined by an ethic. This accounts for some of the unusual juxtapositions associated with the Holocaust. Things that to outsiders living in a normal world look completely out of place were somehow held together in the minds of many of these people. A marvelous example is found in the diary of a camp doctor, Hans Herman Kremer, and demonstrates the way in which morally hideous acts can be compartmentalized and trivialized:

Sept. 6, 1942: Today, Sunday, excellent lunch: tomato soup, half a hen with potatoes and red cabbage (20g fat), sweets and marvelous vanilla ice cream . . . in the evening at 8:00 outside for Sonderaktion [an execution].

Sept. 9, 1942: This morning I got the most pleasant news from my lawyer, Prof. Dr. Hallerman in Muenster, that I got a divorce from my wife on the first of this month (note: I see colors again, a black curtain is drawn from my life!). Later on, present as a doctor at a corporal punishment of eight prisoners and an execution by shooting with small-calibre rifles. Got soap flakes and two pieces of soap. . . . In the evening present at a Sonderaktion, fourth time.[8]

The writings of Kremer make a nice contrast with those of Hoess cited earlier. Hoess struggled with the awfulness of what he had seen. He told us again and again, honestly I believe, of how revolted he was. Kremer, on the other hand, acted as if nothing terribly wrong was happening. He described prisoner beatings and meals in the same tone. The divorce from his wife brought him great joy, while watching a Sonderaktion appears to have had no effect. Yet on another level both men displayed a very similar reaction. Both denied that what they saw was ultimately wrong, Kremer by pretending it was normal, Hoess by suppressing his real feelings. Each found a way of accommodating his everyday life to the utter evil he was perpetrating.

The effects of this double life on Einsatzgruppen commanders took their toll in physical ailments: stomach problems, severe recurring headaches (Hoess), alcoholism. Many, as we said, applied for reassignment, albeit while still carrying out their duties. The case of Franz Stangl is illustrative. Franz Stangl was the S.S. officer who commanded Sobibor and later Treblinka. His story is particularly instructive because, like many others who operated the death camps, he claimed afterward (in 1970, while serving a life sentence in Germany for war crimes) that he had had no choice.[9]

As a civilian police officer, he was inducted into the S.S. shortly after the Nazis assumed power and later assigned to administrative work in the euthanasia program. Early in 1942 he was ordered to Poland, where General Odilo Globocnik put him in charge of building what he thought would be a supply camp at Sobibor. Upon receipt of orders placing him under the command of Christian Wirth, who was then commander at Belzec, Stangl reported to Belzec camp and learned the truth: "Oh God, the smell. It was everywhere. Wirth wasn't in his office. I remember, they took me to him . . . he was standing on a hill, next to the pits . . . the pits . . . full . . . they were full. I can't tell you; not hundreds, thousands, thousands, thousands of corpses . . . oh God. That's what Wirth told me—he said that was what Sobibor was for. And that he was putting me officially in charge."

Stangl protested. Wirth ordered. Stangl went to Lublin to protest to Globocnik but was unable to see him and so returned to Sobibor. He claims to have considered deserting but rejected the idea for fear of what might happen to his family. In the end he decided to stay and keep trying for a transfer.

When the camp was nearly completed, in May 1942, Wirth arrived unexpectedly one day and quickly organized the trial gassing of twenty-five Jewish prisoners. From then on, the killing went forward rapidly. Stangl's reaction: "At Sobibor one could avoid seeing almost all of it—it all happened so far away from the camp buildings. All I could think of was that I wanted to get out. I schemed and schemed, planned and planned."

To no avail. In July, Globocnik ordered him to take over Treblinka, and his attempts to get transferred failed again. While at Treblinka, he said, he avoided direct contact with the killing as much as possible and only tried to see to it that the operations ran smoothly. When questioned on this point, he explained that he was able to function by compartmentalizing his thinking: since he had no wish to harm the Jews, and the killings were not his fault, he felt no responsibility or guilt, only disgust and horror at being forced to oversee such terrible activities.

Stangl, like Kremer and Hoess, was a high-ranking and influential person in the Nazi hierarchy. He achieved this status by his apparent belief in Nazi principles and ideals. These men held the positions they did as a reward for their service to the system. They in turn made it possible for the system to continue running. What is surprising is that these people, committed to making the system work, found it physically revolting. This insight reveals a frightening reality operating behind the Holocaust: the very perpetrators themselves were victims of their own ethic. They were as trapped in their roles in some sense as the victims were in theirs. Both victim and perpetrator, although in different ways, wanted to escape but could not. The Nazis had released a monster that took on a life of its own that dominated its creators. The system became a juggernaut, carrying in its wake victim and perpetrator alike. This is not to say that all Nazis were revolted by what they were doing. To the very end, even to this very day, there are Nazis who fully applaud what was happening. They are not so much our problem. Our problem is the ordinary people thrust into leadership positions who were morally or emotionally disgusted with what they saw and yet did their job because their ethic demanded that it be done. They made the whole thing possible.

The lesson is that people's moral inhibitions are easier to overcome than we might hope. According to Herbert Kelman, the recipe is easy. Moral inhibitions against atrocious violence will be overridden when that violence is given official authorization by those in power, when it is given ethical sanction. People committing the violence may at the beginning feel some moral resistance, but this will almost always be compartmentalized, trivialized, and then ignored.[10]

I have taken time to discuss the psychology of the Nazi movement at this point because I believe that sometime in 1941 or 1942 an important psychological barrier was crossed. The exact time and place cannot be defined. The change did not hit everyone at the same time. But the Einsatzgruppen indicate that something had radically altered and that the unthinkable was now fully conceivable as a policy. A whole civilization, virtually a whole continent, was enmeshed in a new ethic of racial warfare.

9

The Expansion into
Western Europe

An examination of the character of the Holocaust in western Europe is crucial to this volume because it shows that the Nazi ethic of racial warfare did not have to be applied in a monolithic fashion nor did it need to be adopted homogeneously across political boundaries: like any ethic it could accommodate deviations and allow for shades of gray.[1] What one could do to Poles and Russians (i.e., racially inferior peoples), for example, was unthinkable as regards western Europeans (i.e., the more Germanic peoples). This ability to display flexibility shows how fully cogent and workable the Nazi ethic really was. As we shall see later, the idea of murdering Jews in the context of racial warfare continued to be a functioning ethical category in a wide variety of cultural contexts. There were mechanisms by which other countries could accept the Nazi racial ethic and adapt it to their own realities: the general character of ethical discourse in Europe assisted in the adoption of the Nazi ethic. Country after country found itself drawn, to a greater or lesser extent, into the Nazi web of genocide. It is true that in some sense these countries had limited choices: they were all militarily conquered and were dominated by a ruthless and committed government. It is also true that some local attempts to resist Nazi racial policy began to take shape in a number of these countries. Nonetheless, a significant level of complicity did emerge in virtually every country in Europe. This chapter, then, begins to raise a deeper issue, namely, the extent to which people can be persuaded to give up a traditional ethic for a new one, even one promulgated by its bitterest enemy.

It will be impossible to review in detail the enactment of the Holocaust in each country in Western Europe. Instead this chapter will briefly discuss each country's participation in the Holocaust and will then draw some general conclusions.

NORWAY

Norway was invaded and occupied in 1940. The German invaders immediately installed as governor Vidkun Quisling, a former general-staff officer and head of the pro-Nazi National Meeting party. His government provided the bureaucratic apparatus needed to carry out the Nazi party's anti-Jewish measures.[2]

In fact, the process was slow and incompletely carried out in Norway. For one thing, the Jewish population was small, only about two thousand people. Norwegians appeared to have a hard time imagining this tiny community to be a racial threat. In addition, the Scandinavians seemed far removed intellectually from the central European concern with Jews as ethnic minorities. Quite to the contrary, Norwegians, like the Swedish and Danes, saw Jews above all as Scandinavians. For them, the central concern in retaining Norwegian identity was not to purge Jews but to stand behind these Scandinavians against non-Scandinavians. Because of this understanding, Nazi anti-Jewish activity in Norway met with only moderate acceptance and success. The move against Norway's Jews began late—only in October 1942. (By this time, in contrast, Polish Jews had been in ghettos for two years and were now being sent to death camps.) On that date all Jewish males in Norway were arrested (males alone were seized in order to perpetuate the myth that Jews were being recruited for work details). Although the action was to be kept secret, word leaked out, giving most Jews advance warning. There can be little doubt that the true intent of the Nazi action was known. Special services in support of the seized Jewish men were held in Lutheran churches throughout Norway in November. In late November, the women and children were seized and began to be processed for transport to Auschwitz. In December, the Swedish ambassador offered to provide refuge in Sweden to all those Jews about to be deported. Despite this support for the Jews, however, the German administration slowly struggled to complete its mission, deporting 770 Norwegian Jews to Auschwitz by 1944. Public support for the Jews led the education ministry to sponsor a research project in 1943 in order to "expose" dangerous Jewish influence in the country. Apparently the perpetrators needed some excuse, albeit ex post facto, for the actions they had taken which the Norwegians dared to question.

DENMARK

Denmark was occupied without resistance during the invasion of Norway. Possibly because of its lack of resistance, it was not placed under military occupation.[3] The Danes throughout the war enjoyed a measure of independence that was truly unusual for areas under Nazi control. This explains to some extent how the Danes were able to resist being co-opted by the Nazis. This, taken together with the solidarity displayed by Scandinavians in general with their Jewish citizens and against German interference, gave the Danish Jews the best chance for survival of any Jewish community in Europe.[4]

The Nazi policy started innocuously enough. As in Norway, radical anti-Jewish measures began only late in 1942, when the Germans' Jew hatred, in the face of a stalled war effort, became fanatical. The relative freedom of Denmark's Jewish population was no longer to be tolerated. Yet because of the autonomy granted to the Danes and because of their concern for their Jewish neighbors, the Germans realized that they would have to move cautiously. The strategy begun in Germany was followed in Denmark: remove Jews from positions of influence. In the face of Nazi demands, the Danish government agreed reluctantly to remove Jews from public life, to drive Jewish firms out of business, and to begin the process of arresting Jews. Since Jewish influence in Danish public and business life was almost nonexistent, the first two points of concession in fact yielded only the most limited results. The government worked on the third, but only sluggishly.

By the fall of 1943 it was clear to the Germans that so far their policy of segregating Jews in Denmark had been a failure. Consequently, German administrators began to take a more direct hand in matters. In September, the Nazis began a systematic effort to identify all Jews in Denmark and to make preparations for arrests and deportations. Alerted, the government tried to resist, but was powerless in the face of a determined S.S. At this point the citizens of Denmark joined the efforts to protect Jewish Danes. A vast underground network came into being that smuggled Jews to safe houses, guarded their possessions, moved them surreptitiously to docks, and arranged for their passage to neutral Sweden, which continued to offer haven. On the night on which the Nazis had planned their mass arrests, they managed to lay their hands on only about 480 people (out of some sixty-five hundred). The comprehensive actions on the part of the citizenry to protect their neighbors had sabotaged the best efforts of the German bureaucracy. Denmark was one of the S.S.'s plainest failures.

Nor did Danish efforts stop after Jews were deported.[5] Denmark persisted in inquiring after the welfare of its Jewish citizens even after deportation. The nation's ongoing interest in its Jewish citizens seems to have interfered with the smooth operation of the Nazi machine. Ultimately all of Denmark's arrested Jews were sent to Theresienstadt, which for all its horrors was not a death camp. Even then, Danish inquiries continued. The end result was that only fifty-one Danish Jews died in Nazi hands, virtually all from natural causes! The Danes, by never retreating from their moral ground, had thwarted the Nazi program. Their actions stand out as an example of what could have happened throughout Europe.

NETHERLANDS

The Low Countries were overrun by a blitzkrieg during May and June of 1940. All higher-level government positions were immediately taken over by the German victors. Ernst Seyss-Inquart, the Nazi puppet who had invited German troops to intervene in Austria in 1938, was installed as head of government. Other high official positions were either left vacant or filled with loyal Austrians. Thus, although the civil service was run by the local

Dutch, all top-level supervisory positions were filled by Austrians who already had demonstrated their loyalty to, and had gained experience in, administering Nazi racial policy.[6]

It is probably because of this that the destruction of the Jewish community in Holland was nearly as thorough as it was in Germany itself.[7] There was, to be sure, popular resistance to Nazi racial policies, but the resistance had little obvious effect. The first mass arrests of Jews in early 1941 provoked a series of large-scale public strikes that paralyzed public transportation in major cities such as Amsterdam and Utrecht and virtually closed down the ports. Nazi reaction was swift and brutal. Martial law was imposed and Dutch resistance was broken by the simple means of starving the citizenry into submission. For months Holland was a hell of starvation and death. After this, no effective public protest developed.

With the citizenry beaten into submission and the bureaucracy committed to the elimination of Dutch Jewry, arrests and deportations were quickly organized. By the time the deportations ground to a halt near the end of the war, some 115 thousand Dutch Jews had been deported. It is estimated that about five percent of Dutch Jews survived the war by hiding.[8] The fact that several thousand Dutch Jews could successfully hide out in occupied Holland for four and a half years indicates that they enjoyed a good measure of sympathy and support from their fellow citizens. Dutch concern for civil and human rights was apparently not completely overridden by the Nazi ethic.

LUXEMBOURG

Even Luxembourg has a story to tell.[9] This tiny state was to be annexed outright to the Reich. It was home to a mere three thousand Jews, and another fifteen hundred refugees. Of this number thirty-five hundred managed to flee into France, mostly illegally. Of the thousand or so left, five hundred were shipped, for some reason, to the Łódź ghetto. The remaining four or five hundred survived the war in Luxembourg.

BELGIUM

Belgium was overrun during the same campaign that brought the Netherlands into German hands. But there the similarity ends.[10] Holland, like the Scandinavian countries, was "Germanic" according to the Nazi map of the world. The Germanic countries were to be annexed to, or at least brought under the protection of, Germany. Belgium and France were "Romance" rather than "Teutonic" and so were to be dealt with more harshly. Both were placed under military control and regarded as occupied countries. This had two important ramifications. The first was that there was no attempt to co-opt the bureaucracy of these countries as there was in Holland and Luxembourg. The administration was left in local hands, although under the supervision of the military. The other was that the expulsion of Jews from these areas had at the outset a relatively lower priority, since these areas were not to become part of the Third Reich. It is a good indication of the character of Nazi mania that eventually French and Belgian Jews too seemed to be a threat and became the targets of genocide as much as the Jews living in lands destined to be annexed to the Reich. But the fact that Jews ultimately were arrested and deported reflects the role of the local civil authorities who, although under military control, carried out these policies in their own countries. There does not appear to have been effective obstruction of Nazi policies by the local civil service.

The deportation of Jews proceeded in Belgium in the by now familiar way. But only a small proportion of the Jews in Belgium were actually Belgian nationals. Of the ninety thousand Jews to be dealt with by Belgian authorities, approximately thirty thousand were refugees from Germany and another forty thousand were from farther east.[11] The Belgians, in a pattern we will see repeated by the French, tried at first to save their own citizens by bargaining away the lives of refugee Jews; that is, they apparently deemed Belgian Jews to be Belgian first and Jews second. To some extent this vision influenced results. By the time deportations ended, fully one-third of the refugees in Belgium who had not been able to escape farther south had been arrested and deported. On the other hand, only one in twenty nationals was deported. The Belgians were clearly uncomfortable with the role they were expected to play and tried to mitigate its effects as long as they could and in a way, presumably, that was ethically defensible. Somewhat like the Scandinavians and Dutch, they saw attacks on their Jewish citizens as primarily an attack on Belgians and so were motivated to protect these people to a greater extent than they were motivated to protect outsiders.

FRANCE

The story of France's collaboration with the Germans is a bitter and controversial one. The heroic efforts of villages in the south to protect Jews, villages like Chambon sur Lignon (see pp. 186–90), provide the greatest reassurance about human reactions, while examples of out-and-out co-operation, such as that of the Vichy police, give us some of our greatest models of complicity. France indeed presents a complex and ambiguous picture regarding the Holocaust.[12]

Partly the complexity results from the fact that the war divided France into two. The northern part of France fell quickly to the Germans in the summer of 1940. A pro-German government was set up in the town of Vichy. The relationship here was much like that between the Germans and Belgians: victor to vanquished. The southern part of France, although nominally governed from Vichy, remained militarily unoccupied. Its concern was to avoid provoking a full German attack and takeover. In this it was only partially successful.

The Vichy French treatment of Jews is predictable on the basis of the data we have seen up to now. The French bureaucracy, like the Belgian, was dominated by the German military. Thus, although the French government was under German control, it had a measure of bargaining power—as did the Belgian—since the Germans depended on the French civil service to enforce regulations. That allowed the French, as it had allowed the Belgians, to mitigate anti-Jewish legislation to some degree. In general, the French, like the Belgians, tried to satisfy German demands by arresting and deporting refugees while shielding their own citizens. There was also a measure of popular resistance against the German arrests and detention of French Jews. Finally, Jews in France, whether citizens or already refugees, were able simply to flee to the as yet unoccupied south. In combination, all these factors made the German efforts to destroy French Jewry less effective than they might otherwise have been.

In late 1942, the Italians occupied southern France.[13] The Nazi party demanded that Italy, as an ally of Germany, collaborate in arresting and deporting Jews. The Italians, however, proved to be uninterested in helping, and at times even seem to have purposely blocked German moves against the Jews.[14] With minor exceptions, the Jews in southern France remained relatively unmolested throughout the Italian occupation. When the Mussolini government fell in August 1943, the German army moved in to occupy the lands held by their former ally. Only then did registrations, arrests, and deportations of Jews begin in a systematic and sustained way. During the next year, until the effective end of German rule in the south, about one-fourth of the Jews in southern France were deported to the death camps in the East. A majority of the deportees were apparently not French but refugees from other parts of Europe. Refugees, the pattern of events in western Europe tells us, could expect governments and citizens alike to do little to protect them. If being Jewish did not necessarily condemn them, being stateless and refugees did.

ITALY[15]

As we have already seen, Mussolini did not share Hitler's obsession with the Jews.[16] He was, however, under considerable German pressure to deal with Italy's Jews as Germany was dealing with its own. So several of the policies developed by the Nazis in Germany were gradually introduced into Italy as well. This seems to have been largely a result of Mussolini's need to keep up pretenses rather than of any ideological commitment to the theory behind the laws. In fact, the laws were only gradually enacted and then only slowly and haphazardly enforced. Under continued German pressure, however, enforcement became more systematic, especially after the German occupation of northern Italy subsequent to Mussolini's fall. But even then there was popular and bureaucratic resistance. Almost eighty percent of Italian Jews eluded deportation.

CONCLUSIONS

Several broad observations are possible about the implementation of Nazi strategy in western Europe.[17] First, in marked contrast to Poland, in all these countries there was an initial commitment to resist Nazi demands and to protect Jewish citizens. One reason may be the long tradition of democracy in these Western countries. The authoritarian and racial policies of the Germans simply did not have at first a receptive audience in countries that for centuries had lived according to the Enlightenment principles of human rights and equal citizenship. Though the opposition was unable to block the ultimate implementation of Nazi policy and though registrations, confiscations, arrests, and deportations occurred in all these countries, there were protests and then attempts to frustrate or at least mitigate the effects of the policy on some categories of Jews. The racial theories behind the Nazi ethic were only incompletely assimilated.

Second, in almost every country refugees were sacrificed in order to protect nationals. There were any number of reasons why this happened. For one, the refugees were more conspicuous. Since they often looked and almost always sounded foreign, they were already an isolated and distinguishable group. Moreover, they were generally poor and powerless, lacking the connections available to the native-born. Too, they were alone. They did not enjoy the full legal protection of their host countries and, with the exception of Denmark, their countries of citizenship failed to act in their behalf. There was therefore little political consequence in arresting and deporting refugees.

Finally, as outsiders refugees were beyond the limits of immediate moral concern. Sacrificing them did not involve compromising one's national identity. A Belgian helping a Belgian Jew evade Germans was acting out his or her own sense of Belgian nationality by joining with the victim against a common enemy. By the same token, favoring a Belgian Jew over a refugee strengthened that same sense of national identity by reinforcing the distinction between Belgians and non-Belgians. In other words, if all Jews were treated exactly the same, then the sense of a special Belgian identity and shared destiny would be lost. But for almost every ethic, a sense of communal solidarity and mutual responsibility is central. It was precisely this sensitivity to group identity, so much a part of our ethical thinking, that was the leading edge of Nazi ideology. Once a community could be forced to acknowledge by deed that foreign Jews were of lesser ethical concern because they were outsiders, it had taken the first step toward the next proposition, that local Jews could be ethically distinguished from local Gentiles, the heritage group to which the bulk of the population could be defined as belonging. Once the issue of group identity had been raised as the central ethical, political, social, and economic issue, as it was in Nazi Europe, all that was needed was a convincing argument about who were the real outsiders. As we have seen, the Nazi identification of Jews as quintessential outsiders could draw on deep social, religious, and scientific warrant. It was at this point that the form of Nazi ethical rhetoric joined up with existing modes of moral rhetoric to present itself as the logical outcome of already accepted and known propositions. It was here that people could be induced to accept the content of Nazi ethics as their own.

Several factors, then, determined the strength of the resistance to German policies. First, in those countries where Jews had been regarded as outsiders before the war began, German policies met with more success. The countries with the most ingrained legacy of Jew hatred were Germany, Austria, and Poland; Jewish communities in these three countries were virtually eliminated. A second factor seems to have been political heritage. In general, countries that had long democratic traditions that stressed human, as opposed to racial, rights demonstrated more resistance to Nazi measures than did countries that favored only particular economic, social, or ethnic groups. Again, the three countries in which the destruction of Jewry was most complete are the three that had the weakest democratic traditions: Germany, Austria, and Poland. The important exception here is Italy, which had little experience with democracy and was in fact controlled by an openly fascist government, yet consistently resisted implementing German racist policies. Countries with strong democratic traditions, such as Norway, Belgium, the Netherlands, and France, generally tried to protect their Jews, at least at the beginning.

The third and last factor that seems to bear some significant correlation to the extent of Jewish destruction is the amount of control exercised by the German Nazi party. Germany, Austria, and Poland were completely dominated. They also had the highest Jewish casualty rates. The Netherlands, Norway, Belgium, northern France, and later Italy were dominated militarily but were not absorbed into the Reich. Jews had a markedly better chance of survival in these areas. The Jewish communities with the greatest survival rates were those in Denmark and in southern France. Although both areas were occupied by the German army, neither was under tight military control. In short, the extent to which the Nazi ethic was accepted seems to have been a function of a number of factors, including the importance of Jews in terms of national identity (low in Scandinavia and the Low Countries, high in central and eastern Europe) and commitment to legal and human rights (higher in the West, lower in the East). Given administrative room to maneuver, prior convictions materially affected events. Yet to the extent that the Nazis' ideology engaged popular prejudice and ethical values, it was able to govern the flow of events.

10

The Final Stage:
Including the Balkans

The Balkans were the last area of Europe to be engulfed by World War II. By the time the conflict reached these countries, the Nazi racial war had reached full maturity. Some time in 1941–42, with the creation of specially designed and constructed killing centers, the mass extermination of a targeted population became a realized policy. So internally consistent had the Nazi system become that it developed an aura of self-evident truth. That is the only way to account rationally for the utter devotion and self-righteousness with which the Holocaust was now pursued. It also explains the great difficulty many ex-Nazis had, and still have, in seeing what they had done wrong. They had begun to live in an entirely new ethical universe. It was into a world governed by this universe that the Balkan states were drawn.

THE ETHIC THAT NOW OPERATED

What are the implications of claiming the existence of a new ethic? The fact is that in Nazi Europe from 1942 onward, the extermination of Jews was seen as serving a higher good. This helped create a whole array of social and political organizations that saw to it that those who participated in the pursuit of the higher good enjoyed social and economic rewards whereas those who refused to go along were regarded, and treated, as criminals. In fact, the impressive array of scientific, philosophical, and historical warrants mustered by the Nazi world view made helping Jews unethical as well. Rationality then demanded that one remain at least neutral, acting in accord with public standards, even if one had personal doubts. As in any ethic one truly had to be an outsider or social deviant to defy the system and help society's victims. This logic came to dominate not only social policy within Germany and the territories it occupied but also international relations. The Balkan countries' failure to deal harshly with their Jews left them out of the mainstream of what had become European thought, and so at a distinct disadvantage when trying to negotiate with the dominant power in Europe, Germany.

No good cause was served by protecting Jews, who were at any rate often regarded with suspicion by significant portions of the population. On the other hand, to collaborate with the Germans offered many benefits, not least of which was a sense of national identity and political independence. There were, to be sure, elements in all these countries that wanted to protect Jews. But the long tradition of anti-Judaism in these areas and their short tradition of democracy, not to mention the overbearing military presence of Germany, all worked against successful resistance to Nazi ethical demands. Susceptible to the rhetoric of the Nazi system, many of these countries eventually acquiesced to some degree: their Jewish populations were offered to the Germans. Acquiescence had by this time, however, a much more drastic meaning than it had had for western Europe. For the Germans had by 1942, as we have seen, themselves crossed a significant threshold in their treatment of Jews. They had made the imaginative leap from Einsatzgruppen to death camps. The result was that the Balkan Jews went straight from their houses to places like Auschwitz.

The immediate predecessors of the death camps were the Einsatzgruppen (see chap. 6), which represent the first step in developing a mechanism for the outright mass killing of Jews. This first crude effort, involving the direct shooting of civilians, had several severe shortfalls, as we have seen. But the ethical commitment to mass murder had been made, and there could be no retreat. So the killings in Russia went on while the bureaucrats back in Berlin searched for more efficient means. The final solution the Nazis stumbled upon combined the mission of the Einsatzgruppen and the administrative organization already in place in the concentration camp.

The concentration camp was really a huge prison designed to hold undesirable elements of the population. Technically, the first such camp was Dachau, operated by the S.A. as early as 1933 to house political prisoners.[1] As Nazi power was consolidated, the number of prisoners the system generated grew dramatically. Soon the camps were housing a wide range of undesirables: the Jews, of course, but also socialists, opposition leaders, homosexuals, members of certain religious groups like the Jehovah's Witnesses, and so forth. The S.S. camp system expanded accordingly. When war broke out in 1939, the number of political and racial prisoners (as well as POWs) grew astronomically. Holding and transient camps were established all over the conquered territories—in Poland, Holland, Belgium, and France, as well as in Germany and Austria. The ghettos in Poland, we know, were themselves part of that burgeoning system. They were to serve as holding areas for setting Jews apart until resettlement areas became available in the Russian steppes. When the new areas of settlement failed to open, the Jewish prisoners became an administrative and economic burden. It was in this context that the Einsatzgruppen were formed. The point was to ensure that the three and a half to four million Soviet Jews would not be added to the already overwhelming imprisoned Jewish mass.

The killing centers grew out of these two already existing institutions, the concentration camps and the Einsatzgruppen. Their union in the killing centers apparently came about at first almost by accident in response to the negative effects the Einsatzgruppen's actions had on their own soldiers, especially when it came to killing women and children. The problems appear to have come to a head in Serbia when the local Nazi leader wanted some Einsatzkommandos to eliminate his Jewish population:

> Attending to the more immediate problems of the operation Boehme issued "special instructions for the implementation of shootings." These instructions equal in detail any orders the Einsatzgruppen ever got. The shooting detachments were to be officer-led; the shootings were to be carried out with rifles from a distance of eight to ten yards; there was a provision for simultaneous aim at head and chest. "To avoid unnecessary touching of corpses" Boehme ordered that the candidates for shooting stand at the edge of the grave. In mass shootings, he said, it would be appropriate to have the hostages kneel facing the grave. Each *Kommando* was to be accompanied by a military doctor, who was to give the order for any mercy shots. Clothes and shoes were to be handed over to the local military officer, and under no circumstances were personal effects to be handed out to the population.
>
> The army's experience with the shootings was similar to that of the Einsatzgruppen in Russia. We have a report on such an operation by a company commander, Oberleutnant Walther, whose unit was engaged in extensive killings at the Belgrade camp. When Company 9 removed hostages from the camp enclosure, the wives of the Jews were assembled "crying and howling." Baggage and valuables of the victims were collected and delivered by truck to the NSV (Volkswohlfart - Welfare Agency). At the killing site three light machine guns and twelve riflemen were posted as security. "The digging of ditches takes a long time," observed Walther, "while the shooting itself is very quick (100 men, 40 minutes.)". . . .
>
> As for the effects of the shootings on his own men, Walther had this to say: "In the beginning my men were not impressed. However, on the second day it became obvious that one or another did not have the nerve to carry out shootings over a lengthy period of time."[2]

Clearly, new methods would have to be found, especially after the men hostages had all been shot and the troops had to face women and children. Someone proposed that small groups of people be loaded onto vans (later to be disguised as hospital ambulances). The exhaust of the vans would be routed back into the rear section into which the prisoners were locked. The vans were to drive to the prearranged mass burial area. When the van arrived, their human cargo was of course dead. Einsatzpersonnel would need merely to remove the corpses and toss them into the mass grave. This technological solution seems to have met with some success. The vans were used to finish the destruction of the Jews of Serbia and then were sent back to Russia for service in mopping-up operations there. The first step in institutionalizing mass murder through technology had taken place.

THE BEGINNINGS OF THE DEATH CAMPS

The second step occurred shortly thereafter in the district of Chelmno. The *Gauleiter* (Nazi district leader) there wanted his area rid of Jews. On December 8, 1941, an Einsatzkommando equipped with gas vans was dispatched to begin the operation. Now, however, a new refinement was tested. Rather than transporting the victims in the vans, the vans remained parked; the victims were simply marched inside. After the engines had run for a predetermined time, the van was opened and the corpses removed. This made much more efficient use of the unit's time, since the engines were run only for the time needed actually to kill the victims and there was no time taken up as the vans returned empty. This makeshift "death factory" succeeded in eliminating from the Warthe-Gau some two hundred thousand people in a fairly short time and with little of the negative impact on troops reported from the Russian front. This second death camp experiment had been an administrative success.

The experiment at Chelmno was watched with some interest by members of the German government. The chancellery had been sponsoring research for some years in eugenics. Part of this program involved the development of techniques for mass sterilizations, in part aimed at eliminating the Mischling population. Another part of the program, however, called for developing a means of administering death on a large scale to selected undesirable populations in Germany: the insane, for example, or "asocials" such as homosexuals. The idea here was to "purify" the Aryan genetic pool. When the Chelmno pilot program became known to the scientists connected with the chancellery euthanasia program, a new administrative interest in this technique of mass killings developed.

By this time the masses of incarcerated Jews in the ghettos of Poland had become an increasingly difficult administrative problem. When the Russian front stalled and then gradually began to recede, it was clear that new and drastic measures would have to be taken to deal with the millions of ghettoized Jews the Reich was supporting. The results of the Chelmno operation brought a solution into focus. The Chelmno concept would be expanded through the building of regular concentration camps with preplanned parking stations for the gassing vans. Since the construction of concentration camps was by now a routine matter, this presented no technical problems. By that summer, the summer of 1942, three such gassing camps were in operation: Belzec opened in March 1942 in eastern Poland to receive and kill Jews from the districts of Lvov and Lublin; Sobibor, ready in May, operated in the Lublin district but received Jews from other parts of Poland, as well as from Holland and France; and the most notorious, Treblinka, north of Warsaw, was originally a Polish slave labor camp but was converted for use as a killing center to help in the liquidation of the Warsaw ghetto. It, like Sobibor, continued to operate until late in 1943. Belzec, the smallest of these camps, shut down in the spring of 1943. In addition, the gas vans at Chelmno continued to operate on and off throughout the war. They were mothballed in the spring of 1943 but then were briefly recalled to service in the summer of 1944 to handle prisoners from the Balkans. Together these camps accounted for the extermination of over a million people in just over a year.[3]

But this was not the only kind of death camp. The concentration camp at Majdanek, which was established as a slave labor camp, was converted to a death camp in 1942. Here, however, death was to come not through gassing but through systematic undernutrition, combined with hard physical labor. Although no gas chambers were constructed, the treatment of the camp's workers produced the same results: some two hundred thousand deaths over the course of its operation, more than at the death factory at Chelmno and only slightly less than at Sobibor. This camp represented an alternative philosophy at work in the Holocaust, and one that came increasingly to the fore. It was that camps could serve an economic as well as a merely racial function. That is, the theory of racial warfare was here combined with the idea that non-Germans were destined to serve as slave laborers for Aryans. Rather than killing the racial enemy outright, camps could exploit their labor first, killing them only when their economic use to the Germans was ended. This practice, tested at Majdanek, was further refined and developed at Auschwitz, which contained a formal killing center as well as a number of satellite "industrial" camps.

AUSCHWITZ

Auschwitz was, in fact, a first in many ways. Chelmno was begun as an experiment that proved to be only partially successful. The three death camps built next (Lublin, Sobibor, Treblinka) moved beyond Chelmno by providing specifically built gas chambers. The technology that was used was still the same, however: asphyxiation by carbon monoxide. But this method was somewhat slow and primitive and not totally reliable. There were occasional problems in starting the engines, and sometimes victims were not totally dead when the chambers were opened. That not only created a problem for the S.S. personnel but could lead to outbreaks of hysteria among the watching and waiting victims. There was clearly a need to develop a more efficient system.[4] And a new system, based on the pesticide Zyklon B, was in fact developed by the bureaucrats in Berlin and became the basis for what was to be the most modern and technologically sophisticated death factory the world has ever seen: Auschwitz.

Auschwitz was new in other ways as well. It was by far the largest camp, being in fact a conglomerate of three camps: Auschwitz I, the main administrative portion, along with several industrial concerns exploiting the camp's slave labor; Birkenau, the death-camp portion; and Monowitz, a slave labor camp run by the industrial conglomerate I. G. Farben in which their synthetic rubber, Buna, was to be manufactured. Auschwitz also had the distinction of being constructed, supplied, and even partially run by private profit-making firms. By the time of its construction, slave labor had become simply good business and death a commodity to be sold. The sheer capacity of the gas chambers was also unprecedented. The camp was designed to make as efficient as possible the movement of people to the chambers and then the transport of the corpses to giant crematoriums. The efficiency was necessary because of the tremendously large number of corpses the camp was slated to produce. There were five crematoriums in all. It is estimated that at one point the camp was able to "process" nine thousand people, the population of a small town, in a twenty-four-hour period.[5] In fact, the gas chambers could handle many more people; bottlenecks developed only at the crematoriums. There were some attempts to increase the capacity of the crematorium retorts to accommodate a greater number of bodies, but technical difficulties intervened. The camp was eventually forced to resort to open-pit burning to keep up with the output of the highly efficient gas chambers. Some one and a half to two million people were killed in Auschwitz during its nearly two years of operation, enough people to constitute a small country.

Auschwitz represented not only a quantum technological leap over the older-style camps of Belzec and Sobibor but also a large-scale incorporation of the slave labor industry exemplified, for example, by Majdanek. Prisoners arriving at Auschwitz were divided into two groups. Those who could provide useful labor were sent to one of the industrial concerns or the Buna works. There they were worked mercilessly and systematically underfed until they died. In this way an important need of the Reich was met: the Jews (or other prisoners) provided labor in a time of increasing manpower shortages in Germany. Those not deemed able to work (the old, women, children) were sent directly to the death camp at Birkenau. We know in incredible detail just how this massive project worked. In general, trains were scheduled to arrive with their human cargo early in the mornings, sometimes even before dawn. Selections were made immediately, and killings and burnings would proceed all day. The final removal and burning of corpses would be completed by late afternoon or early evening so that the cadre could return home and be ready for the new trains the next morning. It was possible for a prisoner to arrive at the camp, be processed, undressed, gassed, burned, and buried within an hour.

An account of what the camps were like has been given by Kurt Gerstein, a gas specialist who visited Belzec and Treblinka as part of the program leading to the adoption of Zyklon B. His description was reported to the Swedish ambassador in August 1943 and later to the papal nuncio in Berlin. Neither seemed particularly interested:

> A small special station with two platforms was set up against a yellow sand hill, immediately to the north of the Lublin-Lemberg (Lvov) railway. To the

south, near the road, were some service buildings and a notice saying: "Waffen-S.S., Belzec Office." . . . We saw no dead that day, but a pestilential odor blanketed the whole region. Alongside the station was a large hut marked "Cloak Room" with a wicket inside marked "Valuables." Further on, a hall, designated "Hairdresser," containing about a hundred chairs. Then came a passage about 150 yards long, open to the wind and flanked on both sides with barbed wire and notices saying: "To the Baths and Inhalation Rooms." In front of us was a building of the bathhouse type: left and right, large pots of geraniums and other flowers. On the roof, a copper Star of David. The building was labeled: "Heckenhold Foundation." That afternoon I saw nothing else. Next morning, shortly after seven, I was told: "The first train will be arriving in ten minutes." A few minutes later a train did in fact arrive from Lemberg, with 45 wagons holding more than 6,000 people. Of these 1,450 were already dead on arrival. Behind the small barbed-wire windows, children, young ones frightened to death, women and men. As the train drew in, 200 Ukrainians detailed for the task tore open the doors and, laying about them with their leather whips, drove the Jews out of the cars. Instructions boomed from a loudspeaker, ordering them to remove all clothing, artificial limbs, and spectacles. Using small pieces of string handed out by a little Jewish boy, they were to tie their shoes together. All valuables and money were to be handed in at the valuables counter, but no voucher or receipt was given. Women and young girls were to have their hair cut off in the hairdresser's hut (an S.S.-Unterführer on duty told me: "That's to make something special for U-boat crews").

Then the march began. On either side of them, left and right, barbed wire; behind, two dozen Ukrainians, guns in hand. They drew near to where Wirth and I were standing in front of the death chambers. Men, women, young girls, children, babies, cripples, all stark naked, filed by. At the corner stood a burly S.S. man, with a loud priestlike voice. "Nothing terrible is going to happen to you!" he told the poor wretches. "All you have to do is to breathe in deeply. That strengthens the lungs. Inhaling is a means of preventing infectious diseases. It's a good method of disinfection." They asked what was going to happen to them. He told them: "The men will have to work building roads and houses. But the women won't be obliged to do so; they'll do housework or help in the kitchen." For some of these poor creatures, this was a last small ray of hope, enough to carry them, unresisting, as far as the chambers of death. Most of them knew the truth. The odor told them what their fate was to be. They walked up a small flight of steps and into the death chambers, most of them without a word, thrust forward by those behind them. One Jewess of about forty, her eyes flaming like torches, cursed her murderers. Urged on by some whiplashes from Captain Wirth in person, she disappeared into the gas chamber. Many were praying, while others asked: "Who will give us water to wash the dead?" (Jewish ritual).[6]

The massive scale of operations at Auschwitz seems to have made the conduct of its business less difficult on its staff than was the case in the smaller, more intimate camps such as Chelmno. There were other administrative difficulties, however, in keeping such an operation working at respectable efficiency. One major and recurring concern at a large-scale operation such as Auschwitz, it seems, was sadism. The concern was not so much with the pain of the victims but with the purity, we might say, of the staff. Pain itself was understood to be a reality of everyday life for the prisoners. They were systematically starved, inadequately clothed—especially for the harsh Polish winters—overworked, and forced to live in filth. On top of this there was a strictly enforced system of rules that could bring their own punishments, such as flogging. Added to the physical pain were psychological tortures: the loss of family, the constant fear of being selected for medical experiments, the constant sight of the crematoriums belching out their smoke. The staff was also allowed to engage in controlled "sport" with the prisoners as a means of relieving tension. But random and unauthorized acts of sadism were not tolerated. That would be counter to the Nazi ethic of law and order; violence controlled by the state and imposed in the service of a higher good was permissible, but *individual* acts of vengeance of Jew baiting were to be suppressed. It is fully in line with Nazi ethics that in Auschwitz the administration should be concerned with the moral development of its cadre.[7]

THE JEWS OF THE BALKANS

It was into this world that most of the Jews of the Balkans vanished. The Balkans in fact offer an interesting insight into the ethical quandary of Europe at this time. On the one hand, although these countries had never particularly tolerated Jews, they all showed an initial reluctance to bow to Nazi demands. Most seem to have felt that German designs against their Jews were an affront to their own sovereignty. Their nationalistic feelings, especially given the deterioration of the German front lines in the East, meant that Germany had to exert considerable pressure on the governments in order to have anti-Jewish ordinances enacted and enforced. When Nazi pressure reached a certain level, however, these governments gave way, with the result that trains full of hysterical victims streamed northward. On the other hand, when German pressure ebbed, the flow of Jews correspondingly decreased. It is in these countries that we see most vividly the struggle of choosing one ethic over another. Those who stayed within the older ethic hoped to outwait Germany. For them, attacks on Jews were attacks on national sovereignty. For others, eliminating Jews was the most effective means for furthering social goals. In each country, then, there developed a particular and complex interaction of forces, and in each country a particular resolution emerged. In general, the pressure of Germany was too great to be fully resisted, and the Russians advanced too slowly to save the Balkan Jews. The result was that all the Jews in the Balkans were caught up at some point and to some extent in the Holocaust process, although the proportions that were actually deported varied considerably from country to country.

Bulgaria, Romania, and Hungary present three different courses that events could take.[8] Bulgaria turns out to have been the most consistent in protecting its Jews. Under the leadership of its king, who represented the common destiny of all Bulgarians, the Bulgarian government routinely delayed passing anti-Jewish laws and, when such laws finally had to be passed, procrastinated in enforcing them. Although Bulgarian Jews, because of relentless German pressure, were required to wear stars and were even organized into forced-labor battalions, nothing near complete compliance with anti-Jewish laws was ever achieved. By sticking to his principles and putting the rights of his citizens first, King Boris's influence largely frustrated the Nazi plans for Bulgaria's Jews.

Romania presents exactly the opposite case. It was virtually the only country outside greater Germany to implement fully the entire spectrum of anti-Jewish policies. Even Romania, however, made important distinctions. German intervention in Transylvania resulted in that territory's being ceded to Hungary. The Jews there shared the fate of the Jews in Hungary. The Jews in Bessarabia were driven out after this area was recovered from Russia. Russia refused to accept any Jewish refugees, and Romania refused to accept Bessarabia's Jews as citizens. As a result, these Jews, rendered homeless and superfluous, completely perished. The Jews of Old Romania, however, were offered some protection by their government and, thus, largely survived. This indicates that even the Romanians had doubts about adopting Nazi policy fully, especially as regards the authentic Old Romanian Jews. Historical events seem to reflect their ambivalence. The height of anti-Jewish actions against the Jews of Old Romania occurred in 1941–42. By the middle of 1942, when the possibility of a German defeat was already on the horizon, the Romanian government began to show less vigor in its anti-Jewish measures.

HUNGARY

The most unusual case of all is Hungary. Hungary remained free of outright German military control until March 1944, just months before the Russians advanced into eastern Europe. Two factors seem to have played important roles in the final German co-option of Hungary. First, within Hungary itself there had been a political bloc that consistently shared the German hatred of Jews and pushed for an alliance with the Nazis. This bloc drew strength from Hungary's struggle to develop and elevate Magyar nationalism after centuries of domination by Austria. Support for the bloc's views came also from other politicians who hoped to gain some territorial concessions for the Hungarian state from the Germans as a reward for their support. Second, on the German side, there was a real and gnawing fear that Hungary was about to side with the advancing Russians and declare war on Germany. The only way to ensure that this would not happen was forcibly to occupy the country. With this thought in mind, German politicians staged a major desperate push to help the pro-German parties already active in Hungary to take over the government. Their effort bore fruit in March 1944. Along with the military occupation came the Nazi war against the Jews. Under the supervision of Adolf Eichmann, the S.S. began an immediate program of arresting and deporting Hungary's large Jewish population. Russian soldiers entering Hungary hardly six months later found virtually no Jews. Only an insignificant few had somehow eluded Auschwitz, so concerted was the German effort to rid Europe of its Jews.

The liquidation of Hungary's Jews is of interest because of its unusual circumstances. First, the entire extermination process occurred when the defeat of Germany was not only clearly inevitable but also imminent. It was perpetrated in the very face of defeat. Second, although the Jewish community in Hungary remained essentially intact and functioning until the spring of 1944 and was surely aware both of what was happening in Auschwitz and of the German designs on Hungary, it was totally unable to organize or mount an effective resistance when the German deportations began. Finally, the deportations were carried out at a time when their true character could no longer be concealed. The killings at Auschwitz were by now an open international secret, and the Hungarians knew it as well as anyone else. There was no attempt to hide what was happening under the label of "resettlement." Despite a clear knowledge of what was being done, despite the full survival of the Jewish communal structure, and despite the imminent defeat of Germany, the entire community was arrested, deported, and gassed.

The fact that this could be done so thoroughly, openly, and quickly in a country not committed to an alliance with Germany, and to a community that was aware of what was about to happen, and while the world watched in full awareness shows how overpowering and persuasive the ethic had become. The destruction of the Hungarian community tells us how committed to their ethic the Germans were who at the end of their Reich continued to carry out acts of genocide with complete devotion. It tells us about the moral co-optation of Hungarian functionaries who in sight of the German defeat collaborated in this horrible labor in the pursuit of nationalistic goals. It tells us about the Jews who became victims without mounting any effective resistance. And it tells us about the ethical confusion of the world that watched silently as the trains rolled across Europe bringing the Jews of Hungary to the death camp at Auschwitz.

The case of Hungary throws into relief the force of the new ethic promulgated by the Nazis. Its power was so overwhelming that it left even its victims immobilized. Collaboration was simply the most rational choice. But even the German perpetrators, I want to argue, were victims of their own system. Eichmann was not a psychotic or a sadist. He was a middle-level bureaucrat doing his duty to serve what he honestly came to believe was a higher good. In this he was no different from any of us. In pursuit of his ideal he organized hundreds of train transports to carry Jews to Auschwitz, trains desperately needed to carry ammunition and supplies to the ravaged German troops trying to halt the Russians' advance. Eichmann and his superiors were apparently convinced that this was a better use of the train. There could hardly be a clearer proof of how fully the Nazi state had become a victim of its own fanatical view of the world.

Our task in the following pages is to understand how the system worked. We want to examine its internal logic and structure. We shall then be able to begin to answer the larger questions of the nature of ethical systems and of how they can be manipulated and recast in the modern world.

PART THREE

ETHICS AND THE SHAPING OF SOCIAL INSTITUTIONS

We have so far reviewed the intellectual background of the Nazi ethic of genocide and have traced the development of this ethic as it became institutionalized across Europe. My reason for pursuing this diachronic study is to examine how a formal ethic takes on specific content as it is forced to engage and organize an ever-expanding circle of reality. The preceding chapters reveal that the Nazi ethic was flexible enough to be adapted to different cultures while retaining its central integrity of presenting Aryans and other nations and races as engaged in a necessary war against primarily Jewish racial enemies. The analysis so far, then, has looked upon the Nazi ethic as a dynamic and developing system of thought centered upon a basic grid of foundational convictions.

In the following chapters the same evidence will be examined from another angle, namely, from a synchronic point of view. That is, I now wish to look at the Nazi ethic as a system of actions that was able at a given time to generate and sustain a certain institutional expression across the expanse of modern culture. Through this examination I hope to explore how the entire political, intellectual, and economic structure of Nazi Europe was shaped in the image demanded by the Nazi ethic. Our concern shifts away, then, from ethics as a system borne forward by its own dynamic and toward ethics as a force that gives character to the institutions and people living under its influence.

11

Ethics as Partisan Ideology

The Nazi party provides the institutional context within which the Nazi ethic grew from a vague and general orientation toward the world to the ruling ideology of Germany. The particular content of Nazi ideology from 1933 on cannot be understood apart from the intellectual legacy discussed in part 1 as shaped by the specific political and social realities of Germany. This chapter will show how the formal, intellectual characteristics of pre-Nazi thinking were shaped into particular proclamations and prescriptions as the party achieved political prominence in Weimar Germany. Until 1933 at least, the most important factor in the shaping of the content of Nazi ideology was the mind of Adolf Hitler. His activities in fact provide a model case study of how the move from formal orientation to concrete policy and ethic is effected. This chapter, then, traces the genesis of the Nazi ethic as first of all an ideology of a party.

THE EARLY YEARS OF THE NAZI PARTY

The Nazi party has its roots in the political matrix of post–World War I Germany. It developed out of the German Workers' party, one of the small radical parties that had sprung up throughout Germany in 1919 and 1920 in reaction to the establishment of the Weimar government and the recently published stipulations of the Treaty of Versailles. Hitler discovered this party while serving as a corporal in the Army News Bureau. When political anarchy threatened in 1919 and 1920, he, like many other military personnel, was assigned to monitor some of the radical splinter groups that were emerging. One of the parties he was asked to observe was the German Workers' party.[1]

This small group for some reason impressed Hitler deeply. He later claimed that he found there a group of loyal German citizens who were not afraid to identify openly the enemies who had brought on Germany's humiliating defeat. Hitler joined the party. It was not long, however, before he became disenchanted with the lackadaisical leadership of Anton Drexler, the party's founder. The party was little more than an expanded Bavarian drinking club and seemed unable or unwilling to grow beyond that. Its total financial resources consisted of some eight marks.[2] This, for Hitler, would never do. The important truth seen by the group of drinking associates had to be broadcast. Too, Hitler's latent ambitions began to emerge: he wanted a strong and effective organization through which he could galvanize public opinion, and accordingly he began badgering and bullying Drexler to expand party activities. When Drexler continued in his sluggish ways, Hitler simply took matters into his own hands. Within a year, he had managed single-handedly to raise party membership to one hundred. The timing was crucial, because the first serious political challenges to the Weimar Republic were just emerging. In February 1920, the most threatening of these erupted, the so-called Kapp putsch. Although it eventually failed, the coup almost succeeded in Bavaria, where Hitler and the German Workers' party were active. Hitler now saw clearly that the Bavarian populace was dissatisfied with the status quo and ready for a change. In his typically rash and audacious style, Hitler rented a huge lecture hall and proposed to stage a massive public rally under the sponsorship of the German Workers' party.[3] Despite the misgivings of the party's old-timers, the gamble paid off: the hall was nearly full. The German Workers' party had suddenly emerged into the public arena. In less than a year, Hitler had transformed the party from an obscure drinking club into a political force to be reckoned with, at least in Bavaria.

Hitler had by this time initiated a number of important changes within the party as well. First of all, he was now clearly the effective leader of the party. Acting in that role, he changed its name to the National Socialist Workers' party and initiated a vigorous campaign to recruit new members. In this he was apparently aided by the growing revolutionary atmosphere of Munich, for party membership increased dramatically. Among new recruits was Ernst Roehm, a captain in the Army District Command in Munich. Roehm brought into the party a number of former soldiers who were now members of one of the many private militias (*Freikorps*) that had begun to roam the streets of German cities. Out of these people, Roehm put together the party's first paramilitary security unit—the *Sturmabteilung,* or S.A.[4] Such a force was a necessity at this time to keep order at party meetings, to enforce party discipline, and to prevent opposition parties from disrupting rallies. Later, Roehm persuaded Hitler to purchase a small newspaper to serve as the party organ. This paper, the *Völkischer Beobachter,* eventually became an important tool for building a national audience.[5]

By 1921, then, most of the recognizable features of the emerging Nazi party were in place: the party had a mass following, a newspaper, and a tough security force. Its intellectual and material resources were also in place: discontent with the existing state of affairs, a self-righteous moral fervor to effect change and restore German honor, and a cadre of ex-soldiers used to living within the moral universe of combat. All that was needed now was a catalyst that could propel the party into national attention. That catalyst was now fortuitously provided by outside events.

In the previous national election, in the summer of 1920, the moderate, pro-Weimar parties suffered a significant electoral loss, throwing the government into temporary disarray. Then in April 1921, the Allies announced the final sum of reparation payments to be demanded of Germany: 132 billion gold marks! Public despair and anger were broad and deep, setting off a series of assassinations, including that of one of the leaders of the moderate wing, Matthias Erzberger. This was followed a few months later by a plebiscite in Upper Silesia calling for the area to be reunited with Germany. In October, the angered and radicalized German public learned that the League of Nations had decided to ignore the plebiscite and award the territory to Germany's archenemy, Poland. Germany, it seemed, was being systematically humiliated by its neighbors while the Weimar government stood by helplessly.[6] Then, to add to the government's troubles, the economy flew out of control. When Germany, as a result, fell behind in reparation payments, the French army moved in and occupied the Ruhr industrial valley. This only deepened the economic crisis, fueling unprecedented inflation. With the economy in a shambles and the lower classes wiped out, with Germany being dismembered and the government caught in political gridlock, it is no wonder that fringe parties such as Hitler's became desperate to act.

While these events were occurring outside, the party was becoming radicalized from within. The S.A., originally designated to protect Nazi party meetings, had slowly become more aggressive. Members began to disrupt opposition-party meetings and then to rough up their leaders. At the same time, party rhetoric became more and more extreme. To support his new aggressive stance, Hitler, in 1923, turned the party paper, the *Völkischer Beobachter* into a daily. Finally in November he decided that the time had come for the party to act before others seized the initiative. The party attempted its first coup. Although the coup ended in dismal failure, it is interesting because it taught Hitler that he had to prepare the ground carefully before making another radical move. It foreshadows the tactics Hitler used to gain and extend his power. It is worthwhile, then, to dwell on Hitler's first attempt to take over the government of Germany.

THE BEER HALL PUTSCH

Bavaria seemed to be ripe for revolution anyway. The longstanding Bavarian ambivalence toward the central government in Berlin was augmented by the apparent collapse of the Weimar government. There had already been widespread talk of secession. Hitler, by now prominent in the radical political scene in Munich, urged the Bavarian government to initiate military action against Berlin. The Bavarian government refused. Frustrated at the government's inaction, Hitler decided to take matters into his own hands.[7] Accompanied by several of his S.A. troops, Hitler stormed into a beer hall where several government officials were speaking and at gunpoint demanded that the government then and there secede from Germany. The officials, to their credit, refused to be bullied. Hitler then did the unimaginable. While holding the government members hostage and incommunicado, he himself announced that they had "decided" to secede from Berlin and hand over power to a government to be formed by General Erich Ludendorff and himself. Leaving the government ministers under the watchful eyes of armed S.A. members, Hitler triumphantly marched to the town hall to accept leadership of the new government. This bold maneuver failed when, somehow, one of the hostages slipped away and reported that no such decision had been made. Alerted, the local police quickly mustered and broke up the march. Hitler was arrested and charged with treason. Thus ended the so-called Beer Hall Putsch. With it seemed to end all hope for a Nazi takeover of Germany.

REBUILDING THE PARTY

Hitler's trial took place in 1924 and surely marked the nadir of Nazi fortunes. By this time the Weimar government had been able to gain some control over the economy and halt the inflation. There was also an end to the wave of assassinations that had swept Germany. In fact, the next four years, until the depression of 1929, were relatively peaceful and prosperous. No new foreign-policy disasters occurred. With both the domestic and the foreign situation of Germany improving, the overheated revolutionary atmosphere began to cool down. At the same time, the Nazi party itself had proved to be a spectacular failure: its coup had failed, its leader was in jail, and the party had begun to come apart.

Yet Hitler managed to turn even these discouraging events to his own advantage. He used the trial to gain a national platform from which to proclaim his ideas. By the time the trial was over, Hitler had managed to make himself a nationally known figure.[8] He was sentenced to jail and the party was banned, but by the end of the year he had been released, and the ban on the party was lifted shortly thereafter. Even the time he spent in jail was not wasted. During that time, Hitler wrote *Mein Kampf*, his meandering ruminations on Jews, Germany, economic theory, and politics. Thus, less than a year after the trial began, Hitler was free, had a public audience, and with more experience, was able to turn to rebuilding the shattered party with renewed energy and conviction.[9]

Hitler's success in rebuilding the Nazi party during these years is told just by the numbers. The remarkable increase in membership must be seen as a stunning testimony to Hitler's organizing ability and popular appeal. There was a public ban on rallies during the years 1925–27, so the increase was due solely to advertising by word of mouth. The party Hitler returned to in late 1924 had about twenty-five thousand members. In

1926, membership had doubled to nearly fifty thousand. In 1927 it had increased to over seventy thousand, in 1928 to nearly 110 thousand, and in 1929 to an astounding 178 thousand.[10] For a party this large, careful organization was needed. In fact, Hitler seems to have spent a good deal of thought and energy organizing his party. Its early organizational scheme is interesting because it reveals how Hitler viewed the party's mission. The party had two principal divisions. The mission of the first was to devise policies and procedures for undermining the Weimar Republic. The second main division had the task of constructing a countergovernment, one that would be ready to take over the reins of government when the first unit had successfully accomplished its task. Here already the seriousness of Hitler's dream of remaking Germany is evident.

The party had other divisions as well. There were, of course, the official party police, the S.A. The S.A. itself had by this time grown to monstrous proportions. It claimed something like a hundred thousand members, a force bigger than the German national army. In fact, the S.A. was so big that Hitler no longer felt he could fully trust or control it. He thus created a new "elite" guard within the S.A.: the *Schutzstaffel,* or S.S.[11] There was also a Youth Corps to indoctrinate younger members of the party and to train them to become leaders in the new Germany the party was to create. To support all of this there was a women's auxiliary. Hitler had even seen to it that the party had a court system to enforce party discipline. The party was being forged into a powerful, unified ideological machine so that when the next crisis appeared, Hitler would be in a position to exert his will.

He did not have long to wait. A new depression began to develop in late 1929. All of the fears of five years earlier were revived. This was a time that demanded clear and decisive leadership. Yet this is precisely when the Weimar Reichstag became most ineffective. The rising number of anti-Weimar delegates in the Reichstag effectively paralyzed the government. It is in the context of the new economic crisis, accompanied by a growing paralysis in the government, that Hitler was finally able to lift his party into power.

The remainder of our story can be quickly told. In the 1930 election, the Nazi party received some six and four-tenths million votes, making it the second-largest party to send delegates to the Reichstag, with 107 representatives. In some ways this says less than it seems, because the vote was divided among so many parties, none of which commanded anything near a majority. The Nazi party was second-largest only in an array of small parties. Yet this was still an impressive electoral accomplishment. The party now controlled just under twenty percent of the seats in the new Reichstag, a not insignificant number. Its penetration of the Reichstag is especially startling in view of the rapidity of the party's rise: a mere five years earlier it had seemed to have no future. It did even better in the next election. In the summer of 1932, it returned to the Reichstag 230 delegates, something over a third of the total. This made the Nazis the largest single bloc in the Reichstag, and so all but essential for any coalition. This fact was not lost on Hitler, as we shall see in a moment. It is interesting, however, that the election in the summer of 1932 represented the high point of the party's electoral popularity—until the actual takeover, when the election results were no longer necessarily reflective of how people felt. The next election, held at the end of 1932, saw the Nazi party drop some fifteen percent, losing thirty-four seats.[12]

What was behind the party's popularity? Its membership now stood at four million, and its paramilitary units, the S.A. and the S.S., totaled four hundred thousand, making it by far the largest uniformed military organization in the country. Nazi popularity sprang from a number of sources, its platform being probably of only minor influence since it is doubtful that most people really grasped its implications. Of greater importance, apparently, was the deteriorating economic situation and the paralysis of the Weimar government, on the one hand, and Hitler's forceful call for a new political order, on the other. Germany had undergone four years of devastating war and fifteen years of semianarchy. During that time Germany had seen its government driven into gridlock by the electoral successes of dozens of rival parties, had stood by helplessly as its lands were occupied, and had undergone terrible economic crises. The desperate need was for someone to take control. The Nazi party had gained for itself the reputation of being capable of what was needed. It had a charismatic leader, an insistently proclaimed ideology, a clear blueprint for the future Germany based on a need to respond forcefully to Germany's unjust humiliation, a strong organization, good discipline, and a reputation for being able to get things done. These strengths guaranteed it some electoral success.

Important material support was now coming from powerful sectors of German society. Hitler began actively recruiting soldiers in 1920. His own army background, along with his calls for rearmament and the regaining of lost territory, made the military a natural audience for his rhetoric. The wooing of the army is significant because the army was from the beginning a major supporter of the Weimar government. Its gradual neutralization not only spelled trouble for the government but removed a major potential obstacle to the Nazis themselves. German businessmen began to see the Nazi party as alone having the potential to create a rational business climate. Business in Germany, after all, needed political stability and a predictable economy to survive. Hitler, of all the politicians crowding the German scene, seemed to have the requisite vision and toughness. For perfectly understandable reasons, then, business contributions became a major source of funding for Nazi activities during these years.

None of this was lost on the German political leadership as they surveyed their options after the elections in 1930, and then again in mid-1932, and yet a third time in late 1932. They were truly caught in a bind. On the one hand, coalition partners had to be found in order for a centrist government to be formed. The centrist parties were so weak, however, that they could not by themselves sustain a coalition government. On the other hand, the failure to form a centrist coalition would either leave the country without a government coalition or—an equally bleak alternative—give the initiative to the extreme left or the extreme right. Since neither of these alternatives was palatable, the centrist parties had to find what allies they could, fully aware that any party brought into the coalition would have its own preconditions. With this in mind, President Hindenburg vainly tried to find a combination that would keep the moderates in power.[13] The spectacular rise of the Nazi party could not be ignored. Although it is clear that Hindenburg did not want to include the Nazis in a coalition, it is equally clear that by the end of 1932 he had no viable alternative. Hitler's price was the chancellorship, the interior ministry, and a ministry without portfolio. His demands were unpleasant but not impossible. In January, when no other solution appeared, and when there was a possibility that the fifth national election within a year would have to be called, Hindenburg made the fateful decision: he opened negotiations with Hitler. On January 30, Hitler accepted his terms.

TAKING CONTROL OF GERMANY

The selection of Hitler did not mean that the Nazi party controlled Germany. First of all, Hitler controlled only one other vote in the cabinet besides his own, that of Wilhelm Frick, who became minister of the interior.[14] This position was relatively unimportant since in Germany, unlike most other European governments, the ministry of the interior did not control the police. Since the conservatives held most of the important cabinet posts and since Hindenburg remained president, it seemed that Hitler's room for maneuver was sufficiently restricted. Moreover, the election results of December 1932 indicated that the Nazi party's electoral appeal was waning. Thus, Hindenburg reasoned, Hitler was weak enough to be controlled by moderates in the government. The president did not reckon, however, with Hitler's political cunning. Hitler was determined to use his office as chancellor first and foremost to gain more seats in the Reichstag for his party. The first step was to create a need for a new election. This Hitler did by entering negotiations with the Center party, negotiations that were designed to fail. When coalition negotiations with the Center party collapsed, Hitler did what he had to as chancellor and called for new elections. At the same time he made sure that the Nazi party exploited its position as effectively as possible to increase its share of the votes. Business leaders were shaken down for contributions; party officials viciously attacked the leaders of opposition parties; newspapers that spoke out against the Nazis were vilified; opposition leaders were beaten by the S.A. It was to be a no-holds-barred fight for votes. Then, on February 27, 1933, a full-blown crisis played into Hitler's hands. A fire, apparently set by a leftist revolutionary, gutted the Reichstag. It appears today that the fire was the work of a single Dutch communist, but in the atmosphere of the time rumors of revolution were taken seriously. Hitler seized upon this news to create an atmosphere of mass hysteria.[15] It was, he said, the beginning of the dreaded leftist revolution. Immediate steps had to be taken to protect Germany and her citizens from the "bolshevik" insurgents who were even then poised to take over Germany. Badgered relentlessly by Hitler and facing the prospect of mass hysteria, President Hindenburg signed a bill entitled "For the Protection of the People and the State." Its stipulations included a check on democratic freedoms:

> Restrictions on personal liberty, on the right of free expression of opinions, including freedom of press; on the right of assembly and association; and violations of postal, telegraphic and telephone communications; and warrants for house searches, orders for confiscations as well as restrictions on property are all permissible beyond the legal limits otherwise prescribed.[16]

In other words, the government was just before a major election given virtually unrestrained police powers. This was, of course, made to order for Hitler's purposes. It allowed Hitler legally to gag opposition parties and to arrest members of major centers of opposition to Nazi rule, such as the Communist and Social Democratic parties. The government alone had access to the media, which Hitler spurred into stirring up even further fear about a revolution. At the same time, the S.A. went on a rampage of terror against anyone speaking out against Nazi policies and programs. It was at this time, not coincidentally, that the old abandoned factory at Dachau first came into use as a Nazi prison for political prisoners. The Nazi party was suddenly an immense, virtually unopposable, force.

Given the atmosphere in which elections took place a few days later, it is not surprising that the Nazi party showed considerable gains. It won forty-four percent of the Reichstag vote. From another perspective, however, the vote was disappointing. The entire election had been manipulated: major opposition parties had been driven out of the election, and Paul Joseph Goebbels, the party's propaganda chief (he would be named propaganda minister a week after the election), had unlimited access to the media. Even so Hitler fell short of the majority he needed. Clearly other tactics had to be employed. Hitler concluded that legislative authority had to be taken away from the Reichstag.

The occasion for withdrawing legislative authority was to be the convening of the Reichstag in Potsdam, the traditional imperial capital, on March 21, 1933, the anniversary of Bismarck's Second Reich. The choice of Potsdam on this date was a stroke of political genius, apparently suggested by Goebbels, for it symbolized in a powerful way the government's dedication to re-creating the German Empire and reestablishing Germany's honor in Europe. The first order of business, Hitler decided, was to deal with the forces trying to destroy Germany. In coalition with the right-wing parties, Hitler bullied the Reichstag into passing what was in effect its own death decree. Legislative authority was renounced for a period of four years to enable the government to deal vigorously with the crisis at hand. This bill has come to be known as the Enabling Act. Through it Hitler legally gained unrestricted control of the government for four years. By 1937, when the bill technically expired, Hitler was in a position to ignore it totally.

Events unfolded quickly after this point. Indeed, it is easily forgotten how quickly events moved. By the time Hitler had been chancellor for barely two months, the federal government had been effectively destroyed and the major opposition parties abolished. By the summer of 1933, the full apparatus of the Nazi state was in place.

The policy that was now implemented over the next few months is known as the *Gleichschaltung*.[17] This word, like so many Nazi euphemisms, is an engineering term. It refers to the coordination of power between AC and DC. In Nazi parlance, it meant the realignment of the German government to bring it into line with the structure demanded by the Nazi party, that is, the remaking of the state in the image of the party. The first step in *Gleichschaltung* occurred in March 1933 with the abolition of state governments. Each state was now to be governed by a Reich governor appointed by the party; naturally, all appointees were party members. The next major change came at the beginning of April, with the reform of the civil service. This reform called for all "non-Aryans," as well as any other civil servants whose loyalty to the party was questionable, to be retired.[18] Taken together with the abolition of state governments, the reform of the civil service had the effect of Nazifying the entire police, judicial, and bureaucratic apparatus of the state. In effect, the entire power and resources of the government were now working in the service of the party.

The traditional Labor Day observance in Europe is on May 1, and the German workers' parties held a huge rally in 1933 to protest the arrogation of power by the Nazis. That provided Hitler with an excuse for abolishing workers' organizations, which had now publicly demonstrated their inability to work with the Nazi party. On May 2, all labor unions were banned (in a curious move for a politician who rose to prominence through a workers' party). In July, the circle was closed as all political parties were banned. There was no longer any effective center of opposition to the Nazis.

It seems that at first the impact of these moves was not felt by most Germans. Unless one was a prominent opposition politician or an outspoken newspaper editor, he or she was probably not immediately and materially affected. The problem only gradually became evident as more and more people found themselves defined, for whatever reason, as state enemies. These people discovered that they were truly prisoners in a country in which they, and anyone who wished to help them, were powerless. The police had been co-opted, as had the government bureaucracy; the courts offered little help; no organization could serve as their champion. For them, especially the Jews—who were defined as enemies—the die was cast. It took another ten years for the "final solution" to achieve full institutional expression; the labor battalions and death camps were years away. But the process that began now was inexorable and unstoppable. Within the first three months that Hitler was chancellor, all effective means of legal redress were rendered impotent.

The character of the government that now had a monopoly on all power can be illustrated by one event, the Roehm purge.[19] In this bloodbath, the party "purified" itself of undesirable elements. In seeing what the party was willing to do to its own, we get a grim insight into what the party would be willing to do to its sworn enemies. The Roehm purge is so called because its chief victim was Ernst Roehm, longtime commandant of the S.A. Behind the purge of the S.A. lay a number of motives. For one, the organization had become a center of power of its own, making it somewhat independent of Hitler. It could not be trusted in the way the smaller S.S. could be. Second, it had earned itself, and so the party, a bad reputation during the 1920s. It was commonly, and correctly, perceived as a band of thugs. The more conservative backers of Hitler, especially the business people, wanted it brought under control. By destroying it, then, Hitler could both remove this element of independence in the party and satisfy the demands of his important supporters. Finally, the S.A. seems to have been truly revolutionary. It wanted to sweep away all the existing German institutions. But by now Hitler was the establishment. He needed to end the revolution and begin a period of consolidation and rebuilding. To achieve this, the S.A. had to be stopped.

The S.A. had already established itself as an unusually brutal force. It showed no hesitation in breaking up opposition political meetings in the twenties or, later, in brutally assaulting people with whom it disagreed. Its activity at Dachau, one of its private prisons, illustrates the nature of this Nazi militia. The S.A. operations at Dachau prison began in 1933 in order to provide housing for political prisoners arrested in the first few months of Nazi rule. In the first year, some five to six hundred prisoners died while under S.A. control. In the next year, almost twenty-seven thousand prisoners died, mute testimony to the brutal nature of the S.A. cadre. At the same time that the S.A. was becoming more violent, it was also growing beyond all manageable limits. At the time of Hitler's nomination to the chancellorship, it had about three hundred thousand members, a large force by any measure. In 1934, it had ballooned to three and a half million.

There is in this purge yet another element: that of the intraparty rivalry that was taking shape among the various second-echelon leaders. Foremost among these infighters was Heinrich Himmler, the commander of the elite S.S. Because Himmler wanted control of the party military apparatus for himself and his S.S., he actively encouraged Hitler's plans to destroy the rival S.A. The purge finally occurred on July 3, 1934, as Roehm and his leadership cadre vacationed at Bad Wiessen. Himmler had thoughtfully compiled dossiers and death lists ahead of time. Arrests and assassinations were coordinated to occur throughout Germany simultaneously. Roehm was sent to Dachau and allowed to commit suicide. Hundreds of other S.A. officers were shot, either at Bad Wiessen or at their homes. The S.S. used the occasion to eliminate many of its rivals and even to settle some old scores. In the chaos of the purge, possibly as many as one thousand civilians, including a number of prominent government officials and members of the Reichstag, were summarily executed with no pretext of arrest and trial. Gustav von Kahr, for example, who had played a major role in putting down the Beer Hall Putsch in Munich ten years earlier was found hacked to death near Dachau.[20]

The utter control that Hitler by now exercised is shown by the reaction to these outrages. When ten days later Hitler reported to the Reichstag, it offered only the mildest of protests. The army and business interests stuck by the party. The brutal execution by the party of thousands of people, including members of the government, had been accomplished just on the whim of Hitler and provoked no significant public protest. Hitler's emerging modus operandi had been tacitly validated. The entire government had accepted some of the foundational demands of the new ethic.

12

The Bureaucratization of the Ethic: The S.S.

By the time the party came to power, it had already developed fully the framework of its just-war ideology and had gained experience in using that framework to shape a number of diverse party institutions. The period from 1933 to 1939 was taken up in extending that framework from the party to the state's government apparatus as a whole. The process of articulation, of matching party theory to the realities of everyday governmental life, developed on two levels, the public and the party. In the public realm, of course, was the transition of Nazism from party to government. This was the *Gleichschaltung,* the aligning of state institutions with party ideology. At the same time there was considerable internal development of party thought. That internal change was driven primarily by the S.S. The party's elite paramilitary corps saw itself as the truest organizational expression of the Nazi ethic and struggled to impose its values on the party as a whole, and through the party on all of Germany. To understand the development of Nazi ethics from 1933 to 1939 and beyond, then, it is necessary to look at the S.S.[1]

THE CONSOLIDATION OF POWER

The channel through which the party expressed its vision was the normal state bureaucracy, which provided the organization and the technical expertise necessary to carry out government programs. This does not mean that all bureaucrats in the German government suddenly became convinced Nazis. It was necessary only that the policy governing the functioning of the bureaucracy become Nazified. Government workers then either had to make their peace with the new reality or risk losing their jobs. This takeover of the bureaucracy was possible because the Nazis never saw themselves as revolutionary; they had no overt interest in sweeping away the entire existing structure in order to erect their own. Rather, they were perfectly willing to work through existing structures, provided that these could be arranged to carry out the Nazis' program. All that was needed for this was control of a few top positions. The average office workers in the various government ministries saw little overt change at first; they did the same thing when they went to work on February 6, 1933, as they had done the week before. The only tangible difference was that there was a new chancellor. Party policy flowed down the normal, familiar channels of authority.

These first steps in the Nazi takeover, the *Gleichschaltung,* worked so smoothly because bureaucracies are not designed to make laws, or even to question laws, but only to administer them efficiently. Once a party arrogates to itself the lawmaking initiative, the bureaucracy in effect comes to work for the party. Civil servants can go about their appointed rounds, filling in forms and signing documents, with no break in pace. As before, they are simply administering the laws of the land.[2]

With legal initiative arrogated by the party, the gradual control of the social, economic, and cultural activities of the state automatically followed. In fact, the first year of Nazi rule can be summed up simply as a matter of consolidation and the extension of control. Institutions of German society were dissolved (opposition parties, labor unions), co-opted (the government agencies, e.g., the police), or regulated (the railways). By mid-1934 the alignment of party and state was virtually completed; the party was no longer in opposition but was now the establishment. The purge of the S.A., the front-line "shock troops" of the party, marks the transition.

The destruction of the S.A. came at a crucial time. It allowed the party to consolidate its own strength to take advantage of one of the most significant political events in Germany at this time. On August 2, 1934, Hindenburg, the president of Germany and the one person still potentially capable of controlling the chancellor of Germany, died. Hitler, with the full weight of a unified party behind him, took the office of president himself, thus combining the two highest offices in Germany. Now the only source of power in Germany that stood outside Hitler's direct control was the army, but the army too was to be co-opted. As Hitler was inaugurated as president, the armed forces were required to renew their oath of loyalty, although now with a new twist. Loyalty was pledged not to Germany or to the constitution but to the person of Hitler. The *Gleichschaltung* had been an overwhelming and complete success. From here on, all that was needed was the careful working-out of details, the regulations that would turn ideology into policy.

It is important to note that, from within the government, little had appeared to change. The civil service remained largely intact, even if a few Jewish office workers had been retired early. The civil servants still went about their daily duties in the usual manner. They continued to administer the law in a regular, neutral, objective, and nonarbitrary way, as they had been trained to do. What had changed was the character of the law. The law now became an expression of party ideology and discretion. The institutions of the state, in short, became operating agencies of the party. The new relationship between party and state was cemented in small but significant ways. In some cases, the top bureaucrats in a ministry were also party regulars. In other cases, dual appointments or agencies were created so that the government agency was overseen by, or was in competition with, the party's parallel bureaucracy. Individuals who supported Nazi policy found their government careers advanced; those who expressed doubts tended to lag behind their peers in promotions.

Behind all this there loomed another unarticulated threat. The S.S., with its burgeoning system of camps, was already a frightful factor to be considered. There is no question that by 1934, Germans were living in a society based on subtle but real terror. Any open criticism brought swift and at times incredibly brutal punishment. The more influence one had, the more closely one was watched by the S.S. Loyalty and patriotism came to mean performing one's job well and effectively while expressing righteous indignation at what alleged traitors to the German race were doing.

POLICY MAKING IN THE PARTY

The complexion of the Nazi state as it developed in the thirties and forties under the increasing domination of the S.S. cannot be understood apart from the peculiar way in which policy was to develop in the Nazi party. First, the remarkable power Hitler had over people's minds cannot be underestimated. By all accounts, Hitler was a spellbinding speaker and exuded a charisma that overwhelmed all who listened to or had contact with him. Through sheer words and bravado, he created around himself an aura of unimpeachable knowledge, power, and historical destiny. It is astounding to read the accounts of the men surrounding Hitler who for thirteen years or more never questioned the rightness of anything he said or did. He held mature people in his utter control for well over a decade. His knowledge was tacitly recognized as supreme: he designed weapons systems for the military; he approved architectural plans for the new Berlin (to be capital of the world); he led the war; he lectured diplomats on German history; he restructured academic disciplines. More strikingly, through sheer charisma, he made his fantasy world real for millions of people. Masses of otherwise rational and mature individuals actually believed that there was a race war, that Jews had concocted a conspiracy to take over the world, and that Germans were the only truly cultured people in the universe and everyone else was a barbarian. What Hitler's mind assembled out of the debris of the past a whole nation accepted as a general truth; what Hitler wanted a whole bureaucracy accepted as legitimate law. Later in the war, all Himmler needed to do was suggest that something was the "Führer's wish" for it to be accepted and acted on. Hitler came to live the racial myth of the fascist: he was the spokesman of an entire race.

It was Hitler's charisma and rhetoric that provoked the country to cross into the new ethic we are describing. Hitler's articulation of his fantasies became a new reality that millions of people were compelled to live out. There was, of course, no real racial war in Europe, but Hitler inaugurated one.

There was no conspiracy on the part of Jews to take over the world. Hitler, and his army, tried to do just that. There were no stashed billions in Jewish gold, yet Hitler and the party systematically plundered Jewish homes and businesses, becoming wealthy in the process. It was, of course, not true that of all the peoples on the globe only Germans were cultured, and yet under Hitler they became barbarians to prove just that. It was a fantasy to think that all true Germans were blue eyed and blond haired, yet hundreds if not thousands of innocent victims became human guinea pigs to find a technology for producing such a master race under the leadership, ironically, of a dark-haired, dark-eyed Austrian with French blood. Reality in this strange world became a weird sort of fiction, while fantasy and wishful thinking became remarkably real.

The readiness of most people to be lulled into this strange world of ideas in which reality was fiction and fiction fact can be traced also to the intellectual presumptions Hitler was able to draw upon. That is, Hitler's influence lay partly in his ability to articulate a myth of racial struggle and superiority that drew on traditional patterns of thought in Europe. In the desperate times of the early thirties, the claims of Hitler made sense. He promised what all Germans wanted: stability, economic growth, and respect. He identified as enemies people that the Germans had always mistrusted: the Jews, the Gypsies, the social misfits, the Russian bolsheviks. He explained how these diverse enemies fitted together: bolshevism was Jewish (as proved, albeit superficially, by all the Jewish leaders in the socialist movements); social misfits represented the degradation of the German race through racial downbreeding (look how many Jews married and bred with "pure" Germans); the Weimar Republic itself was a Jewish invention (was not one of the chief architects of its constitution Hugo Preuss, a Jew?). Finally, he could explain why the Jews wanted to overthrow Germany in the first place: they were engaged—whether consciously or not is beside the point—in a racial struggle for survival. He could explain how their war was being waged: through mongrelization, through the co-optation of German institutions, through the suppression of the genius of the German Volk. And he could articulate the cure: rid Germany of its Jews. The articulation of this program was Hitler's grand achievement. He was much less able to deal with the details of how to implement it. This he left to the bureaucracy and to the initiatives of his warring underlings. When no clear direction came from above, ambitious department heads proposed their own.

The bifurcation of initiative that developed in Nazi Germany thus provided a second mechanism for the implementation of extremist and brutal policies. Hitler, for his part, never had to come face to face with the consequences of his rhetoric. He could simply expound visions and issue directives without having to consider what these would mean in the real world.[3] His underlings, on their part, had surrendered their right to make judgments about what they said or did. They simply accepted the policies and directives as granted and beyond appeal and acted accordingly. When it came to actually arresting, deporting, and killing people, they could pretend that the responsibility was not theirs because they did not produce the policy. Thus the policy maker was spared contact with reality, and the implementers were spared control over policy. The result was that the ideology of the Nazi state was free to develop along its own lines without the friction realities might be expected to impose.

A third factor in the peculiar way policy developed in the Third Reich was Hitler's refusal or inability to make decisions in matters of policy implementation. The result was that initiative passed to the second level of government in which advisers and government ministers vied for power and control. There was, it appears, a constant jostling among the second-echelon leaders around Hitler to gain power by arrogating new areas of policy to themselves. Interagency competition became especially fierce by the forties, when Hitler grew noticeably more morose and indecisive while the possibilities for immense international power and wealth—from the economic plundering of Jewish property—grew exponentially. Ruthless and power-hungry men high in Nazi ranks struggled with one another to devise ever more grotesque policies designed to earn for their agencies new areas of influence. Internal competition was apparently the engine that drove Nazi Germany toward ever more radical policies. As we shall see presently, Himmler, the commandant of the S.S., became a master at this game. He became involved in bitter competition with almost every other government agency at one time or another. Through his ideological commitment and his ruthlessness, the S.S. gradually gathered to itself a vast amount of power. By 1944, it was by far the most powerful single entity in the party and, in fact, we would argue, it had overtaken Hitler as the vital center of Nazism.[4]

THE RISE OF THE S.S.

The rise of the S.S. to preeminence is a good case study, then, of just how the second-echelon process of policy formation worked in the Third Reich. The S.S. began, we have seen, as an elite guard within the S.A. By 1933, it had grown to immense proportions, with about a hundred thousand armed members, and had already earned a reputation for ruthlessness and terror. The S.S. had self-consciously structured itself around the myth that it was the resurrected incarnation of the ancient Teutonic tribes: it often held meetings in medieval castles; it adopted the language and rituals of ancient Teutonic warlords; it created its own structure of ranks with names like Stormleader and Leader of the Storm Colors; it stressed purity of language in an attempt to rid Germany of all foreign, and hence corrupting, words; it held awesome torchlight parades; it adopted ancient symbols such as the swastika and other runic devices. In short, it self-consciously clothed itself in the mythic image of the ancient, and therefore authentic, Teutonic war-lord bands that once roamed the forests of Europe. Accordingly, the S.S. despised liberal democracy, with its emphasis on individual rights. Rather, it stressed the virtues of conformity, submergence of the individual in the group, and ruthlessness in battle. The individual warrior was the real hero, and this is what the true S.S. member was trained to be. Anything that smacked of weakness or compassion had to be destroyed. Any ideology or movement that found virtue in non-Germanic values was declared inauthentic and dangerous.

With the accession of Hitler to the chancellery, the S.S. took upon itself the mission of destroying all institutions associated with non-Teutonic ideals like liberalism and democracy. These, of course, were precisely the institutions fascist political thinking had labeled state enemies anyway: bolshevism, socialism, democracy, Jews, and Western religious organizations (such as the Catholic Center party, which was pro-Weimar). Thus the S.S. could easily forge an alliance between current political theory and its ethic of racial warfare. By October 1933, it had taken over the operation of the political prison at Dachau and turned that city's name into a byword for brutality unlike anything Germans had yet experienced. The prisoners were treated with unbridled hatred and contempt. But Dachau also served as a training base for preparing new recruits for the S.S.'s Teutonic elite. Corporal punishment of prisoners was carried out by teams of S.S. men in front of guards and prisoners so that any sign of weakness could be instantly seen and subjected to public ridicule. Good solid, unflinching punishment, on the other hand, was rewarded. Thus prisoners became training devices for the S.S. and served as guinea pigs for the early attempts of the S.S. to develop as brutal a camp atmosphere as possible. It was here at Dachau that the S.S. refined its policy of endless roll calls, exhausting marches, demeaning salutes, and the like.

Dachau also became the base for another Nazi program. Training at Dachau did manage to create a warrior elite purged of all pity. But Himmler had higher aims. He wanted the S.S. to be a racial army, one made up of true-blooded German warriors. It was here, therefore, that the foundations of the eugenics programs were laid. Prisoners were to serve as racial guinea pigs in the Nazi attempt to re-create and breed the pure, authentic Teuton out of the highly mongrelized German population.[5]

The first major competition the S.S. faced was the S.A. The Roehm purge of 1934, which essentially destroyed the S.A., was the first important victory of the S.S. over its rivals. The purge of the S.A. had many advocates in Hitler's inner circle. But Himmler was one of the more outspoken advocates of the purge, and he was only too eager to make his troops available to help carry it out. In 1934, with the demise of the S.A., the S.S. emerged as the most salient and trustworthy military arm of the party.

Its new status, however, brought it into conflict with other elements of the party—in particular, with the police now under the leadership of Goering. The conflict between these two uniformed services simmered for four years until the *Krystallnacht* riots of 1938. As we have seen, those riots were organized by Goering in an attempt to gain control over the party's anti-Jewish policies. But Himmler, not Goering, gained wider authority to handle Jewish affairs. In the aftermath of *Krystallnacht* came the first systematic arrests of Jews, who were sent to prison and released upon the promise to leave Germany immediately. *Krystallnacht* represents, among other things, the victory of the S.S. over the police.

With the S.S. in charge of the Reich's Jewish policy, clashes with other government agencies struggling for their own share of Jewish loot became inevitable. We have already taken note of conflicts with the finance ministry, as Gestapo agents began skimming off prized Jewish possessions from confiscated apartments before the finance ministry's people could arrive. Another area of conflict developed over labor. When labor shortages began to be severely felt throughout the German war economy by 1942, the finance ministry wanted to use the camps' vast inmate populations as slave laborers. The S.S., on the other hand, wanted to eliminate these people as soon as possible on the theory that they were racial enemies. In the heated ideological battle that raged, a compromise was worked out. The inmates were allowed to work as slaves (a victory for the finance ministry) but under conditions that rapidly killed them (an ultimate victory for the S.S.). Later, when the S.S. was even more powerful, it disregarded the compromise. Labor camps, such as the Łódź ghetto, were liquidated, over the bitter objections of the finance ministry. Finally, near the end of the war, the S.S. came into conflict with the army itself. This conflict began in 1940 with the Einsatzgruppen. The regular army did not want these troops in its way as it pushed through Russia. Furthermore, the army was upset with the mass murder of civilians, because that ran counter to the military ethic and adversely affected army morale. Despite repeated complaints, however, the S.S. persisted. As the war gradually turned against Germany and the army had to give ground, Hitler was persuaded to create S.S. military units called the Waffen-S.S. These troops were sent to the front to bolster regular army units, thus representing the first successful party co-optation of the military sector. Had the war continued, there is little doubt that the S.S. would have eventually brought even the army under its control.

The remarkable strength and cohesion of the S.S. was due in part to its inbred brutality and in part to its members' incredible loyalty to its ideology. As the S.S. rose in prominence, Himmler took pains to present the S.S. as the role model for all "good Germans." Its particular character is captured in a description:

> Later Himmler frequently spoke on these lines. He would demand unconditional obedience, but it was obedience to a command given, not upon official matters but on ideological matters. It was not therefore obedience in the sense

of the soldier doing his duty, the obedience which might be demanded from a citizen; it was the obedience of the ideological fighter based upon loyalty; as Himmler was so fond of saying, its implication was that a man must *do more than his duty.* One of Quinton's aphorisms was: "The hero acts not from duty but from love"; the thinking is similar to that of Himmler when he said that loyalty was a matter of the heart, not of the mind.[6]

This loyalty was, of course, enforced. In their training at Dachau, S.S. men learned that any act of moderation or compassion would be noted and could lead to punishment or dismissal. As the S.S. grew, its internal discipline became more professional. The terror that the S.S. imposed throughout Germany operated all the more within its own ranks: people who showed no compassion for others knew that they could expect none from their peers. The S.S. became its own best guarantee of loyalty to Himmler. Its seems probable that by 1942 or 1943, even Hitler could not have stopped the S.S. had he wanted to.

The final result of the S.S. takeover was the suspension of even the pretense of legal order. The party had earlier co-opted the legal mechanisms of the state and then ceded legal authority to the Führer as the charismatic spokesman of the Volk. Hitler's wish simply became the equivalent of law. With the ascendancy of the S.S., ideology came to replace even Hitler's expressed wish as a source of authority. The S.S. simply determined what Hitler's wish "must be" and acted accordingly. Himmler could simply announce that such and such was the Führer's wish, and it was so.[7] Since Hitler's wish represented the Volk and since the needs of the Volk defined the locus of the ethical, the system was completely self-contained:

> The hallmark of these ideological orders, unmistakably recognizable as such at the time, was that they were based upon no official regulations and that no attempt was made to bring them ostensibly into line with the normal system, even *post-hoc.* In fact, existing legal regulations and moral norms were discarded or expressly suspended; such orders were legitimized solely by non-official, ideological and political considerations. In these cases no attempt was made to gloss over the incompatibility between these orders and the normal code of existence; the gulf was allowed to remain and both the issue of orders and their execution took place outside the rule of law—as Hitler no doubt intended.[8]

This description needs to be corrected in only one detail. Orders were not carried out "outside the law." In fact, the ideological orders of the S.S. created a new metalaw that transcended explicit positive law. A good example is provided by a court case that occurred on June 9, 1943. The Supreme S.S. and Police Court on that occasion handed down maximum punishment to an S.S. Unterstürmführer whose men had murdered hundreds of Jews in Alexandria. The murders occurred not in a camp or as part of an action but on the whim of the commander. In 1943, when Auschwitz was already operating, an S.S. officer could be sentenced to prison because he "succumbed to the temptation to commit atrocities unworthy of a German or an S.S. Commander. . . . The accused allowed his men to become so brutalized that, following his example, they acted like a barbarian horde. The behavior of the accused constitutes the most serious danger to discipline imaginable."[9] The rule of law still stood, even within the S.S. The rationale is explained:

Motive is the deciding factor in the question whether, and if so what, punishment should be imposed for *unauthorized* shooting of Jews: If the motive is purely political, there should be no punishment unless such is necessary for the maintenance of discipline. In the latter case, depending on the situation, judicial punishment can be imposed under paras. 90 or 149 of the Code of Military Law, or alternatively disciplinary action can be taken. If the motive is selfish, sadistic or sexual, judicial punishment should be imposed for murder or manslaughter as the case may be.[10]

There can hardly be a clearer example of how a bureaucracy could come to serve an utterly pernicious ideology under the full protection of the law. And it is also clear that the idea of ethical behavior was not abandoned. It operated here in recognizable form. Thus law, in the midst of Nazi Germany, retained its character as the political expression of a culture's deepest ethical convictions.

13

The Politicization of
the Ethic:
The German Government

Now that we have seen the channels through which Nazi ethics developed, it is necessary to turn to the kind of behavior the ethical norms led to in common citizens and administrators. This chapter examines the bureaucratic procedures that operated in the dominated countries of western Europe for isolating, imprisoning, and finally killing the racial enemies of the S.S.[1] What I examine here is the pervasiveness of the Nazi ethic throughout German and European society. A vast range of organizations and institutions systematically pursued the good defined by the S.S. ethic with a dedication that is startling both for its concern for detail and the apparently widespread consensus it enjoyed. The success of Nazi policy was not a matter of only the party or the S.S. but of the entire bureaucracy and population of the German state.

UPROOTING

We have seen the problems that Nazi planners faced in defining who was a Jew. Nazi theory demanded that there be clear Aryans and clear Jews. Reality proved to be much more complicated, however. There were many people of Jewish ancestry who were now Christian, and some people of non-Jewish ancestry who were now Jewish. There were also large numbers of people who had mixed blood of varying proportions; a whole new racial category, "Mischlings," was created to deal with such ambiguous types. Thus, we might say, reality was forced into the grid provided by ideology. But this solution only raised new problems in that it created a whole new population to be dealt with.

The creation of a definitional scheme, however awkward, was only the beginning of the problem. Once the definition was made and a series of courts established for assigning status in disputed cases, there was the problem of what to do with the people tagged. Many Jews and Mischlings were married to "Aryan" spouses, and many Mischlings were the parents of what were by law Aryan children. The problem was one of extricating the Jewish or Mischling family member while preserving the rights of the Aryan parents, spouses, children, and other relatives. Again it seems that the Nazi fantasy imagined a world of pure Aryan and pure Jewish family units. When reality refused to conform, the rightness of the theory was not seriously questioned. Rather, bureaucrats asked only how best to apply the theory to the facts at hand. The result was a long-term intramural debate in which two different theories emerged. On the one side, probably best represented by the party, stood those people who wanted to exorcise Jewish blood fully from Germany. For these people, even first-degree Mischlings (people with one Jewish grandparent) posed sufficient racial danger to warrant their expulsion. The rights of Aryan relatives would simply have to be sacrificed. On the other side, probably best represented by the civil service, stood people who hoped to preserve Aryan rights as much as possible even if this meant compromise on racial issues. These people wanted Mischlings to be treated as Aryans. Gradually a working agreement was reached in which first-degree Mischlings were allowed to live and work in Germany as Aryans but not to procreate. The chancellery established a eugenics program to research and develop ways of effecting mass sterilization programs for this population.

Once the definitional problems were brought under control, new problems arose. Not even all pure Jews could be arrested and carted off willy-nilly. Many were veterans of World War I, some even wearing high German military medals. One surely had to treat these German war heroes with some respect even if they were Jews. Then there were the internationally prominent professors, scientists, and artists. The incarceration of such people would certainly lead to international protest. One possible solution was to maintain that the deportations were not arrests but represented a policy of resettling the Jews in villages in the East. This explanation for the disappearance of Jews was in fact the official public line of the party. But how could it be maintained when the S.S. was arresting and transporting elderly couples and people from retirement homes? They were certainly not being sent to work farms in Russia! Nonetheless, Nazi ideology called for the removal of these people from society. Rather than question the whole rationale of the policy, policy makers simply devised a scheme for handling awkward categories. A special camp, Theresienstadt, was established and billed as a kind of retirement village to house special Jews. Even though this camp was modestly better than the regular concentration camps, it was definitely a concentration camp and its population was eventually murdered. The solution of establishing a special camp, however, allowed the policy of deportation to continue without the need to address the moral issues seriously.

But this was not the end of the problems that government bureaucrats faced in trying to implement Nazi ideology. There were Jews who, for instance, played important roles in German industry—even in the arms industry. Such people could not be removed without bringing some harm to the projects with which they were associated. Later, as Germany began to face a severe manpower shortage, Jewish workers of any kind became a significant economic resource. Aryan manufacturers wanted to hold on to any skilled workers they could find, even Jewish ones. Thus the force of circumstance forced Nazi bureaucrats to establish a system of temporary deferments for certain individuals. One of the ironies of this phase of the Holocaust was that when German industrialists were persuaded to release Jewish workers for deportation on the promise that there would be Russian slaves as replacements, the Russian peasants that became available were generally unskilled and made poor substitutes and the manufacturers had to cull the Russian prisoners for Jewish workers, since the Jews in Russia were on the average better educated and more skilled. Thus, while the S.S. was busy identifying and deporting German Jewish workers, the manufacturers were surreptitiously identifying and importing Russian Jewish workers.

In addition to the special Jews and the deferred Jews, there were other categories to be dealt with: resident Jews who were foreign nationals, for example, or Jews in the legal custody of institutions like jails or psychiatric hospitals. In no case do we find the intricacy of the problems ever leading policy administrators seriously to question the rightness or workability of the overall policy. Each problem only served as an occasion for bureaucrats and lawyers to exercise their technical ingenuity.

ARREST

The process of arrest presented relatively few obstacles in Germany once the definitional problems were resolved. This was, after all, the home ground of the Gestapo. In many cases Gestapo members were arresting Jews who were their neighbors and fellow townspeople. There were, in addition, relatively few Jews in Germany. Even by the generous definition of the Nuremberg citizenship laws, which included many Germans who would not have considered themselves Jewish, there were no more than half a million, just under one percent of the population.

In the process of identification and arrest, the Gestapo worked through the existing Jewish communal organizations. In Germany, church affiliation was not purely voluntary but was rather a matter of law. Each citizen was required to pay a religious tax that went to the upkeep of the communal institutions and to the salaries of the clergy of the denomination with which the individual asked to be identified. Under this law, all Jews were enrolled in their local Jewish communities regardless of their level of Jewish identification. These communities were administered by prominent local community members. One of the functions of the council was to maintain an up-to-date record of its membership. As a result, the Gestapo had a ready resource for the identification and arrest of the Jews in any particular locale. The council in each city was charged with the task of providing the names and addresses of all Jews in its jurisdiction and so became, in effect, an arm of the S.S. This scheme proved to be so successful that the S.S. subsequently *created* Jewish councils in the ghettos of Poland.

There has been a good deal of comment on the role played by these organizations in aiding and abetting the Holocaust. There is no question that they collaborated with the Germans and made the initial process of identification and arrest easier. But there is serious question, I believe, over how much practical choice there really was. The most rational thing to do in a world dominated by Nazis was to cooperate. Resistance materially reduced the chances of survival. Besides, no one in 1934 or 1935 could possibly see how far matters were destined actually to develop. The explanation given by Leo Baeck, a rabbi in Berlin, about why he agreed to cooperate illustrates the awkward position in which communal leaders found themselves:

> I made it a principle to accept no appointment from the Nazis and to do nothing which might help them. But later, when the question arose whether Jewish orderlies should help pick up Jews for deportation, I took the position that it would be better for them to do it, because they could at least be more gentle and helpful than the Gestapo and make the ordeal easier. It was scarcely in our power to oppose the order effectively.[2]

Baeck lays out the problem exquisitely. The order was given in any case and would be carried out one way or another. The only choice was whether the Jewish communal organizations would play a role. Given the facts of the case, most of us would probably make Baeck's choice. A new ethical universe had been entered, and those who hoped to survive had to play by the new rules.

It was, of course, possible to hold on to one's old ethic, but that meant becoming a fugitive. To pull this off, however, one had to have an unusual combination of resources, steady nerves, presence of mind, and a good measure of luck. Those who did—referred to as *U-boote,* or submarines—also had to have the assistance of "Aryan" Germans. Such assistance was hard to find, because it drew the Aryan into the murky world of outsiders and exposed him or her to tremendous danger. Such people had to avoid suspicious neighbors, the ever-present Gestapo, bounty hunters, vigilantes, and the pervasive party network that controlled rations, food distribution, public welfare, housing allocations, and so forth. Chances for hiding successfully seemed somewhat better in the occupied countries in the West, such as Holland, Belgium, and France, where Nazi control was weaker and resistance to its ethic more solidified. The chance for this kind of evasion in the eastern European countries, where Jews were already a distinct and despised group, was almost nil.

TRANSPORT

Once arrests and deportations began, transportation became a consideration. Because of the large number of people to be moved, railroads were especially important. Careful arrangements were made with the German railroad system to haul prisoners. In most cases, whole trains were devoted to the purpose, the prisoners being packed, standing, into freight cars. There exist anguished accounts by survivors of these nightmarish train rides. Whole families were crammed into crowded cattle cars, where they spent days without food, water, or latrines as the trains made their slow way into the Polish countryside. In the summer the cars were stifling hot; in the winter, freezing. Without latrines and with nowhere to move in the packed carriages, prisoners soon were covered with their own filth. The pain of standing, the stench, the crying of hungry children and infants, the groans of the dying, the wailing of bereaved parents drove many to near-insanity even before they arrived at the camps. Each car arrived with dozens of dead people, some still standing in place. Each train carried on average a thousand human beings.

Careful administrative arrangements had to be made to ensure the smooth operation of this massive transportation effort. The full cooperation of the railway, as well as of several ministries, was essential simply to make the trains available. The trains, after all, were heading east, toward the front. They should have been used to transport military supplies to the German armies, especially those on the crucial Russian front. To use the trains for another purpose took coordination and, no doubt, some political clout. In fact, the first massive movement of prisoner transports—some fifty trains carrying people to the ghettos in Poland—coincided precisely with the great winter offensive against Moscow in November and December of 1941. Yet, as before, the practical problems associated with the massive deportation effort did not translate into questions about the appropriateness of the Nazi policy as a whole.

Not only did the trains have to be procured but they had also to be guarded and paid for. The guards were usually supplied by the police. They were paid out of funds allocated to the Reich Security Main Office (RSHA). This office also reimbursed the railway for expenses incurred in operating the trains and paid for food for the guards. The RSHA itself was reimbursed by the finance ministry from money collected from confiscated Jewish properties. Thus, the victims themselves ended up financing their own deportation. The creation of a separate "Jewish economy" in Germany reached macabre proportions.

The transportation of hundreds of thousands of people also meant, of course, that some arrangements had to be made to receive them at the destinations. This, too, proved difficult. The first transports were organized before the death camps had fully come into operation; they took the prisoners to ghettos in the East, especially in Riga, Minsk, and Łódź. Chapters 7 and 10 discussed the problems of overcrowding plaguing the ghettos. The arrival of German Jews increased the problems not only because there were more people to feed but also because the arrivees were generally middle-class professionals who were not able physically or emotionally to deal with arrest and imprisonment in such conditions. It was the growing character of the ghettos as hellholes of disease and death that led to more radical solutions. The early deportees who survived in Riga were eventually shot by the Einsatzgruppen. The deportees who managed to stay alive in Łódź were eventually sent to the newly organized death camps of Chelmno or later Auschwitz. Later transports bypassed the ghettos entirely. If they contained deferred or exceptional Jews, they might go to Theresienstadt. Otherwise they traveled directly to Auschwitz.

The German population was, of course, aware of these activities. Popular unrest was forestalled through the impression that the transports were merely taking the Jews to pleasant resettlement areas in the East. There was enough truth in these rumors (the Jews after all *were* being resettled in the East) to allow those who wished not to question matters to assuage their consciences. Nor by this point was protest likely to do much more than bring the protester into the circle of the victims. Bernard Lichtenberg, a Catholic priest, for instance, openly prayed from his pulpit for the welfare of the Jews. Not surprisingly, he was eventually denounced. A search found a sermon in which he claimed that the Jews did not want to kill all Germans. He was arrested, tried, and jailed. After his release, he was arrested again and sent to Dachau, where he died. It was only lone and ineffective voices such as his that protested the hideous transports of German Jews.[3]

CONFISCATION OF JEWISH PROPERTY

Once a Jewish family had been arrested and placed on the transport, there was the problem of what to do with the possessions left behind. This was not an incidental problem but leads us to the center of the perpetrator's concept of the Holocaust. The drive was not only to remove Jews but also to reappropriate their wealth. The Holocaust was, among other things, a systematic effort in the economic reallocation of resources (see chap. 14).

Even at the earliest stages, the bureaucracy was making the assumption that the owners of the property would not return. Thus arrangements were made for the "legal" confiscation and disposition of what had in effect become abandoned property. The bureaucrats of the German government became, in effect, executors for the legacy of an entire community. They had a bewildering array of assets to evaluate and dispose of: personal possessions, apartments, bank accounts, goods in customhouses, securities, firms and real estate held in trusts, credits and debts, pensions, insurance, inheritances, and of course, the full array of communal property from buildings to office furniture to Torah scrolls. The problem of bringing order to the disposition of assets was generally left to the finance ministry, which developed a skilled bureaucracy for this purpose. The legal basis for the bureaucracy's activity was finally promulgated on November 25, 1941 (in the eleventh ordinance to the Reich Citizenship Law). In general, all the prisoners' property was to be expropriated by the state. The two major exceptions were the personal baggage the prisoners were allowed to take with them in order to create the illusion that this was legitimate resettlement, and communally held property of an intermarriage. The personal baggage was confiscated at the camp; the communal property went to the non-Jewish spouse.

The disposition of the remaining property illustrates the complete amorality of a bureaucracy going about its job in as efficient and correct a way as possible. Legal and administrative niceties were respected to such a degree that one utterly lost sight of the macabre nature of the overall project. Pensions paid out by the government were stopped, for example, but it was deemed unfair to stop privately paid pensions. Why should certain companies who had dealt with Jews receive an unfair advantage? Consequently, the companies were required to continue paying owed pensions, but now to the state. An even touchier problem was private life insurance. The same logic would be expected to apply—namely, that companies that dealt with Jews should not be allowed a windfall but should be made to pay the benefits to the state. But to enforce that requirement, there would have had to be proof of death for both the insured and all the named beneficiaries. That, however, would have entailed an embarrassing public admission on the part of the party about what it was really doing with its Jews. Rather than furnish these proofs, the government allowed the benefits to go uncollected. No effective means was found to prevent the insurance firms from realizing their windfall profits.

Another rather sticky problem turned out to be the communal property of the now-extinct Jewish communities: the synagogue buildings, libraries, liturgical vessels, and the like. Since the community was a corporate entity, it could not legally die or emigrate. Nor could its property be legally confiscated unless that was authorized by a community representative. But improvidently, no arrangements had been made, prior to shipping out the last members of the community, legally to liquidate the corporate entity. Thus the status of the communal goods remained in a sort of legal limbo. Finally, it was decided that the property should be transferred to the *Lebensborn* program, an S.S. project designed to aid destitute German families. The legal theory was that such a lateral transfer was possible since both the Jewish communities and the *Lebensborn* program were under Gestapo control. How carefully legal niceties were observed regarding these goods while their human owners were being deported, shot, and gassed!

The empty apartments and their furnishings became the subjects of sharp bureaucratic infighting. The apartments themselves were the focus of a struggle between the party, on the one hand, and the civil service, on the other. Each claimed the right to allocate the much-sought-after living spaces. The furniture was also a source of interdepartmental greed. In general, the furniture was not to be sold on the open market, lest it depress prices and hurt the furniture industry. Rather, the seized furnishings were to be given to charity or kept for the government. To ensure that no one derived undue profit from trafficking in such items, the arresting Gestapo agent was to prepare an inventory. All household goods were listed. As the family left, the key was deposited with the building custodian. It remained in the custodian's care until agents of the finance ministry arrived to take formal possession of the apartment. These agents checked the inventory and then tagged for government use any needed items, such as desks and typewriters. The remaining furniture and clothing were signed over to the party welfare organizations. Precious metals or coin collections were given to Berlin's municipal pawn shop; securities were returned to the treasury; phonograph records to the propaganda ministry; sewing machines to the Łódź ghetto, which had been turned into a textile plant using forced labor from the ghetto's population. Any Jewish cultural items were given to the Rosenberg Foundation, which intended to create an anthropological museum of the vanquished Jewish race.

Gradually, interagency greed began to interfere with the smooth operation of policies. Originally, as we have seen, the apartment and all its furnishings were to be disposed of by the finance ministry. The S.S., ever jealous of its prerogatives, began to protest and soon instructed its Gestapo agents to pick out the choice pieces before filling out the inventory sheets and turning the keys over to the custodian. When the finance ministry discovered what was happening, it protested, with the result that the Gestapo was restrained. Later the administration of the eastern sections tried to obtain the right of first refusal for badly needed desks, chairs, and other office equipment. It apparently mounted a convincing argument, because the bulk of the looted property was eventually shipped east.

As the hapless victims of the party's ideology were being packed onto trains, their homes, property, and personal possessions were becoming the subject of an interagency greed that reminds one of vultures over a body. The great issue no longer was the ethical propriety of what was being done—that was assumed—but who would get the spoils. Within days of arrest, a family that once was a part of the fabric of German life was as if it had never been. Its apartment was allocated to someone else, its furniture and household goods scattered, its bank accounts emptied, and its securities redeemed. The family's excision from human society was complete and done with surgical care, yet with no anesthetic for the victims. Family after family after family was painfully ground to nothing by the relentlessly turning wheels of the bureaucracy, which were greased by the labor of thousands of unquestioning clerks, typists, and managers.

14

The Ideal Institution
of the Ethic:
Auschwitz

The final outcome of the S.S.'s ethic and the bureaucracy's acquiescence to it was the Nazis' unique system of death camps. These were by intent and design large factories of death. Built in collaboration with the Reich chancellery's euthanasia project, they grew out of nothing more than a process that occurs everyday around us: the pooling of government resources to address particular problems. In this case the project happened to be the extermination of a bureaucratically defined group of people rather than the delivery of medical service or the disposal of industrial waste. But institutional logic is remarkably the same regardless of the project undertaken. Special programs are routinely devised by middle-level bureaucrats. Once an idea receives a certain level of general acceptability, and once funding is available, it takes on a life and dynamic of its own. Programs and institutions that begin modestly somewhere in the bureaucracy always have the potential of growing to unmanageable proportions. The progression that led to the death camps was no different. Had the war not ended when it did, many other populations in Europe would have been drawn into the system to be exterminated. Like any governmental bureaucracy, it had grown too big to control and had the support of too many special-interest groups to be ended. It would always need victims.

THE ORGANIZATION AND MANAGEMENT
OF DEATH CAMPS

We can actually trace the origins of the death camps to the period before the Nazi party came into power. This is not to say that their emergence was implicit in the very doctrine of Nazism. To say that would be to absolve everyone along the way of moral responsibility. It is to say that we can trace a more or less single institutional and ideological dynamic at work from pre-1933 days down to the liberation of Auschwitz. Many crucial decisions were made along the way. But when the decisions are taken together, we can see a course of development characteristic of any bureaucracy, namely, a gradual expansion of turf, an atomization of authority, and an attention to procedure rather than to moral evaluations. Not that all German administrators were immoral or amoral, but in the course of their individual jobs, their concern was rightly with efficient operation within their sphere of control. We rarely ask more of any bureaucrats.

The organization that planned and managed the death camps was the S.S. The S.S. served as both the ideological engine of the party and its company of front-line racial warriors. Throughout the process of the *Gleichschaltung,* culminating in *Krystallnacht,* the S.S. took virtually all police power to itself. Thus, it succeeded in centralizing all important national police functions in what was called the Reich Security Main Office (the RSHA), including the criminal police (KRIPO) and the secret police (GESTAPO) as well as the security apparatus of the party. Clearly this organization gave the S.S. a powerful base from which to dominate the entire party. As we know, Himmler saw this possibility and exploited it.[1]

The motto of the new police hierarchy might well have been one of Goering's statements: "Right is that which serves the German People."[2] This, in fact, became the standard to which all organizations were to adhere and the normative yardstick of everything that was to follow. Of course, what is good for the state is a subjective judgment. But the S.S. came equipped with a complete and detailed vision of what the state should be like. Through the various police organizations it controlled, it set out systematically to align reality with its ideal vision. This involved two complementary administrative programs. The first was to provide training for the new racial ruling elite (see p. 129). S.S. personnel were to exhibit to the highest degree the virtues of the mythic Teutonic race that Himmler imagined. We have seen that Dachau played an important role in this. The second program was to eliminate all obstacles to this process of alignment. The S.S., through the police, would thus develop itself as the core around which the citizenry would be refashioned, while simultaneously purging the population of elements incompatible with this vision. To cast this into the racial grid we have already examined, we can describe the S.S.'s view of matters as being that the resurgent Germanic people were in the midst of a vicious battle for their life against the hordes of racial degenerates who had adopted a strategy of overthrowing Aryan civilization by mongrelization of the genetic pool. The S.S. proposed to combat the threat by preserving a core of racially pure Germans and by using its police powers to exorcise the racial enemy through arrest and deportation. Although this course of action would require sacrifice, it was the only way to ensure the survival of the Aryan genius. There was to be a fight to the death. The mode of thinking of the S.S. unleashed an unprecedented wave of barbarism that was intellectually and ethically justified in the name of the highest ideals.

The ultimate weapon in the racial warfare came to be the death camps. These served a number of different purposes implicit in the S.S.'s overall strategy. First of all, they functioned as training grounds for the rising leaders of the reborn Teutonic hordes. Here young officers and enlisted personnel were indoctrinated and trained for the ruthless war that would have to be fought. People who could not operate in a rigorous environment had little future open to them. Second, the camps were used to exploit the slave labor of their prisoners. This not only benefited the Reich materially but also involved what was seen as a transfer of wealth and work back to the "Germans" from groups who had lived illicitly on German resources. Third, the camps provided a pool of racial guinea pigs for the S.S. or Reich chancellery to use in their eugenics research. Inmates at Auschwitz, for example, were often made available to Josef Mengele and his staff, who were searching for ways to breed pure Aryans. Twins were of special interest to Mengele. Finally, and most important, the camps administered the S.S. doctrine that called for the extermination of all racial enemies of the Aryan people. During the camps' relatively short period of existence, rather less than two years, they were responsible for the deaths of some eleven *million* people—six million Jews, the prime racial enemy, and some five million others.

The camp system did not begin with all of its goals and procedures fixed. As with everything else in the Third Reich, here too policies developed with experience over time. The camp system started as little more than an unusually brutal prison system for incarcerating political opponents of Hitler. From 1933 through the early years of the war, the system gradually expanded in size and mission while the S.S. ideology itself was developing. The camps and the ideology behind them thus grew up side by side, each in some way reinforcing the other. By the time Auschwitz was built and operating, the camps had become the supreme institutional embodiment of the S.S. ideology, and the S.S. ideology had become a self-enclosed and self-referential rationalization for the camps. This explains why so many people from within the system could no longer see that what they were doing was wrong: it all fitted together so perfectly. It is precisely the nature of this moral revolution that interests us here. The growth of the camp system provides us an opportunity to see in detail how a desensitizing moral revolution might be effected.

THE EMERGENCE OF THE SYSTEM

The camp system began as a series of prisons run by the old S.A. to house political opponents of the regime.[3] Generally, the early camps were located in old factories, deserted army barracks, and the like. As the prison population grew beyond the capacity of these installations, specifically designed and built prisons or camps came into being. The real development of the prison camps into something radically new was the work of the S.S. It was responsible for turning the prison-camp environment into an arena of racial warfare. For the first few years after the camps were taken over by the S.S., however, they continued to hold mainly political prisoners: opposition leaders (Roehm was imprisoned and died in Dachau), communists, labor organizers, and their like. To be sure, larger numbers of Jews entered the camps during these years, but relatively few remained permanent prisoners. Jews were generally released on parole upon the promise to leave Germany. Yet even at this early stage, prisoners were shocked by the brutality and sadism they witnessed and experienced in the camps.

Because the camp system developed gradually and deliberately over the next twelve years, disintegrating only with the defeat of Germany, it developed an ideological and institutional stability. Had the war not been lost, the system would most likely have continued indefinitely. We can trace the system's growth during its twelve years by distinguishing five periods: (a) from 1933 to 1939, (b) from the outbreak of war until the spring of 1940, (c) from the spring of 1940 until mid-1942, (d) from mid-1942 until the spring of 1944, and (e) from the spring of 1944 until the defeat of Germany.[4]

From 1933, when Hitler came to power, until the outbreak of war in September 1939, there was little substantial change in the general character of the camps. They were used mainly to house political prisoners, and they were notorious for their brutality and sadism as early as 1934. The camp system, of course, expanded and became more professionalized, but its overall character did not undergo major development. The first seven or eight years, then, were a period of consolidation, growth, and training. By 1939, a widespread and well-trained administrative cadre was routinely running a virtual archipelago of unusually brutal prison camps.

A major turning point, inaugurating the second period, occurred with the outbreak of war. For a period of about a year, until the spring of 1940, the prison-camp system entered a period of material and managerial decline. This was due presumably to the needs of the war effort. Scarce resources were shifted to the army, and able bureaucrats were needed to help establish control over the newly conquered territories. For a period of eight or nine months, the existing camp system was largely neglected.

By the spring or summer of 1940, official attention seems to have turned back to the camp system, signaling the third period of their growth. This period is characterized by the framing of a new theory of how the camps were to be used. The war, of course, had brought a vast number of new prisoners into the system, in particular racially "inferior" people from the conquered territories. But now there was also a growing concern in the economic ministries over the labor shortage that Germany was beginning to experience. To industrial planners, the vast populations of the camps began to appear a good source of cheap labor. In the third stage of the camp system's development, then, many camps mounted slave labor enterprises. There were even arrangements whereby private industries could draw on camp inmates as slave laborers, reimbursing the S.S. at a fixed rate per diem.

The camps ceased to be mere prisons and began to fill an economic and racial role in the emerging German Empire.

A fourth period of development of the camp system was inaugurated in 1942, when the RSHA and the Reich eugenics were brought together to create the massive killing programs that were to be administered in the camps. This joint effort came about under the impetus of the ideological commitment of the S.S. to killing its racial prisoners because of the racial warfare it saw itself engaged in. In this context the S.S., which controlled vast populations of racially "inferior" peoples, and the Reich eugenics program, with its experience in mass eugenics, made logical allies. The introduction of the death camp created some unanticipated problems, however.[5] The finance ministry had come to depend on the slave labor that the S.S. was able to provide. The S.S., on the other hand, had come to see the camps as primarily a means of killing people. Clearly, dead people could not serve as slaves. Bitter battles thus arose over whether Jewish prisoners should be killed outright, as the S.S. wanted, or kept alive and used as laborers, as the finance ministry and business interests preferred. Auschwitz, the last major camp to be built, was a compromise. It is known primarily as a killing center, and in fact was the site of more deaths than all the other death camps combined. But it was also part of a vast industrial complex that included some of Germany's most prominent manufacturing firms. Auschwitz could satisfy everyone's needs: the S.S. tolerated slave labor, and industrialists tolerated the killing center in their midst. In fact, the killing center could even serve some of the manufacturer's needs. When the slaves were no longer productive, they could be transferred conveniently to the other part of Auschwitz, where they were gassed, burned, and buried as a sort of industrial waste.

The last phase of camp development is the period from about the spring of 1944 through the end of the war. This was an era of disorganization and disintegration. In the face of advancing Allied troops, not only were many camps, especially those about to be overrun by the Russians, shut down but attempts were made to dismantle them entirely in order to hide the fact of what they were. Because of the complexity and interlocking nature of the entire support system, however, many camps continued to receive prisoners who were already "in the pipelines" until the very last. The camp administrators thus had to abandon camp with hundreds or even thousands of prisoners still in their custody. Such was the S.S. sense of responsibility, however, that the pathetic, beaten, and starved prisoners were not simply left to be liberated by the Russians but were marched back into Germany to be jammed into already overcrowded camps further in the interior. The consolidated camps, of course, were utterly unprepared to deal adequately with the streams of prisoners marching into them from the eastern areas, especially given the fact that the camps were caught up in the general collapse of organization that gripped the Reich in the last months of the war. Eventually even the S.S. realized, or was forced into accepting, the hopelessness of further retreat. They stopped trying to organize orderly decommissioning and dismantlement of the camps. Allied armies from the West began to come across fully intact camps, with dazed prisoners still locked in barbed-wire enclosures. But the more thorough camp administrators machine-gunned whomever they could before fleeing themselves.

What is surprising about this system, especially from 1940 to early 1944, is its sheer size. There is general awareness of the huge death camps: Auschwitz, Treblinka, Sobibor, and Belzec. People are also usually aware of the great concentration camps in the West: Dachau, Mauthausen, Buchenwald, Bergen-Belsen, and the woman's camp at Ravensbruck. But beyond these, literally hundreds of small, inconspicuous camps housing but a few hundred prisoners were scattered all over Europe. If we add to these the various "private" slave labor camps—the rocket manufacturers in Nordhausen, the Krupp works in Essen—we get a sense of the vastness and ubiquity of the system. Tens of millions of people of every description passed through the system in one way or another, although it is doubtful that more than one million living prisoners were under control at any one time. Most of the prisoners died from mistreatment, malnutrition, or gas.[6]

THE OPERATION OF THE CAMPS

An exhaustive study of the camp system is beyond the limits of this book. Instead, a general characterization of the camps and how they operated will enable us to appreciate the extent and intricacy of the administrative machinery required to organize and run such an enterprise. Thus, what is said here is not necessarily true of all camps, or even of any one camp during its entire history.

After the prisoners' arrest, transport, and arrival at camp, they were divided by category. The oldest category, that of political opponents, included members of religious opposition groups such as the Jehovah's Witnesses. Next came the "racial prisoners," almost exclusively Jews and Gypsies. Many of the camps also housed common criminals. Finally, there were the "asocials," generally homosexuals. These categories of prisoners were distinguished from one another by various colored patches in the shape of a triangle, pointed down. A red triangle indicated a political prisoner; a stripe above the triangle signified a second offense. A green patch meant a criminal; a purple patch marked Jehovah's Witnesses; asocials wore black triangles; homosexuals wore pink; Gypsies, brown. For Jews a second triangle was superimposed on the first, forming a six-pointed star. These were yellow. If the offender was arrested for a violation of the race and purity laws, the star was bordered with a black band. Within the star was placed a letter indicating the wearer's country of origin: F for France, for example, or N for the Netherlands. In a kind of bizarre logic, people who had tried to escape sometimes wore in addition a red and white bull's-eye! The patches created the possibility for social stratification even within the world of the camps. Aryan criminals were often given positions of authority over other prisoners. This was so not only because they could be trusted to be ruthless but presumably because their crimes were of a lesser nature than the others, not involving any compromise of Aryan racial purity. Jews, needless to say, ranked at the bottom. It should also be mentioned that as many as fifteen percent of the prisoners were under the age of twelve.[7]

The labor camps, and certainly the death camps, were routinely located in inaccessible spots: in a forest, for example, or by a swamp. Only rarely, and then usually in the West, were camps located in or adjacent to population centers. Yet the camps required outside logistic support. So, though isolated, they were generally within a reasonable distance of a village or town, and the bigger camps were surely near a rail line. This allowed supplies, and prisoners, to be brought into the camp, manufactured goods to be removed from the camp, and an area where the camp administrators could go for relaxation and recreation. In some cases a single large camp, such as Mauthausen in Austria, would spawn a series of smaller work camps around its periphery. The larger camp would then serve as a logistics base for the satellite camps. The general placement of the camps followed, in short, a logic that has been standard for locating military camps for centuries.

The camps were constructed according to a fairly consistent pattern. There was the headquarters or administrative area, where the administrative buildings, the S.S. barracks, senior-officer housing, and other official camp tenant agencies were located. At the outskirts of the camp was a second area, this one dedicated to housing junior officers, midlevel noncommissioned officers, and other personnel connected with the camp. The second area often consisted of small single-family cottages or duplexes. Finally, there was the prison compound itself. This was usually a vast enclosed area, bordered by electrified fences, numerous guard towers, barren strips of no man's land, and the like. Within this area were crude barracks, mess halls, laundries, hospitals, sometimes jails, brothels for the camp cadre, and latrines, as well as open spaces for roll calls and area for public floggings and executions. Some of the camps had fenced-off subcamps that were used for segregating certain prisoners or for administrative punishments of various sorts. If the camp had no gassing facilities, prisoners could be locked up in a subcamp to die of starvation, for example. This pattern was repeated in all its essentials in camp after camp.[8]

The administration of the camps followed a fairly standard pattern. At the top was the commandant and his staff. Depending on the size and function of the camp, the commanding officer could bear a rank from that equivalent to a first lieutenant to that of a full colonel. He was responsible for the overall supervision of the camp. The prisoners came under the command of a subordinate officer or group of officers in charge. These officers supervised roll-call officers who, in turn, had control over block leaders in each barracks. Under the block leaders were detail leaders who were responsible for the individual work teams that were sent out each morning. The detail leaders and block leaders were usually chosen from among the prisoners themselves. They were usually common criminals who had a reputation for brutality and ruthlessness. In return for their services, the block leaders—called *Kapos*—were often given special privileges, such as private rooms in the barracks and better rations. A detail leader who failed to fulfill his block leader's expectations or a block leader who disappointed his roll-call officer faced certain demotion to prisoner ranks and, very possibly, administrative punishments and death. The recruited leaders were under tremendous personal pressure to keep things running smoothly. There would certainly be brutal consequences for a breach in security or general order, whereas the beating or even the killing of a troublesome prisoner would probably not warrant mention. In light of the fact that the *Kapos* were often criminals themselves, the prisoners found themselves under tight and brutal control. Nor were even the S.S. supervisors left to their own devices. Each camp had its complement of political officers from the Gestapo who kept an eye on the camp cadre and who could be trusted to report to the commandant or even to the RSHA any deviation from policy.[9]

During the first few months of the war, a massive influx of prisoners entered the system while administrative and logistical support was preempted by the army. By the summer of 1940, the camps entered a new period of consolidation and professionalization. Administrative cadres originally sent to camps for temporary duty became permanent. These were organized along military lines—into regiments and battalions—and were equipped with the latest weapons, as well as with trained police dogs for guard duty and for hunting escapees. The system settled into a routine. Matters changed only as the war turned against Germany. Many of the elite S.S. troops were sent to the fronts. Their place was taken by foreign conscripts: Croats, Lithuanians, and Ukrainians. These guards had no commitment to the S.S.'s theory of ideological purity. Semicivilized, the new recruits introduced a level of wanton brutality into camp life that the S.S., at least before the decline of its morale, would not have tolerated.

ARREST

The administration of arrest and deportation has already been described (see chap. 11). The mechanics of arrest and deportation were structured to fit into the larger system; the way prisoners were arrested had significance for the whole course of subsequent events. Thus, we are now in a position to gain a perspective on the entire process of dehumanization and death.

Arrest marked entry into the system. Under the best of circumstances, the first few hours of detention would be a disorienting experience. The Gestapo's detentions were not begun under the best of circumstances.

The arrests were almost always made at night, with little or no warning. Thus, the prisoner entered the system in an already debilitated state that turned resistance difficult and so ensured the smooth operation of the next step: the loading onto trains. The ride to the East was often a journey of two or three days. Prisoners who had been hustled out of bed and assembled at railway depots underwent two to four days of unspeakable horror—jammed into freight cars without food, water, light, air, or latrines. The result was that when the freight cars were finally opened at their destination, the prisoners who were still alive were weak, dazed, and half-crazed. All were hysterical with thirst and hunger and desperate for release from the confines of the freight cars. The train doors were quickly opened, light flooded in, there were shouts to get out quickly, barking dogs—in short a scene of utmost confusion. The prisoners were rushed onto the roll-call field and immediately marched off for their "inprocessing briefing," which was usually given in sight of the gallows. At this juncture one of two things could happen. If the prisoner had been chosen for slave labor, he—rarely she—was given a prison uniform and assigned a barracks space. If the prisoner was to be killed, he or she was usually forced to strip and immediately marched toward the gas chambers. In either case, the prisoner was in the place that was likely to be home for the rest of his or her life.

In Alexander Donat's *Death Camp Treblinka*, there is an autobiographical account of what the arrival experience was like at one camp:

In the Boxcar. Over a hundred people were crammed into our car. The ghetto police closed the doors. When the door shut on me, I felt my whole world vanishing. Some pretty young girls were still standing in front of the cars, next to a German in a gendarme's uniform. This man was the commander of the *shaulis* and the escort for our train. The girls were screaming, weeping, stretching out their hands to the German and crying, "But I'm still young! I want to work! I'm still young! I want to work!" The German just looked at them, and did not say a word. The girls were loaded into the boxcar and they traveled along with us. After the doors had closed on us, some of the people said, "Jews, we're finished!" But I and some others did not want to believe that. "It can't be!" we argued, "They won't kill so many people! Maybe old people and the children, but not us. We're young. They're taking us to work."

The cars began to move. We were on the way. Where to? We didn't know. Perhaps we were going to work in Russia. But some of the old people didn't want to believe this and, as soon as the train started moving, they started to recite the mourners' Kaddish. "Jews, we're done for!" they said. "It's time to recite the prayer for the dead."

Things got worse in the boxcars from minute to minute. It was only about 7 A.M., but the sun was already hot and the temperature kept climbing. All the men had taken off their shirts and were lying half-naked, clad only in their pants or underpants. Some of the women, too, had thrown off clothes and were lying in their underwear. People lay on the floor groaning, tossing from one side to another, twisting their heads and their whole bodies, this way and that, gasping for air. Others lay quietly, resigned, semi-conscious, no longer able to move. We were willing to pay the *shaulises* anything they wanted for a little water.

A little later, at about 10 A.M., we could see through the window the German who was in command. One of us asked him through the window to give orders that we should get some water. The German replied that we should be patient, because in an hour's time we would arrive at our destination, Camp Treblinka, where everyone would get water. He also told us to be calm. In Treblinka, we would be divided into groups and put to work. But our train did not move again until 4 P.M.

After passing the Treblinka station, the train went on a few hundred meters to the camp. In the camp there was a platform to which the train ran through a separate gate, guarded by a Ukrainian. He opened the gate for us. After the train had entered, the gate was closed again. As I was later able to note, this gate was made of wooden slats, interwoven with barbed wire, camouflaged by green branches.

When the train stopped, the doors of all the cars were suddenly flung open. We were now on the grounds of the charnel house that is Treblinka.

The doors of the cars were opened by Ukrainians. There were also German SS men, standing around with whips in their hands. Many of the people in the car were still lying on the floor, unconscious; some of them were probably no longer alive. We had been on the way for about 20 hours. If the trip had gone on for another half day, the number of dead would have been a great deal larger. We would have perished from heat and lack of air. As I later learned, when some of the transports arrived at Treblinka and were unloaded, it was found that all the passengers were dead.

When the doors of our car were opened, some of the people who had been lying half-naked tried to put on some clothing. But not all of them were given a chance to throw on their clothes. At the command of the SS men, Ukrainians jumped onto the cars and used their whips to drive the crowd out of the boxcars as quickly as possible.

"So Many Clothes! But Where Are the People?" We left the cars tired and exhausted. After traveling for so many hours in semi-darkness, we were momentarily blinded by the sun. It was around 5 P.M., but the day's heat was at full strength. As we looked around, we saw countless piles of rags. The sight stabbed at our hearts. So many clothes! But where were the people? We began to recall stories we had heard of Lublin, Kolo, Turek and we said to each other, "Jews, this is no good! They've got us!" They drove us faster, faster. Through another exit, guarded by a Ukrainian, we left the platform area and entered a fenced-off area where two barracks were located.

One of the Germans rapped out a command: "Women and children to the left! Men to the right!" A little later, two Jews were stationed there as interpreters to show the crowd where to go. We men were told to sit down outside along the length of the barrack on the right. The women all went into the barrack on the left and, as we later learned, they were told at once to strip naked and were driven out of the barrack through another door. From there, they entered a narrow path lined on either side with barbed wire. This path led through a small grove to the building that housed the gas chamber. Only a few minutes later we could hear their terrible screams, but we could not see anything, because the trees of the grove blocked our view.[10]

DAILY ROUTINE

We have a general idea of the daily routine of the prisoners. Wake-up was between four and five in the morning (an hour later in the winter). There was a half-hour allotted for waking, dressing, breakfast (coffee and bread), and reporting for roll call. That might be followed by a half-hour or so of calisthenics. Then would come the roll call. This was a deliberately trying ordeal, with scantily dressed prisoners forced to stand at attention for as much as an hour or more while names were called and double-checked. If discrepancies were found, prisoners would remain at attention until matters were resolved. The end came with a salute to the commandant. At this point labor details were called to fall in and the day's labor began. There might be—or might not be—a half-hour for lunch, usually a bowl of soup. Work ended about five, or as late as eight during the summer. The exhausted workers were required to stand for another hour or so of roll call—longer if someone was found to have escaped. Survivors often indicate that the roll calls were one of the most unbearable aspects of camp life. Many prisoners report that merely knowing that the command would force their fellow prisoners to stand through long roll calls deterred them from escaping. When everything was in order, there often followed what was called the "commandant's salute," a period of communal singing or repetition of propaganda slogans, the witnessing of public punishments and finally "dinner"—usually bread with maybe some margarine or jelly. Taps were called between eight and ten at night, with about seven hours of rest before the same routine was faced the next day. This went on seven days a week and in all weather. Given this harsh regimen and the starvation diets, it is not surprising that the death rate among workers was high and that resistance was low.[11]

The better part of one's day was spent in the work details. There was a wide range of jobs to be done, from working in the camp administration to laboring in rock quarries. One's chances of survival were closely linked to the type of job one had. People working in the kitchen had a better chance for survival: the work was indoors, relatively light, and there was always the chance to get extra scraps to eat. Rock-quarry work was probably the most lethal. The quarries were often some distance away, entailing an exhausting march out in the morning, hard physical labor all day, and a long march back at night. The job also had its physical dangers, especially for workers who were exhausted and in poor physical condition. The assignment of job was a matter of sheer luck and, of course, could be changed at any time.

Apart from the slow death of routine everyday life, the hapless prisoners faced other hazards. Failure to keep up with the brisk pace set by the *Kapos* and work-detail leaders could lead to being taken off the work detail and sent straight to the gas chambers. There were punishments for even the most trivial infractions of rules: public floggings, hanging by one's hands tied behind one's back, and other forms of torture. Prisoners could be sent to quarantine areas where they were left to starve to death. Then there were the camp prisons, with cells so small that the occupant could neither stand up nor lie down. Almost anything that made one stand out could lead to punishment. Too, there were the sheer accidents of fate: the arbitrary selection to be the subject of some hideous medical experiment, or selection for execution because the camp was overcrowded. The prisoners lived in physical and mental agony and anguish.

A vivid idea of the character of the lives prisoners were forced to lead comes from survivors' accounts:[12]

> There was one latrine for thirty to thirty-two thousand women and we were permitted to use it only at certain hours of the day. We stood in line to get into this tiny building, knee-deep in human excrement. As we all suffered from dysentery, we could rarely wait until our turn came, and soiled our ragged clothes, which never came off our bodies, thus adding to the horror of our existence by the terrible smell which surrounded us like a cloud. The latrine consisted of a deep ditch with planks thrown across it at certain intervals. We squatted on these planks like birds perched on a telegraph wire, so close together that we could not help soiling one another.[13]

> Many women with diarrhea relieved themselves in soup bowls or the pans for "coffee"; then they hid the utensils under the mattress to avoid punishment threatening them for doing so: twenty-five strokes on the bare buttocks, or kneeling all night long on sharp gravel, holding up bricks. These punishments often ended in the death of the "guilty."[14]

> The first days our stomachs rose up at the thought of using what were actually chamber pots at night. But hunger drives, and we were so starved that we were ready to eat any food. That it had to be handled in such bowls could not be helped. During the night, many of us availed ourselves of the bowls secretly. We were allowed to go to the latrine only twice each day. How could we help it? No matter how great our need, if we went out in the middle of the night we risked being caught by the S.S., who had orders to shoot first and ask questions later.[15]

> At the outset the living places, the ditches, the mud, the piles of excrement behind the blocks, had appalled me with their horrible filth. . . . And then I saw the light! I saw that it was not a question of disorder or lack of organization but that, on the contrary, a very thoroughly considered conscious idea was in the back of the camp's existence. They had condemned us to die in our own filth, to drown in mud, in our own excrement. They wished to abase us, to destroy our human dignity, to efface every vestige of humanity, to return

us to the level of wild animals, to fill us with horror and contempt toward ourselves and our fellows.[16]

Such was life in the concentration and labor camps. There were also the death camps. The older camps, those built according to the model of the vans parked in Chelmno (or Kulmhof), used carbon monoxide. This tended to be slow, and so experiments were carried out to find a more efficient gas, leading to the adoption of Zyklon B at Auschwitz. The procedure for administering the gas was also improved with experience:

Men and women were separated for undressing in barracks. An impression was being created that clothes were to be reclaimed after showers. At Sobibor, one of the SS men, dressed in a white coat, would issue elaborate instructions about folding the garments, sometimes adding remarks about a Jewish state that the deportees were going to build in the Ukraine. At Kulmhof the victims were told that they would be sent for labor to Germany, and in Belzec a specially chosen SS man made similar quieting speeches. In all three of the Generalgouvernement camps, there were special counters for the deposit of valuables. The hair of the women was shorn, and the procession was formed, men first. In Sobibor, groups of fifty to one hundred were marched through the "hose" by an SS man walking in front and four or five Ukrainians following at the rear of the column. At Belzec, screaming women were prodded with whips and bayonets. The Jews arriving in Treblinka, states Höss, almost always knew that they were going to die. Sometimes they could see mountains of corpses, partially decomposed. Some suffered nervous shock, laughing and crying alternately. To rush the procedure, the women at Treblinka were told that the water in the showers was cooling down. The victims would then be forced to walk or run naked through the "hose" with their hands raised. During the winter of 1942–43, however, the undressed people might have had to stand outdoors for hours to wait their turn. There they could hear the cries of those who had preceded them into the gas chambers. . . .

When the Auschwitz victims filed into the gas chamber, they discovered that the imitation showers did not work. Outside, a central switch was pulled to turn off the lights, and a Red Cross car drove up with the Zyklon. An SS man, wearing a gas mask fitted with a special filter, lifted the glass shutter over the lattice and emptied one can after another into the gas chamber. Although the lethal dose was one miligram per kilogram of body weight and the effect was supposed to be rapid, dampness could retard the speed with which the gas was spreading. Untersturmfuhrer Grabner, political officer of the camp, stood ready with stopwatch in hand. As the first pellets sublimated on the floor of the chamber, the victims began to scream. To escape from the rising gas, the stronger knocked down the weaker, stepping on prostrate victims in order to prolong their own lives by reaching gas-free layers of air. The agony lasted for about two minutes, and as the shrieking subsided, the dying people slumped over. Within fifteen minutes (sometimes five), everyone in the gas chamber was dead.

The gas was now allowed to escape and after about half an hour, the door was opened. The bodies were found in tower-like heaps, some in sitting or half-sitting positions, children and older people at the bottom. Where the gas had been introduced, there was an empty area from which the victims had backed away, and pressed against the door were the bodies of men who in terror had tried to break out. The corpses were pink in color, with green spots. Some had foam on the lips, others bled through the nose. Excrement and urine covered some of the bodies, and in some pregnant women the birth process had started.[17]

One account gives as striking a picture as possible of the kind of incidents that the camp system engendered:

It was winter, the end of 1944. A contingent of children were brought in. They were from Shavel, Lithuania, where German patrol cars had picked them up from their homes. In broad daylight six hundred Jewish boys, aged twelve to eighteen, were brought in wearing down-at-heel shoes or wooden clogs. The children looked so handsome, so radiant, so well-built that they shone through their rags. It was the end of October 1944. They arrived in twenty-five trucks guarded by heavily armed SS men. They got out in the yard of the crematorium area. The Kommando leader gave an order: "Take your clothes off in the yard!" The children saw the smoke from the chimney and instantly realized that they were being led to their death. Crazed with fright, they started running around the yard, back and forth, clutching their heads. Many of them broke into frightful crying. Their wailing was terrible to hear. The Kommando leader and his aide hit out ferociously at the children. He whacked so hard that his wooden club broke in his hand. He got himself another club and flailed at the children's heads. Brute strength prevailed. The children, panic-stricken though they were, with death staring them in the face, undressed. Stark naked, they pressed against each other to shield themselves from the cold, but they would not go downstairs [into the gas chamber]. A bold little boy went up and begged the Kommando leader to spare him. He would do any kind of work, no matter how hard. The answer was a tremendous whack on the head with the club. Many of the boys darted off frantically to the Jews of the Sonderkommando, threw their arms around their necks, imploring: "Save me!" Others raced about the yard, naked, running from death. The Kommando leader called in the SS Unterscharführer with his rubber baton to help.

The boys' high-pitched voices grew louder and louder in a bitter lament. Their keening carried a great distance. One was completely deafened and overcome by this desperate weeping. With satisfied smirks, without a trace of compassion, the SS men triumphantly hailed savage blows on the children and drove them into the gas chamber. On the stairs stood the Unterscharführer, still wielding his club and giving a murderous crack at each child. A few lone children were, all the same, still running back and forth in search of a way out. The SS men chased after them, lashing out at them and forcing them at last into the chamber. The glee of the SS men was indescribable. Did they never have children of their own?[18]

We are struck here again with how completely the ethic generated by the S.S. came to rule the lives of its followers. The massive and horrible bureaucracy of punishment and death not only worked but was capable of socializing people into supporting it. It is tempting at this point to fantasize that German Nazis were simply not like all other people in the world. The truth is that they were precisely like everyone else.

The camps functioned more or less smoothly, without internal or external interruption for some two to four years. When they shut down, it was due not to internal problems but to the collapsing war effort. As the eastern front drew into the area of the camps, some attempts were made to dismantle the camps and cover up the traces of their existence. Prisoners from surrounding camps were consolidated into central areas. When a camp was ready to be abandoned, the weak and starved prisoners were forced to march back into Germany. Hundreds and thousands of these prisoners died at the close of the war while marching on pointless processions into Germany. The empty camps were then systematically dismantled. Treblinka was entirely torn down and a farm erected on its site. Similar efforts to erase all evidence were apparent at Sobibor and Belzec. Lublin fell only because the Russian advance was quicker than expected. When the Russians arrived at the camp, its administration fled, letting the camp fall intact into Russian hands without resistance. The *Kapos* and others who had aided the S.S. were abandoned to their fate: the advancing Russians simply hung them en masse.

By July 1944, then, only Auschwitz was still operating, and it operated at full steam until the end: in May, June, and July of 1944, it received the Jews of Hungary; in August arrived the Jews from the Lódź ghetto; in September and October, transports from Slovakia and Theresienstadt appeared. In late October, a revolt broke out in the camp and one of the crematoriums was blown up. With the world collapsing all around, the S.S. reluctantly decided that Auschwitz too had to be abandoned. On November 25, 1944, the order was given for its dismantlement to begin. Work proceeded slowly, depending on the labor of its tens of thousands of exhausted inmates. On January 20, 1945, the Russians moved within artillery range. The camp administration left with a death-march column of some fifty-eight thousand prisoners. The Russians liberated some six thousand prisoners too sick to go on. The remainder either died on the death marches or were liberated a few months later from Buchenwald and the other camps to which they had been dispersed.[19]

15

Scripting the Victim: Jewish Councils

An ethic has the power to bind not only the elite or powerful but also the victims. They too have their assigned place in the ethic and are forced to play out their roles. An investigation of the Nazi ethic, then, would be incomplete without a look at how the victims were forced to respond to the system. The victims, of course, are always in an awkward position. They obviously cannot be swept up in the overall logic of the system, which would be tantamount to accepting their own need to be punished or killed. On the other hand, to try to fight or influence the ethic from outside would amount only to gibberish. The victims must try to exert their influence from within the system, thereby implicitly ratifying its validity. This was precisely the bind in which the Jews of Germany, and then the rest of Europe, found themselves. As the last leader of Berlin's Jewish community, Rabbi Leo Baeck, said, the leaders found influence easiest when working within the system. This, of course, left them open to the subsequent charge of being accomplices. It was they, after all, who carried out the day-to-day administration of Nazi policy: identifying fellow Jews, distributing ration cards, arresting people for deportation, carrying Jewish corpses from the gas chambers to the crematoriums, and so forth. It is as if Jewish leaders acquiesced in their own community's death.

From the point of view of ethical theory, however, the reality was much more complex. There is in fact an increasing body of evidence that shows that there was much more resistance than at first appears. The perception that no resistance was mounted is due in large part to the difficulties of finding evidence of it. The Nazi machinery was so large and complex, and most acts of resistance were so thoroughly crushed, that they remained invisible to all but the immediate witnesses. Furthermore, the people who staffed the Jewish councils had little real alternative. They were caught up in the same system as the people under them and the people over them. It is hardly fair, in the vast scale of things, to lay particular blame on them.[1] They acted in the most rational and considered way that the ethic of Nazi Europe left open to them.

What we are hypothesizing is that in these councils we have yet another example of the power of an ethic to script everyone's behavior.[2]

Jewish councils operated in two contexts. The first was the town and villages of Germany proper. The Jewish councils here were merely continuations of the old *Kultusgemeinde* that had governed local Jewish communal affairs in the German lands for centuries. The second context was the newly established prisons and ghettos of Poland and the East. Here too the concept of a Jewish governing council was not new. Similar communal councils, termed *kahal* or *kehilla,* had been operating in the areas of Poland and Russia for centuries. When the Nazis created the Polish ghettos and installed Jewish councils, they were only reintroducing what had once been—in the Middle Ages—a functioning organization of Jewish communal life. What was unique about the new Polish councils was that they were organized specifically on Nazi initiative and were expected to carry out Nazi policy. They form an interesting subject of study because of the way they adapted to their role and struggled, even as victims, to please their Nazi overlords. To understand the power of the Nazi ethic to co-opt even such institutions as these, then, it is necessary to focus especially on the labor of these councils.[3]

The councils were, in effect, municipal governments of the ghettos. They helped identify Jews, issued ID cards, aided in the process of ghettoization, allocated housing and other resources, posted and enforced S.S. regulations, ran whatever municipal services the ghetto had to offer, and aided in arrests and deportations. They were made up, generally, of respected members of the community, people who already commanded a measure of authority. In the larger communities where Jewish self-government organizations had already been functioning for generations, the existing organs were simply taken over. Thus, from the point of view of the common people, little at first appeared to change.

TRADITIONS OF JEWISH
SELF-GOVERNMENT

The concept of Jewish self-government goes back to the Middle Ages and beyond, with roots in late antiquity. The two Talmuds (the Jerusalem, compiled in fifth-century Palestine, and the Babylonian, compiled in sixth-century Babylonia) reflect self-governing Jewish ethnic communities in the Roman and Persian empires. As Jewish communities became established in Europe, they brought with them their tradition of self-government and a corpus of common law recorded in the Talmud. The fact that Jews did not fall under the jurisdiction of canon law made it altogether natural for them to continue to live in Europe according to their own legal customs. Their legal autonomy was ratified in medieval Europe both by the pope and, later, by secular rules. Jews were understood to stand outside the normal chain of feudal loyalty and so were organized in special corporate entities, enjoying the status of "royal servants," or *servi camerae.* Their separate legal status continued into the eighteenth century. It gave way only under the pressure of the emerging concept of the modern state, which provided for the first time a framework in which Jews could be granted equal citizenship with Christians in the secular state. The implementation of this Enlightenment theory was most fully accomplished in western Europe—in France and England. It was instituted later, and as we have seen, with some resistance, in Germany. It was still largely lacking in the eastern states such as Poland and Russia, although changes were beginning even there by the turn of the twentieth century.

The autonomous Jewish communities of the Middle Ages needed some internal organization to adjudicate conflicts within the community and to represent the community before the ruler. These organizations, the *kahals* or *kehillas,* were generally made up of prominent men in the community: rabbis, successful merchants, or other people of stature who were in effect the Jewish "aristocracy." The councils took care of such matters as collecting the king's tax, organizing the disbursement of charitable funds, supervising the upkeep of the synagogue and other communal property, ensuring proper burials for deceased members, adjudicating disputes, and intervening with the government in behalf of Jewish interests. In sixteenth- and seventeenth-century Poland, a number of the local *kehillas* banded together to create a sort of super-kehilla. This organization, called the Council of Four Lands, coordinated Jewish policy and legal practice across a good part of what are now Poland and Lithuania. It represents the most advanced stage of Jewish self-government in Europe.

Even after the collapse of the Council of Four Lands, the local *kehillas* continued to exercise considerable authority over the daily lives of European Jews. At times they even carried out tasks that prefigured what they were ordered to do as part of the Holocaust. For instance, Czar Nicholas I (1825–56) decided that the mass of Jews settled in western Russia would have to be broken up. One scheme adopted for catalyzing this process was selecting young Jewish boys, some as young as twelve years old, for service in the Russian army. Conscription was for twenty-five years. The theory was that these children, thrown into the harshness of Russian army life and forced to live among soldiers, would be forced to give up their Jewish ways. By the time they were released at age thirty-seven (if they were still alive), they would be completely purged of their Jewishness. In putting this policy into effect, Nicholas established recruitment quotas for each Jewish community. It was up to the local kehilla to select the recruits and present them to the army. Thus, the use of kehillas to identify people for deportation already had its precedent.

THE NAZI USE OF JEWISH COUNCILS

It was through these councils, then, that the Nazis proposed to work. Where councils were already functioning, they were simply taken over; in areas where none existed, they were instituted. An instruction, dated September 21, 1939, from the chief of the security police, illustrates how the councils were constituted:

1. In each Jewish community, a Council of Jewish Elders is to be set up which, as far as possible, is to be composed of the remaining influential personalities and rabbis. The Council is to be composed of 24 male Jews (depending on the size of the Jewish community).

   It is to be made *fully responsible* (in the literal sense of the word) for the exact execution according to terms of all instructions released or yet to be released.
2. In case of sabotage of such instructions, the Councils are to be warned of severest measures.
3. The Jewish Councils are to take an improvised census of the Jews of their area, possibly dividing into generations (according to age)—
   a. up to sixteen years of age,
   b. from sixteen to twenty years of age, and
   c. those above and also according to the principal vocations—and they are to report the results in the shortest possible time.
4. The Council of Elders are to be made acquainted with the time and date of evacuation, the evacuation possibilities, and finally the evacuation routes. They are then to be made personally responsible for the evacuation of the Jews from the country.

   The reason to be given for the concentration of the Jews to the cities is that Jews have most decisively participated in sniper attacks and plundering.

A further instruction concerning these councils throws light on their administrative function:

In accordance with Par. 5, Section 1 of the Decree of the Führer and Reich Chancellor Concerning the Administration of the Occupied Polish Territories, dated October 1, 1939 (Reichsgesetzblatt I.S. 2077), I order:

. . . .

Par. 5: The Jewish Council is obliged to receive, through its chairman or his deputy, the orders of the German official agencies. Its responsibility will be to see to it that the orders are carried out completely and accurately. The directives which the Council may issue in the execution of German orders must be obeyed by all Jews and Jewesses.[4]

The Councils were simply declared to be the agencies of the Nazi state and its members made personally responsible for the prompt and accurate execution of all orders. Any dereliction of duty could entail harsh penalties, including, of course, execution. In assessing the activities of the council members, it should be borne in mind that membership was almost never voluntary. In many cases councils were simply taken over with the current membership preserved intact. In the early years, a few individuals drafted into Nazi service in this way tried to resign, but such resignations were dangerous to submit and almost never accepted. So not many options were open to the prospective council member. A few actually fled; a small number committed suicide; occasionally those who stayed on the council protested until they were arrested and executed. But most saw the futility in resistance and so stayed on to influence matters as best they could. Eventually, however, a kind of negative selection process did set in. Those who refused to do the Nazis' work were eventually eliminated from the councils one way or another. They were replaced by people more willing to do what was wanted. Occasionally even whole councils failed to meet Nazi expectations. We have a few reports of entire councils being summarily executed and new councils constituted in their places, usually through the random selection of "volunteers" from the street. The Nazi system operated in such a way that cooperative individuals would always rise eventually to positions of authority.

Once constituted, the councils were forced to work under constant S.S. supervision and harassment. They were never allowed to forget for a moment that they were under the complete and utter domination of the S.S. In fact, by having an unusual degree of visibility, council members were in a sense more subject to Nazi intimidation than most people in the ghetto. Not only were they well known but so were their families. Further, their work was open to constant S.S evaluation. Their chances for subverting Nazi policy in any meaningful way were next to nil.

The conditions under which council members had to work are illustrated by an account written in the Warsaw ghetto. The events described are typical of those faced by council members everywhere. Also important is the fact that the Warsaw ghetto was a major ghetto located in an important urban center. If this could happen to a prominent and large ghetto in the capital, we can imagine what matters must have been like in the hinterlands, where council members had to face junior S.S. officers operating far from headquarters. The report is from an entry in the diary of Adam Czerniakov dated November 4, 1940:

At 3:30 in the afternoon I heard in my study the entrance door of the Jewish Council building was being pried open and that windowpanes were being broken. A soldier and an officer guided by one Sachsenhausen [a Jewish refugee from Germany who had had some squabbles with the Council's labor office] burst into the building. They beat up Popow [the chief accountant], First [chief of the economic department], Zygner, and Zylberman [?]. I phoned the Gestapo and was told to call one of the intruders to the phone. I told one of them to take the receiver, but he angrily refused and ordered me to follow him. When I came to the office of the labor battalion, the officer fell upon me and beat me so long over my head that I fell down. Then they started to kick me in the head with their heavy boots. When I picked myself up they threw me down the staircase. . . . I was dragged to the truck . . . and together with Silberstein [?] and Popow was driven to Szucha Street, and from there back to the Pawiak where we were interned. The cell was three steps wide and six steps long. One of the prisoners occupied the bed, others lying on thin straw bags. One of the prisoners had become sick with dysentery and relieved himself near my straw bag all night long. After a sleepless night, at six o'clock in the morning came roll call—rise and clean up . . . , then shower and delousing. I had to dress without drying myself because I and my friends were immediately summoned to the Gestapo where our statements were taken down. I sat in the cellar waiting to be summoned before Meisinger [a high Gestapo official]. He saw me at 4:30 in the afternoon and reproached me concerning improper remarks being made about the S.S., etc. In the end, all of us were released. I was given my coat and hat. At night, three physicians and a male nurse were called to treat me (at home). My head, arms and legs were bandaged. I am barely able to move, but I will go to the Council tomorrow.[5]

Other records give further insight into the kind of relationship that existed between the council members and the S.S. The normal practice was for council members to remain standing while addressed by officers of the S.S. It was also common procedure to allow council members access only to low-ranking officers, not the officials who made the actual decisions. Moreover, the council members were subject to periodic and arbitrary harassments: they would suddenly be forced to do gymnastics, for example, or made to scrub floors; often their conversations with representatives of the S.S. were conducted in the presence of armed soldiers. In light of the tremendous human problems with which the council members had to deal, the virtual absence of resources, and the contempt with which they were treated, it is amazing that the councils were able to accomplish anything at all.

THE PERSONNEL OF THE COUNCILS

If there was any benefit to serving on the council, it was that by serving, one turned out to have a slightly better chance of survival despite one's prominent position. About eighty percent of the council members were killed by the Nazis, either before deportation or in the death camps. Taking into account those who committed suicide or died a natural death, it appears that about twelve percent survived the war. This may be due in part to the fact that council members could use their positions to channel scarce resources to their families or friends. They could also act at times to shield people from Nazi deportations by securing for them a job on the council, for example. So despite the extra harassment to which they were subject, council members did enjoy some modest benefits in an otherwise utterly brutal world.

Larger communities required cadres of municipal employees that came under the jurisdiction of the councils. As the councils took over more and more municipal functions, their payrolls expanded correspondingly. Some ghettos, such as the one in Warsaw, ran orphanages, a school system (beginning with nursery school), police and fire departments, hospitals, burial teams, and a variety of social services. The creation of large administrative staffs was of benefit to the ghetto. It offered people jobs, made more families eligible for extra rations, and gave employees a measure of security they otherwise would not have had. Many of the councils seem to have encouraged the growth of their own staffs for just these reasons. As conditions worsened in 1941 and 1942, jobs with the council became not just a nice thing to have but a matter of life and death. With starvation a real possibility, the extra rations given to council employees often spelled the difference between health and illness, life and death. Many councils were faced with the terrifying reality of having to turn prospective employees away, knowing that this condemned whole families to starvation and death.

Why did council members carry on? A number of reasons have been suggested. To begin with, the job afforded some personal benefits. In a situation in which there was mass starvation and disease, the extra benefits were significant. In addition, many of the council members, reluctant as they were to do the bidding of the S.S., seem to have truly harbored altruistic motives. Many hoped that in some way they could help alleviate the pain and suffering of their fellow ghetto dwellers. We have already cited Leo Baeck in this regard, who felt that it would be better for sympathetic Jewish soldiers rather than harsh and unfeeling Gestapo troops to evacuate families. Many council members may have hoped that they could use their positions to negotiate, to bribe officials, or in some other way to influence German policy decisions. They apparently felt that, all in all, ghetto life with the council was better than it would be without the council. Consequently, the councils continued to function, offering their puny efforts in a vain attempt to have some impact on Nazi policy. It does in fact seem that the councils occasionally scored slight and limited victories. They managed in some instances to provide cover for resistance fighters and could at times offer a chance for some of the young to escape. The overall impact of these efforts, however, was pathetically slight. The German juggernaut was too powerful and sustained, and the power of the councils too weak and ephemeral.

To be sure, there were some council members who were driven by greed. The most famous example is Mordecai Rumkowski of the Łódź ghetto. He had made himself virtual dictator of the ghetto, which he had turned into a vast textile factory. He presided over his domain with a haughtiness the equal of his Nazi overlords'. By all accounts he ruled his domain ruthlessly. Yet there may be something redeeming even about Rumkowski's madness. He had turned the Łódź ghetto into a vital economic enterprise for the Nazis. It is possible that by aping Nazi behavior and making his ghetto economically indispensable, he hoped to save his population from extermination. Whether that was his intent we shall never know. But if it was, he almost succeeded. The Łódź ghetto was liquidated near the very end, in the summer of 1944.[6]

On the one hand, council members did collaborate with the Nazis and so did make the Nazis' work easier by imposing a layer of bureaucracy between German policy makers and the people affected by their policy. The S.S. thus never had to deal squarely with the reality of the life in the ghettos that it created. On the other hand, the council members clearly, and with reason, saw themselves as making the best of a bad situation. There is a sort of perverse logic at work here, one we encounter again and again. Had there been no councils at all, the S.S. might not have been able to do what it did. But since there were some councils, any community without a council could reasonably be expected to suffer all the more. So although the phenomenon of councils raises deep moral questions, no single community could afford to do without one. Logic compelled one at some point to play along with the Nazis.

But by serving the Nazis, council members were drawn into the vortex of the Nazi ethic. Yet we must not lose sight of the fact that even in the midst of this ethic, the councils often tried to perform what from the Nazi perspective were perverse acts of goodness. They played a curious double role, like the *Kapos* who warned young arrivals at Auschwitz to overstate their age so that they might be sent to the labor camp and not the gas chamber. Accomplices of the devil, they tried to perform acts of human kindness.

The councils raise starkly once again the question of options. In a system like that of the Nazi Reich, people's choices are necessarily limited. In a system in which torture, starvation, and killing are matters of daily routine, acts of kindness and care are instances of deviant behavior. The council members and their deeds have to be judged in the light of such a reality, the reality of the cosmos in which the councils operated. Seen in this light, they could scarcely have done other than they did. This is the ethical truth the Holocaust reveals, from which there was, and still is, no escape.

16

Rewarding the Perpetrators:
The Economics of
the Holocaust

We have paid considerable attention to the intellectual trends that nourished the Holocaust and that gave the Nazi ethic its aura of credibility and legitimacy. There were, however, other warranting forces at work, specifically the tremendous economic benefits the process of the Holocaust generated for its practitioners. In fact, from an economic perspective, the Holocaust can be described as a massive and systematic transfer of assets from the victims to the killers. Seen from this angle, a new way of understanding the systemic logic of the Holocaust emerges, and with it a new understanding of why the logic continued to be compelling to so many people. The pursuit of the Nazi ethic materially blessed the perpetrators. This simple observation suggests that there is an economic facet to the persuasiveness of an ethic that deserves greater attention.

This chapter will explore the Holocaust from the perspective of the transfer of wealth it effected from "Jews" to "Aryans." At least since the Middle Ages, the Christian West has displayed a pattern of relating to Jews in economic terms. It is, of course, true that war always offers an opportunity for one side to exploit the economic resources of the other. Germany herself was a victim of such an experience after World War I. Yet Europe's perception of Jews in economic terms is unusual in that it was a tradition that had structured relationships between Europeans for centuries. Thus, it was almost inevitable that an economic component would be part of the Nazi persecution of the Jews.

In essence, the Nazi myth of Jewish world domination included the assumption that central to the Jewish efforts was a plot to control the world's wealth. The Nazi program thus called not only for an end to the Jewish racial threat but for a recovery of the wealth the Jews had "illegitimately" taken. Plundering the Jews therefore became a matter of highest principle. Nor should the power of the controlling myth be underestimated. Even after the war, Polish and Ukrainian peasants dug through the ashes of cremated concentration-camp victims looking for the hidden gold and silver the Jews undoubtedly still had with them! From our perspective it is ludicrous to think that the starving prisoners were hoarding precious metals, but the notion of Jewish wealth was so strong that people were driven to search. The drive to retrieve the hidden wealth of the Jews affected the entire character of the Holocaust.

THE ECONOMIC ASPECT OF
GENTILE-JEWISH RELATIONS

A connection formed very early in the consciousness of the West between the Jews and the control of wealth. The roots of this pattern of thought go back to the earliest economic structure of medieval Europe. With the collapse of the Roman Empire, most of the European population was either tribal and nomadic or worked as simple farmers on the vast Roman estates, the latifundia, scattered across Roman Europe. The European masses with few exceptions were tied to the land, and the Jews constituted the most outstanding exception. The position of the Jews was connected with the historical circumstances by which they had come to settle on the European continent. The first Jews in Europe were colonists—administrators, tradespeople, or retired Roman soldiers who settled in the Roman administrative colonies as part of the government's efforts to pacify and control those lands. The Jewish colonists—for not all the colonists were Jews—thus began their careers in Europe not as farmers and peasants but as administrators and merchants in urban centers. A second wave of Jewish migration into the area occurred later, in the period after the collapse of Rome, as traders, craftsmen, and merchants found their ways into Europe. Some of this migration was encouraged by explicit government action. Under the Carolingian renaissance, for example, Jews were encouraged to settle in what is now southern France and along the Rhine to develop trade and commerce. There were Jewish farmers and landowners, but it is clear that most of the Jewish settlers were not engaged in agriculture.[1]

This distinctive social and economic character of early Jewish settlement in Europe was reinforced by a distinctive legal status. Because Jews could not be part of canon law, the ruling authorities of Europe chartered their Jewish communities as distinct legal entities within Christendom. The Jews were usually defined as servants of the king and owed their loyalty to him alone. As the political organization of Europe matured and a struggle emerged between the secular rulers and the church, the Jews constituted in many cases the single most important economic resource upon which many of the secular rulers could draw. They were, after all, the king's servants and so could not be co-opted by the church. As a result, of course, their rights and privileges expanded. The secular rulers saw that the more wealth that flowed into their domain, the more resources they would have with which to build palaces and forts, to levy armies, and to protect themselves from neighboring warlords.

Because of these historical, social, and legal factors, the relationship of Jews in post-Roman Europe to the rest of the population was largely an economic one. At first the relationship was highly beneficial for everyone concerned. The rulers for their part had undisputed control over a significant economic estate on the continent. The Jews for their part occupied a crucial niche in society and so enjoyed a degree of security, respect, and protection. In all, a fruitful and highly beneficial symbiosis was established.

Unfortunately, the symbiosis contained the seed of its own destruction. There is no doubt that the Jews performed their function well. They provided a crucial resource for the economic development of western Europe. But as the emergent European economy took shape, the privileged position of the Jews began to diminish. Rising native firms slowly began to displace Jewish firms. Rulers who had once found loyal subjects in the Jews while fighting the church for authority now turned to loyal Christian entrepreneurs over against Jews. Although Jews continued to play an important role in the urban and economic life of Europe up to the twentieth century, they never again held the crucial position they did during the four or five centuries after the collapse of Rome.[2]

With the erosion of Jewish economic power came a corresponding erosion of legal and social rights. Europe's Jews were, to use a modern phrase, becoming dispensable. It is surely no mere coincidence that the eleventh and twelfth centuries witnessed both the waning of Jewish economic importance and an increased susceptibility of Jewish communities to violence and destruction. The first large-scale attacks on Jewish communities occurred in conjunction with the first crusade, in the eleventh century. By the next century, pogroms and anti-Jewish riots had evolved into overt governmental action across the continent, bringing in their wake the seizure and burning of Jewish religious books and even the expulsion of entire Jewish communities. Europe had come to see Jewish rights in terms of economics. When the Jews had an economic role to play, they were invited to settle, encouraged to build communities, and offered security and protection. When their use as an economic resource was over, they were seen as competitors and outsiders, and their rights were steadily eroded.

As it turned out, the economic growth of western Europe from which the expulsion of the Jews resulted coincided with the beginning of economic development in central and eastern Europe. Thus, the Jews expelled from the West were finding a welcome reception further to the east. The expulsion of Jews from western Europe, combined with the attractiveness of the economic frontier areas in Poland and Russia, set up a migration pattern that by the sixteenth century saw the better part of Europe's Jews located in the eastern half of the continent.[3] Here the pattern of relationships that had developed in the West was largely repeated. At first, the Jewish merchants, traders, and craftsmen performed a crucial economic service and were accorded various privileges. Much of the early Polish lumber and alcohol industry began under the supervision of Jewish monopolies granted by the local rulers. And again, as native firms emerged, these could appeal to nationalistic impulses to drive their Jewish competitors out of business. This time, however, there were no expulsions or new migrations. Rather, the Jewish communities of eastern Europe stayed where they were, sinking into ever-deepening poverty. The Jews became petty merchants, small innkeepers, even subsistence farmers. It is true that a number of privileged Jewish families continued to occupy positions of considerable influence and wealth in Poland into the twentieth century. But by then the overwhelming number of eastern European Jews had been reduced to utter poverty in the economic backwaters of rural Russia, Poland, and Lithuania.

This discussion is not undertaken to trace the economic history of the Jews in Europe but rather to make the point that for a variety of reasons Jewish-gentile relations in Europe were perceived largely in economic terms. This pattern of thought continued to govern relationships long after the economic reality behind it ceased to exist. Two examples will suffice to make the point. The Austro-Hungarian Empire, in what had become a routine European practice, levied special taxes upon its Jewish subjects. At one point, the special levies made sense, since the Jews did in fact constitute a special economic estate within the empire. By the nineteenth century, however, economic realities had shifted significantly, but the view that the Jews were an especially taxable component of the population continued undiminished. So ingrained was the connection between Jews and taxable wealth that as late as the mid–nineteenth century the government continued to try to raise revenues by levying special Jewish taxes even though it had itself classified one of every three Jewish families as living below the poverty line.[4]

If government officials continued to formulate policy according to this mythic conviction, it should come as no surprise to see the same themes at work in the popular imagination. Russian and Polish peasants continued to regard Jews as an economic resource despite the obvious fact that the Jewish villages—the *shetlach*—were sunk deep in poverty. The pogroms or anti-Jewish riots that broke out repeatedly in the nineteenth century, especially in Russia, always included the looting of Jewish homes and stores. In fact, the evidence suggests that the chief focus of the rioters was on plundering.[5] Jews who did not resist stood a fair chance of surviving, although inevitably stores and homes would be ransacked. The pogroms should be thought of, then, as economic raids rather than attempts to slaughter Jews. They represent the same ingrained pattern of Jewish-gentile relations that existed in central and eastern Europe.

THE ECONOMIC ASPECTS OF
THE HOLOCAUST

Against this background, many of the features of the Holocaust take on a new cogency. The first concerted Nazi efforts against the Jews were economic boycotts: pickets around Jewish-owned stores, for example. These were not consumer protests that claimed that Jewish stores cheated customers or sold shoddy goods. Rather, they reflected a gut reaction to what was by then a traditional European pattern of treating Jews as economic competitors.

Krystallnacht is a superb example of how this myth was acted out in real life. True, these riots, curiously replicating the Russian pogroms, destroyed what remained of Jewish communal institutions. But a second important target turned out to be Jewish businesses. The name *Krystallnacht,* "night of broken glass," is derived from the debris left by the shattered glass of Jewish storefronts. Even after nearly six years of brutal Nazi rule, there was little systematic killing of Jews during the riot. But Jewish communal and economic institutions were deliberately and systematically targeted for destruction. And when thousands of Jews were arrested, they were immediately offered release if they would pay a ransom. These facts are not accidents but represent a deep pattern of thinking about Jews in economic terms. In this regard, the government's response to the riot is also highly revealing. In the face of the clear and public destruction of the economic base of the Jewish community, the government insisted that the Jewish community pay for the damage and that an additional fine be levied against the community. In short, the government reverted automatically to the traditional European expedient of extorting money from the Jews. It was simply assumed, even after six years of economic oppression and the destruction of virtually every Jewish place of business in Germany, that billions of Reichmarks were still available to the Jews, that the Jews had endless resources on which to draw. The logic proceeds even further. As we have seen, the payment of fees and fines entirely drained the German Jewish community of its remaining economic resources. Soon the governmental organization of labor battalions and soup kitchens became absolutely necessary to avert mass starvation. Yet even feeding the starving Jews, once members of the German middle class, was done begrudgingly. It was as if there was a lingering suspicion that with each cup of soup the Jews were managing economically to exploit their Aryan hosts. In the face of the starkest reality, the perception of Jews as economic parasites continued to exert its influence.[6]

The theme of economic exploitation can be seen in especially vivid form in the process of arrest and deportation discussed earlier. Arresting and deporting whole families was a matter of administrative routine. At no point did these actions seem to have provoked bureaucratic difficulties. Yet, at the same time, the disposition of the material goods left behind was a matter of considerable attention and heated debate, certainly much more than the killing of the owners. It was more than simply a matter of which agency could get first crack at the obvious booty: clothing, furniture, typewriters, sewing machines, pictures, stamp albums, and the like. Infinite care was taken to bring all of the arrested person's economic resources into the net as well: bank accounts, securities, insurance policies, trusts, even items stored in customhouses. The considerable care taken to identify, legally collect, and then distribute the economic plunder is striking when seen in contrast to the almost nonchalant way in which the owners were dispatched. From the point of view of energy expended, the Holocaust in Germany was not a matter of killing Jews but a matter of appropriating and distributing their property, the murder of the owners being just a step in the process.

The effects of this logic can be seen as well in the treatment of prisoners in the camps. Had the goal been the expeditious killing of people, we would expect the arrivals to have been herded directly from the trains to the gassing rooms as quickly as possible. In fact, there were a number of intermediate steps. The victims were first carefully stripped, and their clothing, jewelry, and eyeglasses were meticulously collected and sorted. Nor were the corpses simply buried or burned. They were examined for hidden jewelry; gold teeth, if any, were extracted by teams of dentists; and even hair was shaved off. Cottage industries developed for weaving fabric out of Jewish hair, making lampshades and other curios out of Jewish skin and—some reports have it—even producing soap out of Jewish body fat. Like buffalo on the American plains, Jews were killed not for the sake of death but for the economic exploitation of their parts. The haul was considerable. One report, dated February 6, 1943, reported the deliveries from Auschwitz and Lublin: VOMI (the Ethnic German Welfare Organization) took delivery of 211 *freight cars* of men's, women's, and children's clothing. In addition, the finance ministry received some thirty-four freight cars of men's and women's clothes, ten freight cars of bed feathers, three *tons* of women's hair, and four hundred carloads of rags.[7] In May 1943, Hans Frank, the governor of Poland, reported the receipts of ninety-four thousand men's watches, thirty-three thousand women's watches, and twenty-five thousand fountain pens.[8]

Nor should it be assumed that the redistribution of this booty was carried out without reflection. It was in fact a carefully managed process. One poignant example involves a shipment of clothes from the Chelmno camp through the Welfare League (NSV) to a relief organization in the Polish district of Poznan. The NSV needed the clothes desperately for ethnic Germans who had been resettled from Poland or elsewhere, and obviously it was able to obtain them from the Chelmno camp at a good price. But when the goods were delivered to the local outlet, there turned out to be problems. According to the report by the welfare workers at the NSV, many of the suits were not suits at all but mismatched jackets and pants. Further, many of the dresses were stained with dirt and blood. Even more troubling, hundreds of items still had Jewish stars sewn on. Because of the condition of the clothes—not because of how they had been obtained—the welfare agency refused parts of the shipments and returned the questioned items to the suppliers, the *Ghettoverwaltung*. The supplier, however, claimed that the spots were not blood but rust so that the clothes were not returnable. Of the 2,750 suits returned, receipt was accepted for only 250. The local welfare office filed an official protest but apparently received no satisfaction. The conflict was not entirely in vain, however; one change did result. Frank ordered that Jewish badges be removed from all confiscated clothing before it was shipped out.[9] Protest could succeed in Nazi Germany if it involved important economic issues—not the killing of Jews but the condition of goods sold to charities.

This is, of course, but one incident in a systematic and complex network dedicated to the distribution of plundered goods, which was carried out with the seriousness accorded to any industry. Carloads of shoes, eyeglasses, watches, wedding rings, fillings and gold caps torn from teeth, women's hair, and children's toys were treated as so many apples and oranges. The condition of these goods upon delivery was of paramount importance, the question of their origin was never a concern. Even a respectable and professional institution such as the Dresdner Bank could refuse a loan request from a textile trading firm not because the firm was dealing in stolen goods but because its goods were shoddy: too many bullet holes and bloodstains on its suits, dresses, and children's clothing.[10]

The persistence of the myth of Jewish wealth led to the unspeakably gruesome. One of the worst episodes was the so-called Treblinka gold rush (see pp. 164–65). The victims of the Treblinka death camp were generally drawn from the Warsaw ghetto, which was especially notorious for its unspeakable living conditions. Malnutrition and outright starvation were the norm there. The inhabitants could thus be lured to the train stations to be shipped to Treblinka merely on the promise of extra rations of bread and margarine. So deep was the starvation and misery of the ghetto dwellers that any hope of relief made it worth trusting the Nazis. At Treblinka, the pitiful victims were stripped and gassed, their bodies searched for hidden jewels, gold fillings, and other valuables, until all that remained was an economically useless corpse of skin and bone. But even then, the victims had no rest. After the camp was abandoned, peasants from the surrounding villages descended on the heaps of human ashes and bones, digging greedily down through the charred remains of whole Jewish communities. They were still searching for Jewish gold.

ARYANIZATION

The economic exploitation of Germany's Jews did not end here. The entire Aryanization project must be taken into account as well. The dissolution of Jewish firms proved to be a bonanza for German businesses. First, there was the obvious elimination of troublesome competitors. Even more important, however, was the chance to acquire merchandise or capital goods at bargain-basement prices. In complex relationships worked out between German banks, business brokers, and German corporate managers, Jewish concerns were identified for takeover, had their market value depreciated, and were then sold to the designated Aryan investors at a fraction of their true value. If a dispute over prices arose, the interested buyers and the lending banks simply settled matters amicably among themselves, announcing their agreement to the hapless Jewish owner, who was powerless to influence matters. Thus, when several German firms became interested in acquiring the Jewish-owned steelworks of Rawack and Gruenfeld, for example, an agreement was reached under the terms of which the two main contenders, Mitteldeutsch Stahlwerke and L. Possehl and Co., would each become half-owners. Each agreed that neither could dispose of its shares without the consent of the other until January 1, 1943. After that each partner could sell shares as it wished, provided that it offered half the package first to the other partner. Here is a good example of how an important economic resource was transferred to Aryan control with no concern for the Jewish owners but with careful attention to the effect the sale would have on the competing businesses who were acting as buyers and on their Aryan stockholders. A similar agreement was worked out among three German banks interested in buying out three Jewish-owned banks. According to the pact agreed to by the buyers, each was to be allotted one Jewish bank. That would prevent any one of the banks from gaining a competitive advantage over the others. Thus the Dresdner Bank acquired the Boehmische Escompte Bank; Deutsche Bank took over the Boehmische Bank; and Kreditanstalt der Deutschen purchased the Länderbank.[11] These examples display the same incredible compartmentalization of ethical concerns seen earlier with the clothing distribution. On the one hand, questions never appear to have arisen about the propriety of major buyers and their financial agents colluding to take over competitors' businesses at a fraction of their market value. But on the other hand, great care was taken to ensure that the Aryan business community was fully protected. No German concern was allowed to emerge with an undue advantage over its peers. It is not that German businessmen did not operate ethically or have a sense of fair play: they most assuredly did, as they demonstrated over and over among themselves. They simply did not perceive ethical barriers when plundering Jews.

Though a somewhat businesslike atmosphere surrounded the plunder of Jewish firms in Germany and Austria, matters progressed much more quickly and with much less concern for legal niceties in the East. After all, those areas were understood to be reserved for German economic exploitation anyway. Businesses there were not bought but were subject to outright confiscation.[12] A whole bureaucracy developed for identifying businesses, annexing their assets, and channeling their inventories to appropriate charitable organizations. This was no small-scale or petty matter. The incorporated area of Poland is estimated to have had some seventy-six thousand minor Jewish firms, some nine thousand medium-sized firms, and nearly three hundred large firms. The Łódź area, in the Generalgouvernement, lost some forty thousand businesses and in the process yielded tons of raw materials, especially textiles, that made up for dwindling wartime supplies. Such confiscations provided crucial raw materials for the German economy, providing literally boxcars full of shoes, hair, fur, clothing, and rags.[13]

SLAVE LABOR

Real profits were made, however, through the use of slave labor. Aggressive private corporations lost little time in investigating the economic possibility of using slaves. It is true that the industries themselves did not arrest or imprison the slave laborers. It is also true that by 1943, German industry was beginning to face real labor shortages. Nonetheless, the apparent ease with which free enterprises, left to their own devices, could accommodate themselves to using slave labor is unsettling. By 1943, major German industrial companies and conglomerates of international reputation, such as I. G. Farben, had begun to establish production facilities in several camp areas.[14] In fact, the larger part of Auschwitz was not taken up by the death camp but was a vast industrial park for private industry. Some of the best-known German companies located plants in the area of Auschwitz in an attempt to reap profits from the cheap labor the camp could provide. Nor, it is sad to say, were slave laborers used only within the S.S. camps. Krupp, the arms manufacturer, had its own private labor camp adjacent to its works in Essen.[15] Albert Speer reports that he saw slave laborers at work at the missile works in Nordhausen.[16] Postwar claims were also launched against such responsible companies as Telefunken and AEG for renting slaves from the S.S. Germany was truly evolving into a slave-based economy. This, incidentally, was hardly unforeseen or unwelcomed: the original "master plan" for Europe called for turning the vast Slavic lands to the east—Russia and Poland—into massive slave-worker reservations. In fact, the systematic execution of Polish intellectuals has been connected to a general policy of downbreeding Poles to serve as day laborers in the Thousand Year Reich. The beginning of a slave labor economy was not an accident but part of the publicly proclaimed platform of the Nazi party. If business could support the party in its rise to power, we can hardly expect it to have had qualms about exploiting the opportunity that the party provided for cheap labor.

The policy of developing slave labor industries seems to have begun, as is the case with so much else, with the S.S. Several industries had been established in the ghettos of Poland by the S.S. to provide basic military necessities. Because the S.S. was not interested in making major capital investments in the Jewish ghettos, industrial activities as there were were limited to simple crafts such as brush manufacturing and weaving. Later, when the death camps were built, each had facilities for housing some modest S.S. industry. Besides building and maintaining camp facilities, inmate laborers were assigned to gravel works in Auschwitz and Treblinka, a granite pit at Mauthausen, a cement plant in Lublin, and food-processing and lumbering operations in Lublin and Auschwitz. Later a metal-recovery installation to be run by inmate labor was established in Sobibor.[17]

As the war progressed, private industry became interested in using slave laborers itself. On the one hand, the military requirements of the war were placing ever-increasing production demands on German industry. Endless numbers of uniforms, guns, tanks, bombs, airplanes, and ships had to be produced. At the same time, most of the able-bodied men were being conscripted into the armed forces, leaving German industries with severe and growing labor shortages. With the S.S. camps crowded with idle people and with the S.S. experience with slave labor industry apparently a success, German businessmen began to see a possible solution to their production bottleneck. With the backing of the finance ministry, pressure was applied to the S.S. to delay the killing of prisoners and to allow them first to be made available as factory workers. The S.S. finally agreed, very reluctantly.

The use of slave laborers was soon growing exponentially. For example, I. G. Farben had been interested in camp labor since 1935. The company apparently had investigated the possibility of locating a facility at Dachau, but the capital investment needed for security and the like was too great. By 1941, however, the economic situation had changed sufficiently for the use of prison labor to be economically feasible. The final agreement with the S.S. grew out of two pressing interests. On the one hand, I. G. Farben owned Buna, the chief German manufacturer of synthetic rubber. Demand for this product was great, and a new production facility was urgently needed. On the other hand, the finance ministry, trying to institutionalize slave labor both to relieve the manpower shortage and to reduce S.S. influence, began pushing Auschwitz as a prime industrial site. In April 1941, the government and I. G. Farben's board reached an agreement by which a new Buna plant would be located at Auschwitz. Eventually I. G. Farben would invest some seven hundred million Reichmarks in this industrial village.[18]

This first experience in bringing outside industry to Auschwitz went so well that the S.S. decided to encourage further development along the same lines. With the help of the finance ministry, arrangements were made to supply companies willing to locate in Auschwitz with the necessary supply and bunking facilities. When Krupp's works at Essen were bombed, that company was induced to move some of its operations to Auschwitz, thus becoming the second major industrial concern to locate there. The Hermann Goering Works also eventually located a plant in Auschwitz, as did Siemens-Schuckert and Union Metallindustrie. Soon Auschwitz was surrounded for miles on every side by industrial concerns exploiting the cheap labor the S.S. was making available.

Auschwitz benefited private industry in other ways as well. A good portion of the killing machinery at Auschwitz was manufactured by private concerns. Companies bid on the open market for the privilege of being awarded construction contracts for this new S.S. camp. Topf and Sons, oven builders, received contracts for work involved in manufacturing the special doors and windows needed for the gas chambers. The gas itself was provided by a private concern, DEGESCH, a firm partly owned by I. G. Farben. It marketed its gas through two suppliers, HELI and TESTA. The actual gas was produced by two independent manufacturers holding contracts with DEGESCH: Dessauer Werke für Zucker, and Chemische Industrie und Kaliwerke AG.[19] An array of private industries and their stockholders profited from the gruesome work of gassing people. Along with the exploitation of slave labor and the sale of confiscated clothing and other articles, the killing of Jews had become big business. Germany had moved well beyond the military approach to ridding the world of Jews that we witnessed with the Einsatzgruppen. A new economic sector had emerged.

The implications of this development did not escape the S.S., which was already receiving some benefit from its own modest slave labor operations and from the sale of confiscated goods. Whole new possibilities opened up. Slave laborers could be rented out at a modest fee per day, and the resulting income from the tens of thousands of slaves the S.S. could provide would more than pay for the extra expenses involved in transporting prisoners and guarding the camps. At the beginning, the S.S. was able to charge a mere one and a half Reichmarks per prisoner per day. As labor became scarcer and the human resources that the S.S. controlled became correspondingly more precious, the price gradually rose to five Reichmarks per day. Even at this price, demand could hardly be met. The S.S. came under increasing attack for providing industrial customers with trainloads of only women, children, and old men.[20] Rather than looking at this as an opportunity to save lives, industrial managers protested the poor quality of the slaves they were paying for. Even at the height of the Nazi mania for killing Jews, then, conflicts emerged over what a reasonable fee for renting Jewish slaves might be. In the midst of Auschwitz, the relation between Jew and Gentile was still gruesomely governed by money relationships.

BLOOD FOR TRUCKS

The bizarre "blood for trucks" deal was floated by the S.S. in the middle of 1944. The negotiations began when someone in the S.S. suggested that it might be willing to trade the lives of ten thousand Hungarian Jews for trucks and other commodities essential to German troops fighting the rapidly advancing Russian army. How serious the offer was shall never be known because the negotiations were not allowed to proceed. As the Jewish contact made his way to the West, the British detained him for a crucial four months, until all the Jews in Hungary were dead.[21] The case is interesting not only for the possibilities it opened for the West to save Jewish lives but also for the mind-set it represented. Under normal circumstances this kind of bargaining with the lives of human hostages is beyond all moral limits. But from the Nazi perspective, it cohered with other streams of thought already routinely accepted by Germans. Jews were economic commodities. They had use for the extraction of wealth and material goods. That the Nazis were trafficking in human lives was, of course, no longer apparent to anyone at this point. And so why not treat Jews as tradable commodities? The "blood for trucks" deal is startling because it was made in such innocence and openness.

The Nazi system for realizing profit from the exploitation of a certain class of humans raises some interesting interpretive possibilities. It has been seriously and convincingly suggested by Richard Rubenstein that it is to be seen in light of the fact that Europe was suffering from an excessive population. There was a need to eliminate some portion of the population. The Nazi hierarchy had simply defined the Jews as that portion. Once the possibility of forcing the Jews to migrate was eliminated, two ways of dealing with them remained. One was to kill them outright. That was the original driving vision of the S.S.[22] The other was to use them as an exploitable economic resource, as a raw material that produced first, work and, then, hair, gold fillings, skin material, and fat. The S.S. state, as it was taking shape in 1943, was in the process of adopting this more "economic" approach.

The institutional workings of the Nazi ethic reveal some interesting patterns that throw light on how ethical systems become empowered. I stated as a working hypothesis at the beginning of this book that ethical systems posit pairs of evaluative definitions (good-bad, right-wrong), the members of which are binary opposites. This means that at a deep, preconscious level, positive and negative evaluations will always be mirror images of each other. I asserted, for example, that the character of evil in an ethical system will always represent the systematic inverse of that same system's notion of good. This implies, of course, that good and evil objects or actions are formally similar; else they could not be binary opposites. Evil acts can be identified and defined only in the terms provided by the good acts of which they are the opposites, and vice versa. By the same token, I can perceive the wrong only if I have a notion of what the right is, and can clearly identify the right only when I have a sense of what constitutes the wrong. Neither concept is effective alone and in isolation. The terms "good" and "bad" define each other, as do "right" and "wrong." An ethical system, on this view, is analyzable on two levels. On the one hand, it provides the basic grid, the terms available for any evaluating of deeds. On the other, it manufactures a content for this grid by assigning evaluations to certain deeds or ideas on the basis of what is already "known" about the nature of good and evil—or of right and wrong—by the system. This, in review, is the theory with which we are working.

The evidence adduced in this section is nicely organized by this theory. What we would expect to find is that the nature of good as posited by the Nazi ethic will be similar in form to the nature posited for evil. In concrete terms, this means that we would expect to find in the Nazi ethic formal similarities between what the Nazis claimed was a locus of evil, namely, the Jewish race, and what the Nazis saw as the locus of good, namely, themselves as representatives of the Aryan race. The material reviewed in these last chapters offers ample evidence of such similarities.

We can begin with the overarching ethical categories of "Aryan" and "Jew." These terms were formally parallel and yet ethically opposite. The Nazis saw the Jews in the Nazis' own self-image, namely, as a national and racial group struggling to achieve political domination. So whatever became true of the Nazis became ipso facto true of the Jews, except with the opposite ethical sign. Nazis saw themselves as dedicated fighters in a bitter racial war, and projected that same status and dedication onto Jews. Conversely, what was perceived to be the way Jews acted in pursuit of what was evil became definitive of how Nazis should act in pursuit of the good. We have just seen that the Nazi myth that Jews were systematically engaged in economic exploitation became the warrant for the systematic Nazi plunder of, first, German Jews and, then, occupied Europe. The need to halt the evil of Jewish domination of the world became the rationalization for the Nazi attempt to carry out strategies of domination themselves. In fact, as Nazi territorial domination expanded, the corresponding parallel fear of Jewish domination increased. That is probably why at the zenith of Nazi territorial expansion, in the control of the Balkans, the pursuit of Jews was carried out almost in a panic. The greater hatred shown to the racially pure, ethnic Jews of eastern Europe surely stems in part from the Nazis' appropriation of the Roman view that Jewish "clannishness" reflected their disdain for other people. The Nazis' response, of course, was a eugenics program of their own. In fact, any number of features of the Holocaust can be associated with the converse views the Nazis held of themselves and the Jews. If Germany represented the height of human civilization, Jews were to be made to live like animals. If German culture was to set the pace for Europe, Jewish culture was to be reduced to a museum exhibition of the Rosenberg Foundation. And finally, if Germans were to live, then their quintessential opposites had to die. What we witness in the Holocaust is the utterly coherent construction of a universe based on the total binary opposition between good and evil. That is why the awful dehumanization of Jews was transformed into an ethical virtue.

Our analysis has thus come full circle. We began by positing a theory that predicted that an ethic would always cast good and evil in terms of each other. We have now reviewed the world of the Holocaust in detail. Looking back on the territory we have traversed, we see that the theory does indeed help account for what we have encountered. Through the theory, and in light of the Holocaust, we are able to see more clearly how an ethic shapes the behavior of people, determining what they will find abhorrent and what they will find worthwhile. The Nazi ethic began with a theory of evil and remade virtually all of Europe in terms of that ideal, ironically but predictably casting Germans and Aryans in the precise role they condemned in others.

PART FOUR

RESPONDING TO AN ETHIC: THE LOSS OF EVIL

I have been arguing that the Holocaust is not the result of absolute evil but of an ethic that conceives of good and evil in different terms. The Nazi state illustrates not the banality of evil but how it is that ethical systems redefine evil. That is why the horrors of Auschwitz could be carried on by otherwise good, solid, caring human beings. As counterintuitive as that might sound, the analysis up to now has shown that such a reading is consistent with the data.

Part 4 addresses the question of how such an ethic might be judged and on what grounds it could be rejected. Because we are speaking of an ethical system, that is, a complete universe of discourse, it follows that any footing for criticism that there is must exist outside the system. To test this conclusion, I have chosen to examine the responses to Nazism of what I regard as three quintessential types of outsiders: individuals who chose to defy the system and become rescuers; the ideological adversaries, such as Britain and America; and the victims, in this case post-Holocaust Jewish theologians. The critiques by all three types of outsiders take shape within the framework of Western culture. What emerges is a new stage in Western ethical discourse that tries to absorb the lessons of the Holocaust and to reshape our universe of discourse appropriately.

In the case of the individual rescuer we shall see what appears to be a common feature of any principled dissent, namely, that the rescuers are deviants, people who are misfits in their societies. The defiance of the German rescuers grew not out of an internal critique of Nazism but out of the rescuers' experience as social and political outcasts. In the cases of the Allies' war trials and the thinking of Jewish theologians, we shall find that a critique is conceivable not on an individual level but only by treating the whole discursive universe of Nazism. In these cases, then, individual innocence or guilt seems hard to assign. Final responsibility is understood to lie, finally, on the framework in which people worked and made decisions. This, I want to claim, reflects the fact once again that in Auschwitz we observe a coherent ethic at work.

179

17

The Perspective of Insiders

The larger theological, historical, social, and economic trends that have been discussed provide the grid or matrix within which individuals take their place. These trends provide the ethical basis for the construction of meaningful patterns of living. Like any ethic, the Nazi ethic produced its few fanatic and self-righteous adherents, its mass of unreflective supporters, and a subclass of dedicated and deviant opponents. In this, Nazism was no different from any other ethical code. Each person would, over a lifetime, establish a certain relationship to the regnant ethic, a relationship that grew not out of philosophical analysis but out of that person's personality, character, and social situation. In other words, conformity or opposition to an ethic is rarely, if ever, a matter of philosophical analysis.[1] It is almost always a matter of accident, of where one happens to find oneself along the way.

That means that it is wrong to judge people as evil simply because they conformed to the Nazi ethic, or as saints simply because they ended up opponents or rescuers. Their activities one way or the other were generally the result of mixed and unreflective motives. In recent years a number of studies have considered the nature—the ethical choices, in our terms—of various individuals in the Holocaust drama. These studies point in many ways to the mixed influences on people who later were labeled paradigmatic evildoers or saints. I shall briefly look at two such people here—at an official in the German foreign office, Martin Luther, who came to play a modest role in the extermination of Jews in order to forward his career, and at André Trocme, a Protestant pastor who stumbled into making the small village in which he lived a center of rescue.[2] Neither man set out to become a paradigm of evil or good, nor would either of them be comfortable with accepting that characterization later. In fact, given the social setting of each, they acted in perfectly predictable ways. Luther was a German struggling to create a career for himself in the government of his country. Trocme was a Protestant preacher in an isolated Protestant village in France, and a pacifist

in the increasingly militant Europe of the 1930s and 1940s. That one of the
two men would work within the Nazi ethic and the other against it is, in
the light of these facts alone, hardly surprising.

MARTIN LUTHER: AN EXAMPLE OF
A PERPETRATOR

Martin Luther, a career officer in the German foreign office, allowed himself to be drawn into the Nazi system as an accomplice. Luther, it must be
clearly held in mind, should not be seen as a single or exceptional case. He
represents in his way a whole range of people who made choices as they saw
fit. Luther is nothing more than an example of how a person makes use
of given opportunities to advance, without deeply reflecting on the ethical
underpinnings of the system at hand.

To understand Luther and how he became what he did, it is necessary to
review the basic environment in which the bureaucracy worked in Hitler's
Germany. The government under Hitler divided itself into a number of competing fiefs. Weak policy direction from the top encouraged the fiefs to com-
pete with one another for turf and power, with the result that there was a
continual drift to more radical policies. For example, the S.S. and the party
combined to decimate the S.A. during the Roehm purge in 1934 (see
pp. 122–23). The process of consolidation led over the next few years to the
emergence of three loci of power within the government: the S.S. under
Heinrich Himmler, the finance ministry under Hermann Goering, and the
party under Josef Goebbels. Of the Nazi leaders, Himmler was the most
ideologically committed to the extermination of the Jews. We have seen that
he made the elimination of the Jews and the concomitant creation of a new
Teutonic elite in the S.S. his primary goal. In his mind, this meant that eventually the S.S. would have to take over all functions of the state. But this
ambition led him into conflict with his two chief rivals for authority—the
party and the finance ministry. By the late 1930s, however, the party had
already lost control over affairs, as was clearly shown when Goebbels failed
to gain control over Jewish affairs through the riots of *Krystallnacht*. The
expanded influence of the S.S. at the expense of the party brought it into
conflict with other government agencies. Eventually, a major conflict developed with the finance ministry. That conflict began over who would have
control in the disposition of "abandoned" Jewish property, and it eventually
developed into the dispute over whether to put the interned population to
death or to use it as slave labor (see pp. 172–74). Before this conflict reached
major proportions, however, the S.S. ran afoul of the foreign ministry because of the S.S.'s efforts to identify, arrest, and deport Jews from foreign
countries. The foreign office rightly felt that such policies fell under its jurisdiction. In the bureaucratic infighting that ensued, Martin Luther saw a
chance for advancing his own career.

The foreign office had not remained uninfluenced by Nazi anti-Jewish policy. By March 1933, two months after Hitler's ascent to power, a foreign-office desk for dealing exclusively with Jewish affairs was established. Known as Referat Deutschland, its purpose was to coordinate Nazi anti-Jewish policy with other foreign-affairs policies—in essence, to encourage Jewish emigration. This was part of the general policy of the *Gleichschaltung* that was discussed earlier; it ensured that issues having to do with Jewish emigration would now be handled by party personnel attached to the foreign office (or by foreign-office personnel taken into the party, depending on one's perspective).

The *Gleichschaltung* seems to have had little direct effect on the actual administration of foreign policy. After all, the definition of Jews, their social segregation, and the confiscation of their businesses were still in these early years a purely internal German affair. Nazi anti-Jewish policy affected the job of the foreign office only insofar as it had to act as public spokesman in defense of German actions and to supervise the routine administration of passports, visas, and the like. At no point does the imposition of the Nazi system seem to have caused any major dislocations for the foreign office.

Matters continued in this vein until November 1938, when the S.S. emerged as a major power in Germany. Germany's treatment of the Jews now became noticeably harsher. In this period the emigration of Jews from Germany had come to a virtual standstill because of the reluctance of other countries to admit refugees. Since for the S.S. the continued existence of Jews in Germany, especially Polish and Russian Jews, was unbearable, other solutions had to be devised. If Jews could not or would not emigrate on their own, the S.S., now in power, was determined to expel them by force. The first expulsion attempt was a move forcibly to repatriate Polish Jews. Several hundred were simply rounded up and sent by train into Poland. But the Polish government refused to accept the expellees and sent the train back to the German border. There it stood, with its passengers unable to detrain in either Poland or Germany, while the bureaucrats negotiated a settlement. Incidents such as this angered the foreign office, which recognized the implications for foreign relations and felt that transfers of foreign nationals, and the associated negotiations, should be carried out by career diplomats or at least in consultation with them. Himmler, as usual, was assuming complete authority to do anything with Jews that he desired. The foreign office was determined to protect this infringement of its authority by outside agencies.

As late as the early 1940s, the foreign office was still hoping to work out a modus vivendi with the S.S. But the S.S., unwilling to yield any control, consistently rebuffed proposals advanced by the foreign office, while continuing to organize mass deportations. By 1941, however, the S.S. had reached an impasse. The war had brought literally millions of Jews under German control and, because of the success of the German armies, there was no place left in Europe to which to expel them. With the Jews of

Serbia, the S.S., having run out of ideas, was finally ready to turn to the expertise of the foreign office. As anxious as it was to rid Serbia of Jews, the S.S. could find no convenient place to send them. The foreign office suggested a distant place like Madagascar and actually started concrete planning along these lines.[3] With the S.S. anxious for a quick solution and with the old career foreign-service officers pursuing the pipe dream of a Jewish colony on Madagascar, the young Martin Luther saw a chance to advance his career. Apparently without the knowledge of his superiors in the foreign office, Luther approached Reinhardt Heydrich at the Reich Security Main Office in October 1941 and suggested that the Jews of Serbia simply be shot. In light of the Einsatzgruppen now beginning to operate in Russia, the proposal hardly broke new ground, but it did show the S.S. that there was at least one official in the foreign office who was sympathetic to S.S. ideals and who had the "requisite toughness" to deal with Jews "correctly."[4] The foreign office was still officially committed to negotiated and legal solutions to the disposition of Serbia's Jews. But Luther had indicated his willingness to join forces with the S.S.,[5] and the S.S. lost no time in taking advantage of this resource. With S.S. backing, Luther secretly began to build his own pro-S.S. power base within the foreign office.

The effectiveness of the S.S. subversion of the foreign office through agents such as Martin Luther is, in fact, indicated by the office's response to the Einsatzgruppen. Upon learning of these units, the head of the Jewish-affairs section of the foreign office, Karl Rademacher, was appalled.[6] He was as proud to be an ethnic German and as anti-Semitic as anyone else in the bureaucracy, but he felt the concept of the Einsatzgruppen was too extreme. Not only was the mass killing of civilians morally repulsive but it could create innumerable problems for foreign relations if word of it leaked out. By all rights, Rademacher in his official capacity should have protested. Yet he chose not to. For one thing, it was not his place. For another, he was presented with a fait accompli. But these were largely excuses. The fact is that the foreign office was already feeling pressure from S.S. sympathizers in its midst, people like Martin Luther. Both Rademacher and his superior, the assistant foreign minister Ernst von Weizaecker, decided this was not the time to challenge the S.S. Both continued to invest time and energy in the doomed Madagascar plan, hoping to outflank the S.S. while, as a consequence, letting the initiative pass to the S.S. Because of people like Martin Luther, they were no longer fully the masters of their own house.[7]

Failing to protest the Einsatzgruppen, and with the S.S. continuing along the lines of the policy it had initiated, the foreign office fell into line by default, ratifying by its silence the ever more aggressive policies of the S.S. When mass deportations of Jews began from the conquered territory of Slovakia, the foreign office still said nothing. The silence continued even through the next escalation of S.S. foreign policy, the arrest and deportation of Jews from the nominally independent countries of Belgium, the Netherlands, and finally, France. In no case was the foreign office consulted, and in the aftermath it offered no protest.[8] It simply did the bidding of the S.S. clearly intimidated by the presence of employees who, everyone now knew, worked for the S.S. Martin Luther, by developing his contacts in the rising S.S., was in effect exercising influence over his own bosses.

In short, by playing the S.S. against the foreign office, Martin Luther built a successful career in the Nazi regime. He had perceived two important truths about the inner workings of the Third Reich. The first was that the road to advancement, influence, and power lay in aligning oneself with the right institutions, and that the most successful institution at this point was the S.S. The second was that the S.S. was looking for, above anything else, a willingness to meet the Jewish question with complete dedication and lack of inhibition. For one wishing to grow with Nazi Germany, then, the key lay in working as an ally of the S.S. in its destruction of the Jews. For Luther this seems to have been a fairly risk-free way of playing office politics. He faced little immediate danger, and as long as he played his cards right, he had a brilliant and influential career ahead of him. Nor did he have to face the real physical consequences of the policy to which he had now adapted. The dirty work was being done by others. Luther simply had to be ready to speak when necessary and then await his bureaucratic reward. He certainly seems no more anti-Semitic or venal than anybody else. He was simply a good player in the political game of bureaucratic advancement. He made the correct choices and for a period of a few years reaped the anticipated rewards of power and influence.

Luther's well-managed rise to power and influence was only temporary, of course. His game finally came to an end in Italy, when the Germans took over in 1943 after the fall of Mussolini.[9] For a number of reasons, the new foreign minister, Joachim von Ribbentrop, and Rademacher considered Italy to be a perfect area to force a final showdown with Himmler. To begin with, Italy had always been lukewarm about anti-Jewish actions. For that reason, S.S. control was less complete there than elsewhere. What is more, by this time the S.S. had come seriously to frighten the older professionals within the foreign office, who were finally ready to take a stand. With their backing, and with S.S. control still untested, Ribbentrop made his move.

A three-way bureaucratic struggle developed in the bowels of the foreign office. The S.S. wanted to institute its radical policies in Italy without any interference from other government agencies. Ribbentrop, committed to re-asserting his control over the foreign office, insisted that deportations could continue only if they were arranged through diplomatic negotiations handled by his office. Finally, there was Luther himself, caught in the middle.

Under Ribbentrop's initiative, the foreign office began to recoup some of its lost influence. It actually took over the negotiations that led to the first deportation of Jews from Italy and then had some success in arranging for the deportation of Jews from Bulgaria. Luther, realizing that his whole career was now in danger, desperately tried to oust Ribbentrop. His coup failed, thus effectively ending his career in the foreign office.[10] In the end, shifting political power left him stranded. But he had played the game well. In fact, the foreign office continued to pursue the policy he helped create, arranging for the deportation of Jews in foreign countries. True, the S.S. had lost some influence to Ribbentrop, but overall, this turned out to be of secondary importance; the foreign office, with its newly regained power, continued to do the work of the S.S. all the same. Luther, apparently never reflecting on ultimate questions of good and evil, achieved his modest success in the system, helping to shape a policy for his government.

ANDRÉ TROCME: AN EXAMPLE OF
A RESCUER

In contrast, André Trocme was an observer who saw no choice but to rescue people threatened by the S.S. Pastor Trocme was hardly the only rescuer, and his village was hardly the only one to become a haven. But he serves as a model for that frame of mind that motivated many others to endanger themselves because they were opposed to the Nazi ethic.

The context of Trocme's "deviant behavior" is, of course, highly relevant. His village of Le Chambon was a tiny, mostly Protestant village located in the mountainous region of southeastern France. The village had survived the religious persecutions of the seventeenth century because of its location in a remote corner of France and up in the mountains, away from the more accessible valley. The land it occupied was inhospitable and the weather difficult, but the village had survived for generations in its rugged setting. In the thirties this little Protestant village received Trocme as its new pastor.[11] Trocme found the village dying. He decided that the vehicle for revitalization would be a new school. In the increasingly fascist and nationalistic atmosphere of Europe in the thirties, Trocme decided that his school, in this remote and different village, would itself have to be different; it would stress pacifism and the value of all human life. The school opened, as fate would have it, across the road from the other important school in the village, Roger Darcissac's boys' school.

Trocme's little school was already well under way in 1940 when France fell to the German army. Although the French government had capitulated, German troops were actually occupying only northern France. The southern part of the country, in which Le Chambon was located, remained technically unoccupied, being subject to a French "government in exile" at Vichy. On paper the so-called Vichy government was free to pursue its own policy but in fact lived in the shadow of the German military presence just to the north. The president of Vichy France, Marshall Petain, thus had to walk a narrow line. Both out of political conviction and out of a need to prevent a complete German takeover, he established a fascist-style government for France in Vichy.

The realities of the new political scene eventually reached even the remote region of Le Chambon. Petain demanded that every school in France conduct a flag-raising ceremony each morning around which the citizenry gathered and saluted the flag. This policy was designed to foster two of the goals of fascism everywhere: nationalism and discipline. Trocme's school would, of course, be expected to conduct such a ceremony. At this point, Trocme made an important and, as subsequent events would show, a fateful decision.[12] As a matter of principle, Trocme simply refused to make his school a party to nationalism. There would be no flag-raising ceremony at his school. He did not openly protest government policy: he simply ignored it. His neighbor across the street, Darcissac, offered a compromise. Darcissac's school would conduct the flag raising on *its* lawn. His students would form a semicircle around the flag. Trocme's students and faculty could complete the circle on their side of the road. In this way, Trocme would be in technical compliance with the law without having to commit himself. Trocme did not endorse or condemn the compromise but simply let matters play themselves out. At first, the ceremony enjoyed widespread support, with Trocme's students dutifully lining up on their side of the road and singing allegiance to Petain's government. But gradually the numbers on Trocme's side of the road began to decline. Eventually, there was only Darcissac's semicircle, and this too began to thin out until there was no flag ceremony in Le Chambon at all. Trocme had refused to compromise his own personal principles and had ended up establishing a tone for the entire village. By 1941, Le Chambon had discovered its moral independence. The village simply continued to do what it had for centuries, namely, chart its own idiosyncratic course.

A second incident occurred at the end of July 1941, the first anniversary of Petain's rise to power.[13] By government decree, bells throughout France were to ring in commemoration. It should come as no surprise to learn that the bells at Le Chambon did not ring. But the story has an interesting conclusion that throws light on what had been developing in the village. As Philip Hallie relates the story, a group of French tourists were vacationing in the area. When they failed to hear the required bell ringing, they marched indignantly into the village and angrily confronted the old woman who acted as church custodian. They demanded that the church bells be rung. Standing in the cold rain that afternoon, the old woman resolutely refused to ring the bells, pointing out that the bells belonged to God, not Marshall Petain. After a lengthy argument, the indignant tourists left in defeat. The bells of Le Chambon, defended by a single old woman, were among the few in France that did not ring in honor of Petain's fascist government.

The next important confrontation occurred later that year with the visit of the French minister of youth, Georges Lamirand.[14] Minister Lamirand was, of course, met with all due protocol in Le Chambon, although he was clearly not regarded as a hero. The villagers knew nothing yet of the labor camps or the early death camps or of the ghettos of Łódź or Warsaw, but they had begun to receive Jewish refugees and so were aware that the Petain government was violating basic human rights. When the Chambonais began questioning Lamirand about the true intent of German policy, he quickly left the village.

Le Chambon's reputation as a refuge for victims had already been widely established by this time. But the village had begun with no such intent. The first stragglers had wandered in during the preceding winter.[15] The first was a barefoot woman who was found outside the parsonage, standing in the snow and the cold, blistery wind of Le Chambon's winter. Although the woman was clearly in need of help, the villagers were reluctant to take her in; it was already dangerous to harbor fugitives from Germany. Magda Trocme, André's wife, was ordered by the town council to send the woman on. Magda refused. To do so, she felt, would be a violation of her Christian duty. Magda took the woman in. Soon other refugees appeared. The Trocmes always received them and always managed to find people in their congregation who were willing to house and feed them. In this informal, ad hoc way, the village soon was supporting hundreds of refugees. When questioned about their activity, the villagers never denied what they were doing: to have done so would have been to lie.[16] Yet the village consistently shielded from the French police the refugees they had taken under their wing. It had somewhere along the line become a matter of pride and principle.

By 1942, the Vichy government, maybe predictably, had become a full partner in the Nazi genocide of the Jews. French police were even arresting Jews and transferring them to the S.S. In 1942, the police, in search of Jews, finally reached the obscure village of Le Chambon.[17] Upon learning that the police were arriving, the students and Boy Scouts of the village hid the refugees in the surrounding woods. The police arrived equipped with motorcycles (for hunting down refugees) and buses (for transporting them to internment camps). When no refugees were turned in voluntarily by the local townspeople, the police in standard fashion began a terrifying and systematic search of every house in the village. Literally everyone and everything was searched. After three weeks of meticulous police work, the effort was given up in frustration. The police had managed to locate a total of two refugees. No one in town had betrayed a single person!

In 1943, the village's defiance of Nazi policy took another step forward. At the Nimes Conference, the American Friends Service Committee—an arm of the Quakers—inaugurated a bold policy designed to save victims of Nazism by providing them with medical certificates that would make them technically exempt from conscription in "labor battalions,"[18] in the hope of at least delaying deportations. Efforts would be directed first at saving the men, since they were the most likely victims of labor conscription. If that failed, the conspirators would try to protect the women, especially if there were children. As a last resort, they would commit themselves to sheltering orphaned children. The problem was where to house the children. Since the reputation of Le Chambon was well known, the American Friends Service Committee approached Trocme to see whether or not he would be interested. He was, but he realized that a commitment such as this would require the endorsement of his presbytery. Although there was opposition, the village eventually agreed to join in the plan. Refugees, mostly children, were received by the village, fed, educated, and when possible, taken across the border to Switzerland and freedom.

Rescue had become so much a part of village life that even after Trocme himself was arrested in 1943, the village continued its work. The villagers had created among themselves an ethic of rescue that was just as self-perpetuating as the obverse Nazi system in Berlin and Vichy. They saw a need and committed themselves to meeting it. Hundreds of human beings were allowed to live because of the simple work of these isolated French villagers. Like Luther, these people did not act out of abstract or philosophical reflection but simply reacted to the reality around them.

These stories demonstrate only how different people reacted to the Nazi world. Each saw an important opportunity open up, and each made what seemed the appropriate choice. For Trocme, the possibility of ignoring the nationalistic demands of Petain allowed him to establish the nonviolent, pacifist, humanistic policies of his school. Through his early choices he took the first steps toward making himself and his village into model rescuers. On the other hand, Martin Luther saw the conflict between the foreign office and the S.S. as an opportunity for advancing his career. By making the appropriate early choices, he began the process of becoming a model collaborator.

It would be comforting at this point to be able to point to Trocme as a kind of saintly hero of virtue, and to Luther as an immoral or unfeeling psychopath. The reality, however, is not nearly so clear-cut. Trocme was no great hero or moral philosopher. He simply performed deeds that were in consonance with his and his village's character. Taking in that first starving and barefoot woman in 1940 was hardly an act of great moral courage. Nor was Luther that different from the tens of thousands of bureaucrats and administrators all over the world who try to protect and advance their careers by taking advantage of opportunities that become available. Both men operated out of the simple impulses that are at work in all of us. In the context of Nazi Germany, Luther emerged as a bright and aggressive diplomat, while Trocme remained a parochial village pastor bucking the mainstream culture in his isolated village. It is only in the aftermath of World War II that we portray Trocme as a great moral hero and Luther as the

epitome of the amoral bureaucrat. The troubling problem is that both characterizations are internally coherent and correct, depending on the judge's
perspective. Just as Trocme could not have conceived of acting differently
than he did, neither, we may suppose, could Luther. Each did what in his
context was the appropriate thing to do.

It is interesting to reflect for just a moment on the divergent routes these
two careers took. If we try to find a particular point of radical action, we
are at a loss. At no point does either career seem to have undergone a
sudden conversion one way or the other. Each career trajectory began in
a simple way: the decision to step into an administrative impasse, the decision not to raise the flag. From these very first steps, each trajectory is
smooth and predictable. The first, almost inconsequential decisions made
by these two individuals set them on tracks that moved in widely different
directions. It is probably fair to say that neither man realized the momen-
tousness of his first innocent decision. Each simply made it and then followed the opportunities its consequences opened. Only in retrospect do we
see clear heroes and villains; only in retrospect can we make evaluations as
to good and evil.

18

The Reaction of Outsiders

The Nazi ethic was able to win broad public acceptance because it bore formal similarity to an already-understood ethic. Older values—some, such as self-defense and justice, positive, and others, such as murder and thievery, negative—continued to operate throughout the Nazi culture. What had changed was their context, how these values were applied. The subtleness of this shift allowed Nazi ethics to override former norms and sensibilities. Although people were often uncomfortable with what was going on, very few apparently saw anything *morally* wrong. Dislodging the Nazi ethic simply could not occur from within; the Archimedean point had to be outside and had to afford sufficient leverage to move a system of ethics that did, after all, materially and psychologically improve the lot of most of its adherents. The obvious place for such a moral fulcrum to be located was in the governments, people, and religious institutions of the West. Yet, as we shall see, the fulcrums that might have been expected failed to materialize. The political and religious institutions of the West found themselves until the very end unable to take a firm stand against the Nazi ethic. That is because they, like the citizens of Germany, were lulled by the formal congruity of the Nazi ethic with their own. The Nazi claims about the supreme value of state sovereignty, about the need to fight "bolshevism," about the alien character of Judaism, and about the need to preserve racial purity all rang true. Nazi Germany claimed, to an extent correctly, that the West's refusal to take in Jewish refugees indicated an implicit agreement with what the Nazis were doing. It remains a fact that until the very end of the war, no move was made by the Allies to protect or rescue Jews or other victims. Germany, for the Allies, remained a military threat. Its ethic, we see, was tolerable, except for propaganda purposes.

THE SILENCE OF THE WEST

The absence of sustained moral challenge on the parts of Britain and the United States and the Vatican and other religious institutions is one of the most striking features of the Nazi period. The absence of challenge was not, as later apologists have tried to assert, because no one knew what was happening. There is now overwhelming evidence that even *public* knowledge about German racial laws, arrests, confiscations, ghettoizations, deportations, camps, and mass murders was accurate, full, and timely. Despite this full awareness, no effective opposition was ever mounted. When Jews could have emigrated, no one wanted to admit them; when Jews were arrested and deported, no one wished to protest; when Auschwitz was in full operation, no one felt compelled to bomb it; when Jewish refugees managed to escape from Germany, they were imprisoned by the Allies and on occasion even returned to Germany. Why was this the case? How was it that the Allies themselves, the United States and Great Britain in particular, chose silence in the face of Nazi genocide?

Because acquiescence on the part of the Allies was so manifest, the following discussion is in two parts. The first briefly reviews the evidence demonstrating that the Allies knew in remarkable detail what was being done to Jews in Europe. The second chronicles how the Allies, by at first ignoring what was happening and then refusing to act upon their knowledge, actually ratified the compelling character of the Nazi ethic.

The theme of this discussion, we might say, is a remark attributed to Judge Felix Frankfurter:

> Judge Frankfurter [sat] in a meeting during the war with Jan Karski, a Polish emissary recently arrived, who told him about the mass slaughter in Europe. Frankfurter told Karski that he did not believe him. When Karski protested, Frankfurter explained that he did not imply that Karski had in any way not told the truth, he simply meant that he could not believe him—there was a difference.[1]

Frankfurter's reaction fits in well with the facts we observe. In the face of the fanatical determination and despite the utter brutality of the Nazis, people were morally immobilized. It took people, even high government officials, years to realize that they were facing something new, if they ever realized it. It then took even longer to fashion a response. By the time a response was conceived, it was, of course, too late. The victims were already dead, and Nazi Germany lay in ruins. Life returned to normal, at least for most, and the need to come to terms with the horrors of the new age the Nazis ushered in had passed.

WHAT WAS KNOWN

Despite concerted efforts on the part of the Nazis to keep their plans and activities secret, we know now beyond a doubt that information about Nazi atrocities was available early and in astounding detail.[2] A good example of the Nazi attempt to suppress information is in a speech of Himmler's in Poznań on October 6, 1943:

That is all I have to say on the Jewish question. You now know the full story, and you will keep it to yourselves. In the distant future it will perhaps be worth considering *whether the German people should be told more on this subject.* I believe it to be better that we—all of us—should carry this burden for our people, and that we should take the responsibility upon ourselves and *carry the secret with us to the grave.* [3]

Of course, some public explanations had to be made as to intentions. After all, Jews were rapidly disappearing. Where were they all going? To camouflage matters and yet offer some explanation, the Nazis developed a dictionary of euphemisms: Jews were sent to "resettlement areas" where they would be "deloused" or given "special treatment."[4] It eventually became possible to discuss the entire genocide of the Jews in detail without ever using an unpleasant word. Yet, even so, the secret could not be totally guarded. As the machinery of destruction expanded, so did the circle of people who knew what was happening. The three thousand executioners in the Einsatzgruppen clearly knew what was going on: they were doing it! The soldiers around them also clearly knew: they were eyewitnesses. (In fact, it seems that the first accounts of these actions were made available to German citizens through soldiers who were serving on the Russian front and came home on leave.) The mass of bureaucrats certainly knew the character of the machinery they were running: they saw the after-action reports. Nor was this sector of the population inconsequential. By the time the camps were built, for example, a substantial portion of the German railway system had become involved in arranging Jewish transports—in allocating rolling stock, establishing schedules, assigning crews, and keeping accounts for subsequent reimbursement from the S.S. Government ministries were also deeply involved in the process, especially the police and the finance ministry. Nor were managers and administrators of the Holocaust limited to the government or the railroads. The disposition of confiscated and abandoned Jewish property was carried out with the full cooperation of bankers and business leaders. Private industry was intimately involved in creating the material plant for the genocide: Topf and Sons successfully bid to build the crematoriums' oven doors at Auschwitz; I. G. Farben supplied the gas through one of its subsidiaries; factories made arrangements with the S.S. to use cheap slave labor, eventually conspiring in the plan to build a huge industrial park around Auschwitz. Nor can we ignore the populations living around the camps and factories. These people had contact with camp personnel, often worked for the support administration of the camp, and surely saw the prisoners. The stench of burned flesh from Auschwitz is said to have been noticeable for miles. Are we to suppose that these people concluded nothing? No. The Nazi genocide effort was too massive, too complex, and too intertwined with the economy to remain a hermetically sealed secret. With so many sectors of the population in direct contact with the enterprise, it is clear that local populations had access to a wealth of data about what the Nazis were really doing.

But there were other witnesses as well, escapees who saw firsthand what was being done to the people around them. When rumors of Treblinka began to circulate in the Warsaw ghetto at the time of the first transports to the camp, one of the resistance groups sent out a scout, one Zalman Friedrich. On his way to the camp, he ran into one of the first escapees from the camp, in Sokolov. The escapee recounted all that he had seen. Friedrich hurried back to Warsaw with a full report. Thus, the first full account of Treblinka reached the inmates in the Warsaw ghetto no more than six days after the camp began operation. Other reports followed. One prisoner, Eli Linder, had managed to hide in a pile of confiscated clothes in Treblinka and so escaped.[5] Another, Abraham Krzepicki, escaped after spending eighteen days in Treblinka.[6] Each of these witnesses arrived in Warsaw and confirmed Friedrich's initial report. Later confirmation came from railroad workers. Villagers around the camp apparently were aware of the function of the camp, recognizing the familiar stench of death. The secret of Treblinka was well known even before the camp had had time to settle into a routine.

Just as word of the true nature of Nazi atrocities became fully known in Germany, so too did it immediately become known to the outside world. The Allies had several sources of information. Several Italian officers while on an official visit to the Russian front, for example, had inadvertently witnessed a unit of the Einsatzgruppen in action. They were appalled and reported to Rome in full what they had witnessed. The Russian army, and later, Balkan troops, witnessed these events too.[7] Nor were Nazi officials always dedicated to keeping the secret. A famous incident is associated with Kurt Gerstein, chief disinfection officer in the office of the hygienic chief of the Waffen-S.S. Gerstein had been sent with a load of Zyklon gas to Belzec to evaluate its use as a possible mass killing agent.[8] On the way back to Berlin, he happened to be seated next to a Swedish diplomat, Baron Göran von Otto. Gerstein used the occasion to relate to von Otto everything he had seen at the camp, and upon returning to Berlin, the diplomat immediately wired the results of the conversation to Stockholm. Thus, the mission of Auschwitz and the details of its operation became available to Allied intelligence even before the camp was fully operational.

The Allied governments were, of course, vitally interested in gathering intelligence on German military, economic, and industrial matters. They established elaborate intelligence-gathering and -transmitting networks in order to gain timely information about events in Germany. Many maintained large delegations or consular staffs in Germany especially dedicated to intelligence gathering: Sweden alone maintained fifty-three offices. Neutral Finland had thirty-two. Even Portugal had twenty. These offices naturally served as intelligence-collection points, and all had access to secure lines of communication to their home governments. Other countries constructed major military information gathering stations, such as listening posts. Switzerland was especially active in this regard. Other listening posts operated in Turkey, Sweden, and Spain. Although Vatican archives are still sealed, it seems certain now that the church too knew of the genocide occurring just across the border. Gerstein, who talked so freely to von Otto, had made contact with the Vatican as well. In short, a steady stream of high-quality information flowed out of Germany and into the hands of the Allies. To claim that, among all this, evidence of the Holocaust failed to surface is absurd.

Finally, there were the resistance activities in Europe specifically dedicated to providing the West with up-to-date information and intelligence. France and Poland in particular had large and well-organized underground resistance movements that maintained lines of communication with the West throughout the war. It was a Polish group, in fact, that sent Jan Karski to the United States. The Polish underground was particularly useful in keeping a steady stream of dispatches describing Nazi atrocities flowing to the West.[9] Nor were the American and British intelligence services idle. Army intelligence had managed to break the S.S. code as early as 1941! From then on it was fully aware of all S.S. communications traffic. Also in 1941, the railroad code was broken. American and British intelligence not only knew what the S.S. was doing but also could trace the rail traffic to and from the camps. It is clear, then, that the actions of the Nazis were not, nor could they have been, a secret. Information was pouring out of Germany and Nazi-occupied Europe like water from a sieve. Significant portions of this information were of high quality: the information was timely and detailed, and it had independent confirmation.

An impressive indication of the quantity and quality of what was known to the Allies is indicated simply by what was in the popular press. The religious press in America, hardly known for its substantial investigative reportage, carried enough news from Germany concerning the Jews to show that full and up-to-date information was easily available.[10] Virtually every anti-Jewish event in Germany from 1933 to the outbreak of the war received due coverage in the American religious press. The *New York Times* reported the same events but in much greater detail. Even during the bitter years of war, the major papers of the United States had available from their press services considerable detailed information about the S.S., the Einsatzgruppen, the labor camps, and the death camps. Simply leafing through the papers of the time will convince even the doubter that substantial information was *publicly* available despite wartime censorship. By simply reading the morning papers, American government officials could have known what was happening to Europe's Jews. Presumably the government had even more and better information itself.

The sad fact remains that despite massive information, there was hardly any outcry or any substantive attempt to save the victims on the part of the

Allied governments. Jewish immigration quotas were not increased; refugees were not taken in even on a temporary basis; rail lines carrying dying prisoners to Auschwitz or Treblinka were never disrupted. Despite the devastation of Germany, Auschwitz remained largely untouched by the war.

WHY THE ALLIES WERE SILENT

We can note five important factors that led to the remarkable lack of action on the part of the Allies. One was caution. There had been a number of atrocity reports coming out of World War I. As it turned out, most were false, crude attempts to sway public opinion. Government officials who had been burned once by propaganda were determined to be more careful this time. The same was true of their audience. When atrocity reports from Germany were released, they were as often as not shrugged off as anti-German propaganda. Pro-German leagues in the United States and abroad provided a steady stream of press resources designed to assure the public of just that. Nor can we fully blame the citizens of the West. The victims in Europe did not themselves believe what was happening.

The second and a more complex factor was Britain's ambivalent position vis-à-vis Palestine and the Arabs.[11] With the fall of the Turkish Empire during World War I, Great Britain had assumed control over the southern Levant. Already in 1917, Great Britain had officially expressed its willingness to the World Zionist Congress to allow Jewish migration into the area. The result was a small but steady stream of Jewish settlers. By the 1920s, however, local Arab leaders, riding a wave of rising Arab nationalism, began to protest Jewish settlements. Tension grew in the area until finally, in the late 1920s, full-scale rioting broke out in British Palestine. As Arab anger increased and as Britain began to contemplate the world in which it would have to operate in the years ahead, cooperation with the Arabs seemed a prudent policy goal. That concern, coupled in the 1930s with the fear of driving Arab leadership into the pro-German camp, compelled Britain to place restrictions on Jewish immigration into Palestine. The restrictions, instituted in 1939, could hardly have come at a worse time for the Jews. Once war broke out, almost no country in the West would accept German immigrants, even Jewish ones. For the increasingly desperate Jews of Europe, the only hope for escape was Palestine. Now that one remaining option had been closed as well. The sheer desperation that this move created is indicated by the constant stream of Jewish refugees from northern Europe over the Pyrenees into Spain, and even the creation of a Jewish refugee community in Shanghai. There were simply no other places for Jews to go.

Zionist organizations, of course, protested the British-imposed immigration quotas bitterly. When negotiations failed to achieve results, some more radical groups organized a series of blockade runs to land Jewish immigrants in Palestine illegally. This, of course, only provoked the

British to tighten their blockade. The result was a gruesome contest of wills. The British found themselves in a difficult position. On the one hand, they had publicly capitulated to Arab demands to restrict Jewish migration into Palestine. They had established a strict quota system and were determined to stick to it.[12] On the other, the atrocities of the Nazis were creating immense pressure on refugees to find a haven, and British Palestine seemed the logical choice. To prevent world pressure, both at home and abroad, from becoming unbearable, the British made the decision to play down the nature of Nazi atrocities as much as possible. To admit that a full-scale genocide was in progress would put them in a position in which they would have little choice but to open the gates of immigration to Palestine. They thus collaborated with their Nazi enemies in suppressing the details of what was happening to the Jews in Europe.

A third factor behind the lack of response from the West was reluctance on the part of the United States to publicize Nazi anti-Jewish atrocities. The reasons were complex. First of all, the United States was experiencing a wave of Jew hatred itself.[13] So virulent was anti-Semitism in the United States in the early 1940s that even American Jewish organizations were fearful of speaking out too loudly. Roosevelt's own attitude toward the Jews is unclear, but he clearly perceived that any overt bending to Jewish demands would be a political liability. Roosevelt's interest was in preparing the United States to enter the war at Britain's side, and to do this he had to lay a foundation carefully. He realized that placing Jewish concerns too far toward the forefront would jeopardize his efforts to have the United States join the war. So the United States, like Britain, had deep political reasons for wanting to suppress the news of Hitler's anti-Jewish atrocities. Despite the unceasing flow of information about the arrests, deportations, and camps, the major Western governments had very little to say publicly. Acknowledging Jewish concerns would have presented a danger to British foreign policy and would have been political suicide in the United States.

A fourth factor in restraining Western response was the ambivalent attitude toward Jews of some of the Allies, especially Poland and Russia. The Poles had suffered tremendously at the hands of the Nazis and were proving to be loyal and useful allies. Why upset the Poles by pointing a finger specifically at atrocities perpetrated against Jews? The same logic could work with the Russian allies. They had borne the brunt of the Nazi Blitzkrieg. They continually claimed that the actions of the Germans were an affront to *all* Russians: to this day Russia refuses to acknowledge any special place to Jewish suffering. Why alienate the Russians by stressing what was happening to Jews over and above what was happening to Russians? Because the Poles and Russians were important allies and traditionally anti-Semitic, and because the Jews were weak and obviously growing weaker, they simply did not seem to rate any special effort or concern.

Finally, we cannot discount the psychological barrier pointed to at the beginning of the chapter. Despite the awful evidence of what was happening, the Allies seemed unable to take a stand against the basic assumptions that underlay the Nazi ethic. They, like the German people and their sympathizers throughout Europe, were caught in the web of their own moral preconceptions about race, state sovereignty, and the demands of war, and so could not form an adequately forceful response to Auschwitz. In war, human life is cheap, and the death of a few Jewish victims was deemed inconsequential within the frame of the larger picture. It is precisely this moral ambivalence that prevented the West from providing the Archimedean fulcrum needed to dislodge the Nazi ethic.

The reluctance on the part of the West to come to the aid of Nazi victims must be itself seen as part of the system of events that made the Holocaust what it was. It, first, forced the victims to remain within the sphere of Nazi influence, thus frustrating the Nazis' attempts to rid Germany of its Jews and leading to the increased radicalization of the Nazi war against the Jews. Second, it played a role in establishing the apparent legitimacy of what the Nazis were doing. The Nazis used the repeated demonstration of the Western Allies that they did not want Jewish immigrants as a way of justifying their own attempts to exorcise Jews from their midst. If other countries found Nazi anti-Semitic policies abhorrent, let them take in the Jews! If they were unwilling to do so, the Nazis propagandists repeated again and again, then such countries had no right to protest Nazi actions. By showing the Allies that they shared many basic values with the Nazis, the Germans undercut the Allies' ability to take a moral stance against the genocide that was occurring. Western morality was portrayed publicly as being in ultimate agreement with what the Nazis claimed to be right.

A premier example of how this worked is the case of the *St. Louis,* a passenger liner that was chartered to convey Jewish refugees out of Germany in 1939.[14] The passengers consisted of some 950 German Jews, many of whom had already been in Nazi camps and had been warned to leave Germany immediately. Some were already being actively sought by the Gestapo. These were indeed people in immediate need of asylum. Nonetheless, they could find virtually no place on earth willing to take them. The ship set sail for Cuba, which was one of the few countries left in the world willing to accept Jewish immigrants. (Latin American countries seemed the most receptive to immigrants at this time, one of the most willing of all being the Dominican Republic.) Nazi sympathizers and agents in Cuba, however, had already begun a sustained campaign to block the acceptance of the refugees. Anti-Semitic broadsides appeared daily in the Cuban press. Public rallies sponsored by Nazi agents were organized. In fact, so much political turmoil was created that the president of Cuba finally decided that he could not afford politically to allow the refugees to disembark. The ship, however, had already arrived in port and so was forced to remain anchored within sight of

Cuba for weeks as negotiations dragged on. In the end, Nazi anti-Jewish pressure prevailed and the refugees were refused entry. The captain had also by now received orders to return the ship and its passengers to Germany. Apparently feeling compassion for his passengers, he reluctantly began the slow trip back to Europe. He deliberately sailed slowly northeast, along the eastern seaboard of the United States, hoping that the Roosevelt government could be persuaded to grant immigration visas to his passengers. In fact, the fate of the ship and its passengers was at that time the subject of heated debate in Congress. As the ship slowly sailed the length of the eastern seaboard and had finally to change course for Europe, the debate in Congress raged. Finally, the United States found itself unable to help. The ship and its 950 refugees sailed back to Europe. In the end, Britain, France, and a few other countries reluctantly accepted most of the refugees, with the clear understanding that under no circumstances would more be accepted. The result of all this was a brilliant propaganda victory for the Nazis. It was now clear to the world that no country, not even the United States, wanted Jews. Anyone who subsequently questioned Nazi policies was simply shown the demonstrated fact that the Allies' protests were insincere. Through its silence, the West was understood by Germany to be implicitly ratifying its policy. It goes without saying that no other such legal refugee ship left Germany for the duration of the war.

THE WEST AND THE REFUGEE PROBLEM

It was only in 1944, when German defeat was assured and most of Europe's Jews were dead, that real international efforts to deal with refugees finally began. Why efforts suddenly emerged then we do not know, although a number of things had happened that might have a bearing on the matter. By 1944, public opinion in the United States had finally found a moral footing that opposed the very basis of Nazi society. Also by 1944, the defeat of Germany seemed close enough that the Allied leaders could begin seriously to consider how to deal with postwar Europe and its masses of refugees and displaced persons. In any case, only at this late date do we find a number of substantive steps being made to deal with the Nazi system and its refugees in a systematic way.

These efforts were met by the Nazis with a curious schizophrenia. It was at this time that German armies, acting with a sort of paranoiac energy, moved into the Balkan countries and shipped out Jews to the killing centers with breathtaking speed. With the war going badly on all fronts, it was almost as if the Nazis hoped that by killing Jews faster, they could salvage the war effort—a perverse consequence of the S.S. ideology that the Jews were the real enemy. It was also the one campaign of the entire Nazi effort that was now moving along with any success. At the same time, however, individual Nazi leaders suddenly appeared willing to make all sorts of deals to save Jews. At last, one true attempt on the part of the West to counter the Nazis

on moral grounds was made, and with some success. This was the halt to
Nazi activities in Hungary.

Hungary was taken over by the Germans late in the war, in March 1944.[15]
The Germans had been negotiating with the Hungarian government for
some two years by that time and had managed to have a series of short-lived
pro-German governments installed. With each new government and with
the gradual increase in German military pressure, the Hungarian government slowly passed more and more restrictive anti-Jewish legislation. Yet it
was clear to the Germans that the Hungarians were going to be at best lukewarm allies. Facing defeat on the eastern front and fearing a Hungarian de-
fection to the West, the Germans invaded Hungary and immediately set in
motion the machinery necessary for arresting and deporting Hungary's Jewish population. By now, however, keeping matters a secret was impossible.
The American War Refugee Board announced over public broadcasts aimed
at Hungary that Hungarians collaborating with the Germans would face certain punishment after the war; the Hungarian head of government, Miklos
Horthy, was besieged by telegrams from the War Refugee Board, the government of Sweden, the Red Cross, and even the Vatican, warning him not to
allow the deportation of Hungary's Jews. Nonetheless, in full sight of the
Allies, the Red Cross, and the Vatican, the S.S. establishment in Hungary, in
a campaign organized almost single-handedly by Adolf Eichmann, proceeded to arrest and deport Hungary's Jews. The Nazi deportation machinery had by now become highly efficient. By June 7, 290 thousand Hungarian
Jews had already been delivered to Auschwitz. Fifty-one thousand additional deportees had joined that number by June 17. By the end of the month
another forty-one thousand had departed. Fifty-six thousand were added to
these by July 9. In short, virtually an entire community of 440 thousand
people disappeared into the crematoriums of Auschwitz in the space of just
over a month! This fully public act of genocide finally broke the West out of
its complacency.

International pressure, in light of Germany's imminent defeat, became
too strong to resist. On July 9, Horthy felt strong enough to defy the Germans and stop the deportations. Eichmann did manage to have one more
transport leave, but Horthy effectively frustrated German efforts to organize further mass-scale arrests in Hungary.

Other forces were now also at work to save the Jews in Hungary. In July,
Count Raoul Wallenberg, a Swedish diplomat, appeared in Budapest. With
sheer bluff and bluster, he threatened Hungarian officials with severe retri-
butions if they continued to arrest, round up, or deport Jews. His efforts had
effect, with thousands of Jews being suddenly awarded "diplomatic" immunity. Wallenberg continued his rescue work into October, when the Horthy
government was ousted by the pro-Nazi Arrow Cross. Under this short-
lived government, new attempts were made to exterminate what remained

of Hungary's Jewish community. The failure of these efforts was due in some measure to Wallenberg's counterefforts. For one of the few times in this dismal story, the German genocide of Jews in Europe met with determined opposition.

The absence of sustained rescue attempts has to be seen as systematically related to the process of the Holocaust as a whole. Rescue was nowhere a priority, because the people who needed rescuing had no effective mechanism for putting forward their claim. With the exception of the revisionist Zionists, no single, coherent group in all of Europe or the United States had an ideology or administrative structure dedicated to the rescue of Europe's Jews.[16] By the very nature of things, victims' interests were *always* secondary to someone else's. Only in the few cases in which their interests were pushed to the forefront do we register even modest results. The Danish government's continued concern for its citizens is unquestionably responsible for saving the lives of much of its Jewish population. Sweden's continued concern contributed to the rescue of thousands of people not only from Scandinavia but also from as far away as Hungary. The reluctance on the part of the Bulgarian, Romanian, and several of the Hungarian governments to implement Nazi policy, at least as regards their native Jews, allowed hundreds and thousands of people to evade Nazi deportation. When the victim's rights were cared for, human lives were saved.

The problem was that there was no single motivation to provoke the countries to take up the cause of the victims. Each country perceived the victims in the frame of its larger interests. Britain continued to evaluate the Jews within the context of its relations to the Arabs in the Middle East. Roosevelt had to deal with the American public's xenophobia and isolationism. Belgium and France worried about the fate of their own citizens, Jewish and non-Jewish, and viewed the fate of foreign refugees in that light. Bulgaria, Romania, and Hungary had to be concerned with their own independence in light of Germany's military might and proximity. So everyone in Europe had priorities that took precedence over, and so helped define, the fate of the victims.

What the Nazis had stumbled onto is the fact that human rights exist only when there is a mechanism for enforcing them. Rights are a legal category. A stateless person has no rights, because there is no institution for guaranteeing or delivering them. When Germany disenfranchised its Jews, making them in effect stateless, it also took away any effective claim they had to human rights. A Jew could be robbed in midday, his store demolished by the whim of a mob, his family murdered, and he had no legal recourse. His rights as a human being disappeared. As long as no other state or agency spoke for that person, he could be handled with impunity.

It is astounding now to look back and realize that a generation ago the leading democracies of the West—the United States, Great Britain, and France—could have been induced to define human rights in such legalistic terms. The fact remains, however, that none of these countries took a strong stand against the Nazi atrocities. They all conceded at some level that Germany had a right to do with its citizens, and then with the citizens of its allies, as it saw fit, especially if these were Jews. So although legal niceties were carefully observed, the killings in Russia and Poland progressed unhindered. The Allies cannot escape the verdict that they too played a role in the Nazi system of genocide.

19

Nuremberg: The Failure
of Law

One area of human endeavor that claims to stand above individual choices and institutional vagaries is the law. In the law, we claim, resides a standard of right and wrong that guards the basic moral character of our societies. As the Holocaust makes abundantly clear, however, the law is in fact a servant of a culture, not its guardian. As we have already seen in ample detail, the Nazi system was one of law. Yet in this case the law made permissible the slaughter of Jews and others in the name of a higher good. The Nazi experience tells that a country's laws are no guarantee against atrocities or Holocausts. But what about a law that transcends individual political structures? Can an "international law" be invoked that might pass judgment on national legal systems that have run amok? An affirmative answer was assumed at the Nuremberg trials. But even international law is no guarantee. Like individual state laws, international law is a creature of politics and cultural norms. International law no more than any other law can transcend its origins. While the postwar trials could address the Holocaust more fully than could any single nation's laws, it could not escape the Western ethical discourse entirely. Thus, the Nuremberg trials constituted at best an ambivalent response to Auschwitz.[1]

THE IDEA BEHIND THE TRIALS

The assumption behind the trials was apparently that "international law" could somehow establish a reference point that would provide the fulcrum needed to prevent similar events. It is also probably true that the trials were motivated at least in part by an attempt ex post facto on the part of the Allies to distance themselves, after years of silence and inaction, from the deeds of the Nazis. The silence of the West was no longer to be taken as evidence of moral acquiescence but was rather to be understood as the result of an inadequacy in international jurisprudence. The argument seems to have been that the West did not protest the treatment of German Jews because it had no "right" to. What a country does to its own citizens is not a matter for outside intervention; it is a purely internal affair unregulated by international law. Since everything Germany did in Germany and the annexed territory was technically legal and much that was done elsewhere was either part of the war or was not specifically prohibited by international law (no one had bothered expressly to prohibit death camps), the United States and Britain could claim that they had no right to intervene. The proper response now that the war was over would be to ensure that international law covered such events so that in the future the Allied powers could respond appropriately. It was largely on the basis of such reasoning that the United States began to push for an international tribunal to try the Nazis on what were to be labeled "crimes against humanity."[2] The truth of the matter, as we shall see, is that the trials hardly made a clear and unequivocal statement; certainly they did not make one that will prevent future Holocausts. Probably the greatest achievement of the trials was to assuage Western guilt by punishing the (mostly) *German* offenders. The problem of Western silence during the Holocaust was, of course, ignored, and even the prosecution of German perpetrators lost impetus as soon as other interests came to the fore. Thus, the trials illuminate in their own way the intellectual difficulties facing the Allied governments in trying to define precisely within the given universe of discourse what the Nazis had done wrong. This chapter will examine the way the trials were conceived and organized, and the light thrown on the cogency of the Nazi ethic by this failed exercise in trying to establish an ethical critique.

It should be said at the outset that the very idea that a trial would be an appropriate response was not self-evident to the European Allies at all. The push for trials came from the Americans and remained largely an American enterprise. This meant that the only international attempt to counteract the Nazi ethic came from that ally that was most removed, both physically and intellectually, from the Holocaust. The result was an important disjuncture between the discourse behind the Nazi ethic and the discourse behind the tribunal that was supposed to respond to it. This is a perfect illustration of the point being argued throughout this book that the Nazi ethic could not be dismantled from within. A viable critique could come only from outside, that is, from a vantage point independent of the European culture that had spawned Nazism. But by its very nature, a critique from the outside could be least understood by the Nazis; it came from a discourse too foreign to their own to make immediate sense. The consequence was that the trials addressed the Nazi world from a fresh perspective, but by that fact they were precluded from being fully understood by those close to, or still within, the Nazi discourse.

Let us first look at how the very idea of a trial came about.[3] The seeds of Nuremberg go back to September 1943 and a plan first floated within the American government by Henry Morgenthau, United States secretary of the treasury. Morgenthau was probably the most outspoken hawk in the

Roosevelt administration, urging early on that America enter the war, and when the government finally committed itself to war, Morgenthau was ahead of everyone else in thinking about the need to punish the perpetrators of the Nazi Holocaust. His original idea was to set up a tribunal that would purge Germany of all Nazis; he used the word "pasteurize."[4] Those convicted would be summarily executed or possibly exiled to obscure parts of the world, in a curious mirroring of the Nazis' own Madagascar plan.

The chief opponent of Morgenthau's original suggestion was Henry Stimpson, the secretary of war. Stimpson raised a number of realistic objections. His main thesis was that the United States should focus efforts not on punishing Nazis but on constructing some sort of viable and just foundation for postwar Europe. That is, he feared Morgenthau's plan would repeat the mistakes of Versailles that had created the fertile ground for Nazism's growth to begin with. He argued along these lines that it would be better for the Germans themselves to take responsibility for punishing the Nazis, rather than making punishment an American project. In this way, the basis for a new, repentant Germany could be laid. This was important not only because of the experience of the Treaty of Versailles but also because he saw a stable and de-Nazified Germany as essential to the economic recovery of western and central Europe and to the defense of the area against the Soviets. For these reasons, he found Morgenthau's plan, with its call for the execution or exile of German leaders, to be politically naive.

The resulting impasse was overcome by a compromise put together by Cal Murray Bernays, a consultant for the war department.[5] What Bernays did, in effect, was combine what he saw as the best features of the Morgenthau plan with the best features of Stimpson's alternative program. In addition, Bernays tried to take seriously the large number of actual defendants, mostly German, with whom such a trial would have to deal. Because of the nature of Nazi Germany, the trial would have to concern itself in some way with virtually every member of the German government and bureaucracy, the entire military, a good part of German private industry, and tens of thousands of foreign agents and sympathizers in countries from Russia and Poland to Belgium, France, Holland, and the Balkan states. If Morgenthau's plan were enacted as it stood, the Allies would have to deal judicially with a fair percentage of Europe's population. To reduce the scope of the trials to a manageable size, Bernays proposed that organizations, not individuals, be put on trial. In this way, the Allies would have to try only certain select groups such as the Gestapo, the S.S., and the Nazi party. If these organizations were judged to be criminal organizations, then all of their members could stand indicted under a "conspiracy" clause without the need for tens of thousands of further trials. Hence a vast number of indictments could be handled through a small number of major trials, drastically reducing the court's workload. In general conception, this became the basic legal theory upon which the actual trials were conducted.

This foundational strategy was not without its deep legal and philosophical problems, however.[6] It hinged entirely on the American concept of conspiracy, a legal notion completely foreign to the Continental jurists. This meant not only that Great Britain, France, and Russia would have to acquiesce in a trial based on legal principles they neither understood nor accepted but also that the Germans would be indicted in a court of law under a legal concept they neither understood nor accepted. Further, it stipulated in effect that underlings in the various criminal organizations to be identified were to be given no due process: once an organization was declared criminal, all individuals associated with it became criminal conspirators ipso facto, without a chance to appear in court on their own. Incredibly, these ramifications of Bernays's plan were not seen as major legal obstacles by its American advocates.

Why was this so? Why did the great legal minds of the American government pursue this strategy despite its obvious flaws? In terms of the scheme developed in this book, the answer is clear. The American jurists struggling to fashion a response to the Nazi ethic were forced to deal with it as a formal system of behavior, and so somewhat on its own terms. We have said repeatedly that the individual participants in the Nazi genocide were not wicked or evil people; they were only acting in accord with a received ethic. Responsibility for the genocide, from this perspective, lies in the system as a whole, not solely in its individual members. What had to be addressed, then, was not so much individual choices here and there but the entire intellectual construct—the ethic—in which the choices were made. It is for this reason, I wish to assert, that the Nuremberg trials finally had to focus not on individual acts of murder but on organizations and "conspiracies." Only at this institutional level could the problem begin to be addressed adequately. From the perspective developed here, even this level of attack would be ineffective, as it in fact turned out to be. The institutions themselves, after all, were merely symptoms of the larger ethic that dominated thinking in the culture at large. In fact, by implicitly identifying the Holocaust as a criminal conspiracy, the Bernays plan effectively blocked any attempt to see its events in a wider context. As criminals, the Nazis could still be handled within the framework of Western legal and moral discourse. Nonetheless, the American jurists did respond properly at least in intent. They shifted focus away from individuals and toward the social and institutional grid within which individuals made their decisions.

EMERGENCE OF THE FINAL
TRIAL STRATEGY

Let us return to the formulation of the trial strategy. Low-key haggling about the trial continued among the Allies into the summer of 1944.[7] By

June, the Americans, sure that victory was imminent, began a frantic drive to organize the actual postwar tribunal. At this time the only serious proposal on the table was the Bernays plan, and so by default this became the center of discussion. With this general scheme in hand, the Americans turned to the task of gathering their allies' support. This proved to be difficult, however. Each of the Allied countries had its own legal traditions and, of course, widely different experiences of, and so perceptions of, the war. The Russians, for example, had been the victims of tremendous German brutality; the Einsatzgruppen decimated their villages, the German armies pillaged their land, the S.S. systematically starved Soviet prisoners of war to death. To add insult to injury, this was all done after Hitler had signed a nonagression pact with Russia. For these reasons, the Russians were much more interested in executing the Germans for war crimes than in establishing a legal precedent in international law for the rather nebulous concept of "crimes against humanity."[8] The British, too, with their experience of rocket attacks, were much more interested in wrongs committed against their citizens as a result of how the Germans pursued the war than in what happened to Jews. The British, in fact, were also seriously considering mass executions of leading Nazi political and military leaders as an appropriate and easy way of administering some justice. The French, dealing with a divided country and a history of accommodation to Nazism, seemed to have little clear idea at all of what their response to Nazis after the war ought to be. Further, all of these countries also had grave misgivings about the conspiracy and criminal-organization clauses in the proposed indictment. The Americans, on the other hand, had not experienced the same level of brutality at the hands of the Germans but had entered the war ostensibly to halt Nazi atrocities. Their primary interest was with crimes against humanity, not necessarily with war crimes. Further, they were perfectly comfortable with the conspiracy clause. The first step toward acceptance of the plan occurred when Roosevelt finally persuaded the British to drop their objections and adopt the American plan. When the French delegates arrived, they found the United States and Great Britain already in substantial agreement. They thus reluctantly went along with Bernays's plan although they had grave doubts about the propriety of prosecuting Germans under a law that was not theirs. The Russians were even more upset.[9] They were especially taken aback at the ex post facto character of the indictment, which they protested bitterly. They also aligned themselves with the French in opposing the conspiracy clause. They thought that the entire scheme was complex, unwieldy, and conceptually unclear. In the end, however, with no alternative forthcoming and the war rapidly drawing to a conclusion, they too agreed to participate under the Bernays plan.

There was also, of course, a good deal of simple political maneuvering, as is bound to be the case in any such international endeavor. A good example is provided by the attempt to elect a president for the court.[10] This was an important event because it marked the transition from theoretical discussion to concrete organization and policy implementation. At this juncture, the British were especially upset at what they perceived to be an American attempt to railroad their own proposals into acceptance and so dominate the trials. The British justifiably felt that after having suffered from Nazi attacks for years, they ought to have a larger say in the trials. The British thus prepared to block the perceived American attempt to co-opt the presidency of the trials. Meanwhile, the American delegation, aware of the resentment of the British, had entered into an agreement with the French to back the British nominee as a way of appeasing the Continental jurists. No one, however, had consulted with the Russians. So at the balloting, the Russians voted for the American nominee and then were shocked to see that the Americans and the French, along with the British, voted for the British candidate. Curiously, this alignment— the Americans, British, and French on one side and the Russians on the other—foreshadowed, or maybe more accurately already reflected, the political division of postwar Europe. (The trials, after all, were being organized just as the cold war was taking shape.) Although the Soviet armies for all intents and purposes had single-handedly defeated the German army on the eastern front, Russia was already being ostracized by the Western Allies in the postwar political structure. Given all the highly complex legal and political issues now at play, it is a significant human achievement that the trials were brought into being at all.

THE INDICTMENTS

By June 1945, the tribunal was finally ready publicly to issue its indictments. The indictments had been largely drawn up by the Americans, partly because only they understood the legal theory behind the Bernays plan and partly because they alone could afford to make the trials a priority in the aftermath of the war. Eventually, three indictments in addition to the conspiracy clause were agreed to:

Violations of the laws of war. In general, this indictment allowed the court jurisdiction for violations of international rules of warfare as articulated in the Hague Rules of Land Warfare and the Geneva Convention. It covered a number of themes about which there could be some general agreement, such as the mistreatment of POWs and devastation beyond "military necessity."

Crimes against humanity. This indictment was created because institutions like death camps were not covered in the first indictment. Among other things, this indictment allowed the court to prosecute German organizations for murder, extermination, and "persecution on political, racial or religious grounds," whether committed "before or during" the war, as long as such acts were undertaken or executed in connection with other acts "under the jurisdiction of the Tribunal." This indictment was obviously the most broadly worded and also the most controversial. Since many of its charges were not technically covered by international law prior to the war, it was, as the Russians insisted, a pure case of trying people ex post facto. In fact, what the Germans did was immoral but, in no sense of the word, *illegal* under either German law or international law.

Crimes against peace. What precisely this means in the context of international law is not clear. International law does not make war illegal; it merely attempts to regulate its "excesses." This appears to have been a general clause to punish the Nazi government for its invasion of Slovakia, Poland, and the Low Countries.

Conspiracy. While not an indictment per se, this section of the indictment charge gives life to the other three. It says, in part, that "all the defendants, with diverse other persons, during a period of years preceding 8 May 1945, participated as leaders, organizers, instigators or accomplices in the formulation or execution of a common plan or conspiracy to commit, or which involved the commission of, crimes against peace, war crimes or crimes against humanity."

IDENTIFYING THE DEFENDANTS

With the general framework of the trial now agreed upon, the delegates turned to the task of identifying the organizations that would be charged as criminal organizations under the conspiracy clause. Drawing up this list was itself a considerable task. Over Russian objections, the German general staff was listed. This alone encompassed some twenty-five thousand people. Then, of course, there was the S.S. (and presumably, all former members of the S.S., e.g., people who had retired), as well as S.A. members (and former S.A. members), the Gestapo, the party, the army, the various government ministries, and the railroad. The range and depth of organizations involved in the Holocaust made the identification of defendants a huge task. Nor was it always clear who was serving the German government in a perfectly legal way and who had crossed the invisible line and participated in "crimes against humanity." But this task was easy when compared with the next step, that of collecting and collating the evidence needed to demonstrate that each of the identified groups was a *criminal* organization in the sense demanded by the indictment. Documents were scattered throughout the length and breadth of Europe. Many had been destroyed, either deliberately by fleeing German officers or as a result of the general devastation of Europe during the last few months of warfare. Court investigators had to search offices and rubble across the continent for archives so as to locate and retrieve what usable documents they could find. Even such a haphazard search, however, yielded literally boxcars of documents. Each document had to be evaluated so that if relevant it could be culled from the mass of essentially routine and uninteresting correspondence that any agency generates over the years. Because of the disarray of matters, this became a monumental guessing game. A batch of documents retrieved in France, for example, might seem totally irrelevant until seen in the light of complementary materials discovered in Poland. To ensure that no vital evidence was lost, an elaborate classification and filing system was necessary. This labor, in turn, was complicated by language barriers: documents appeared in German, French, Polish, Czech, Russian, Dutch, Hungarian, and a dozen other languages. Each document had to be translated into the languages the judges could use—English, Russian, and French—and into German for the defendants. Then it had to be compared with other documents and assigned its rightful place in the case being built. This was a daunting assignment.[11]

It was in this framework, then, that the trials proceeded. We need to review their overall effect in some detail in order to get a sense of how completely the legal response to the Holocaust failed to get at substantive issues. That failure was not due to any lack of energy or commitment on the part of the Allies, who, as we shall see, worked diligently within the agreed-upon framework despite their individual reservations. Rather, I claim, the legal approach failed because the larger ethical issue never became explicit. The trials turned out to revolve around proving individual "criminal" wrongdoing and so faded into the pattern of normal postwar trials in which the victors punish the vanquished. The wider problem of why the institutions became criminal was never really addressed. In fact, the form of the indictments allowed the ethical question to be dodged altogether. The most logical defense against the conspiracy clause was for the defendant to claim that he or she was not aware of what was being planned. Given the care with which the S.S. constructed euphemisms for what it was doing, this became in fact a plausible line of defense. Instead of focusing attention on the systematic nature of atrocities that had been committed under the Nazi system, then, the trials actually encouraged the perpetrators of the Holocaust to argue that they were not aware of what was happening. Efforts were consequently directed toward establishing what people should have known rather than toward the more relevant question of the framework within which the events of the Holocaust could take place at all.[12] Some broader insights did emerge but not nearly to the extent that the atrocities would seem to warrant. We see this in the way the trials proceeded.

The first order of business, as we would expect, was to determine precisely who would appear in the actual docket as representatives of the reputed criminal conspiracy. A number of different classes of defendants were identified. First of all, certain individuals were to be tried for their particular actions. The four primary defendants here were, of course, unavailable: Adolf Hitler had committed suicide in the final days of the war; Heinrich Himmler, head of the S.S., had in fact been captured but committed suicide in his cell; the head of the RSHA, Reinhardt Heydrich, had been assassinated in 1942; and Martin Bormann, Hitler's chief of staff, had disappeared and presumably committed suicide with Hitler in the bunker. Other eminent figures, such as Adolf Eichmann and Josef Mengele, were still at large.

A second class of defendants consisted of representatives of major organizations expected to be declared criminal under the terms of the indictment. These included the S.A., the S.S., the Gestapo/S.D., the Nazi party "leadership corps," all cabinet ministers from 1933 onward, and the military general staffs and high commands. Since S.A., S.S., Gestapo and Nazi party officials operated legally in Germany, their activities could come under the jurisdiction of an "international" tribunal only after war was declared. Therefore, only people affiliated with these groups after September 1, 1939, were covered by the indictments.

A third class of defendants represented organizations that were deemed to be of lesser overall guilt. Nine categories were identified: medical doctors, members of the judiciary, the Flick industrial combine (made up of illegally confiscated industrial concerns), I. G. Farben (for its unabashed use of slave labor), the Reich Security Main Office, the Einsatzgruppen, Krupp (the arms manufacturer, which also used slave labor), minor government officials, and the generals who planned and executed the invasion of Russia.

Fourth, and last, there was that broad class of defendants who did not stand trial but were presumed guilty if they were associated with a declared "criminal" organization. To govern the disposition of these "criminals," a series of de-Nazification laws were enacted. Once the trial itself was over, and their organizations had been duly declared criminal, these defendants were to be dealt with administratively.

RESULTS

The trials have to be seen as a sustained series of generally connected tribunals that were held over a period of several years. The centerpiece, the International Military Tribunal, which judged the major individual defendants, sat from November 1945 to October 1, 1946. The twelve lesser defendant trials (called the Subsequent Nuremberg Proceedings) took place between 1946 and 1949. In addition, there were a number of subsidiary trials held in various countries under the de-Nazification laws. Dutch trials continued into 1952, for example, and German and Austrian de-Nazification trials stretched into 1953. The Russians held occasional trials connected with World War II atrocities up into the 1960s.

During these years, the political contexts within which the trials took place changed considerably. In 1945, the Allies, flushed with victory and still reeling from their first direct confrontation with the atrocities committed by the Nazis, saw the trials as a kind of crusade. They would not only demonstrate the righteousness of the Allies' cause but lay a foundation for future international law. The real impact of the trial was made during the first and most spectacular phase, the phase of the so-called

International Military Tribunal sessions of 1945–46. Here the major defendants—Goering, Hess, Ribbentrop, Kaltenbrunner, Frick, Hans Frank, Seyss-Inquart, and Speer—were tried and convicted. By 1947, however, interest had begun to wane. First of all, the war had been over for two years and its pain was no longer so acute. Second, the prominent Nazi leaders had already been tried and in many cases executed: vengeance had been taken. Now, however, Russian expansion into central Europe was a growing concern, and Washington was seriously considering the possibility of allowing Germany to rebuild so as to serve as a bulwark against expanding Soviet influence (Hitler's Germany was, after all, rabidly anti-Communist). In this context, the work of tracking down, trying, and imprisoning the leaders of German political, economic, and commercial life seemed to be increasingly against the West's best long-range interests. Nor, it seems, were the issues so clear anymore. Passing ill-defined and controversial legal judgments on the activities of second- and third-level bureaucrats was a tiresome business. As we have seen, no clear moral messages were emerging, and in fact the whole legal basis of the trials had never achieved full clarity. To be sure, trials continued, but the energy of the immediate postwar years was waning.

The conduct of all the various trials and tribunals cannot be retold here. We shall have to be satisfied with some brief summaries of their findings. The main trial, the International Military Tribunal, dealt with twenty-one defendants. Of these, eleven were given the death penalty, three more were given life sentences, four were given lesser jail terms (ten to twenty years), and three were acquitted. The Subsequent Nuremberg Proceedings considered the fate of 177 individuals. Of these, twelve were sentenced to death, twenty-five to life imprisonment, and the remainder to lesser prison sentences, although under the Clemency Act of 1951 most were released early. Further trials in the American, British, and French zones convicted approximately five thousand additional Nazis, of whom about eight hundred were sentenced to death and about four hundred actually executed.[13] The United Nations War Crimes Commission supervised the trial of another thirty-five hundred or so German war criminals in the United States, France, Britain, Greece, Holland, Norway, and Yugoslavia. Such was the Allies' response to the Nazi ethic. The most salient perpetrators were sent to jail, and some were even executed. But the underlying cause of the events, the Nazi ethic itself, remained unaddressed.

In the end, it is surely better that there were such trials and that the Nazi program was not allowed to go totally unaddressed. But given the utter brutality by which the Nazis wreaked devastation upon the peoples of Europe, the trials seem asymmetrical. The abstract and rather dubious theory under which they operated, the careful regard to legal procedures, the endless recitation of bureaucratic documents seem utterly removed from the horrors and the agonies of Auschwitz. The vague and forced definition of the Holocaust as a criminal conspiracy hardly catches the nature of twelve years of S.S.-sponsored pogroms. Yet maybe the trials did the only thing they could. They proposed ritualistically to punish some perpetrators and so to purge, as it were, the evil from our midst. The result was that a few individuals suffered punishment while the real root of the Nazi world remained untouched. Nor, for that matter, was the supporting role of Western silence ever addressed. The seminal force behind the Holocaust—the human capacity to redefine good and evil—proves beyond the reach of any legal system, our own as much as the Germans'.

20

Epilogue:
Jewish Theology and the
Rethinking of Ethics

Jewish theologians represent another attempt by outsiders critically to evaluate the Nazi ethic and to find the basis of its power. This chapter examines four of the most prominent Jewish thinkers on the Holocaust in the last twenty years or so: Richard Rubenstein, Eliezer Berkovits, Emil Fackenheim, and Elie Wiesel. Like the framers of the Nuremberg trials, these authors of theological critiques have produced an appraisal of ethical discourse that takes shape within Western culture. The lawyers and judges at Nuremberg, however, were at best only partially successful. They did mete out some punishments and even executed a few dozen of the most notorious perpetrators. Yet they failed to address the intellectual underpinnings of the Nazi ethic. Nazi leaders were treated as criminals, not as people conscientiously conducting themselves according to a new and widely held notion of right and wrong. The meaning of the trials and their sentences thus remains inconclusive and unsatisfactory. One reason for this, I suggested, was that the Nuremberg lawyers were themselves so close in tradition to the defendants that they were unable to step outside the system sufficiently to evaluate it as a whole.

JEWISH THEOLOGICAL REACTION TO
THE HOLOCAUST

The Jewish thinkers we shall now review seem to have had more success. As victims of Nazi self-righteous fury, they have of course had the most pressing need to examine the Nazi ethic from top to bottom. They have also been able to operate without the political considerations that have always colored the Allies' approach to Nazism. Finally, these Jewish theologians could draw on the traditions of a largely non-Western religious heritage as a starting point for a thorough reevaluation of what they experienced. Their intellectual critique is thus much more pointed and incisive. We shall want to look at their reactions, then, to see whether or not they approach their ethic in a way that is compatible with the critique

214

attempted in this study. As I hope to show, there are indeed a number of parallels and congruities.

The motivation behind all these writers, of course, is that of reconciling the horrors of the Holocaust with the traditional Jewish claim to be God's chosen people. The old ways of thinking about good and evil will simply no longer do—this conviction they all share. Yet they differ, at times radically, from one another in the path they decide to follow in the wake of what Nazism has revealed. No consensus has yet emerged, although with Elie Wiesel one may be in the making. What these thinkers do supply, however, is a series of first responses laying out some of the possibilities before us and, so, serving as guides for potentially fruitful reevaluations. We witness in these people a developing intellectual tradition that takes seriously the demise of Western ethical credibility and even conceptions of God in the wake of Nazism and tries to find a new basis for constructing a way of understanding good and evil. This epilogue explores where such speculation seems to be leading.

Two themes emerge in one form or another from all of these thinkers. The first is that, by and large, the people of Europe were not motivated by their ethic to help the Jewish victims. There were exceptions, to be sure. But the exceptions, such as the marvelous conspiracy of rescue carried out by the Danes, or the subversion of Nazi policy by King Boris of Bulgaria, or the brave deeds of hundreds of Polish peasants, simply underscore the complacency that was the norm. In particular, none of the institutions that would have been expected to defend Jews and other victims felt compelled to do so: not religious institutions (with a few minor exceptions like the American Friends Service Committee, the Prussian Lutheran church, and a few Catholic bishops) nor humanitarian organizations nor lawyers nor doctors nor even the Western Allies. When none of these people or institutions can be moved to respond to Auschwitz, something in the Western ethic is terribly wrong. So we have the first common assumption: the fact that so little help was forthcoming from across the continent indicts at some point all of Enlightened Western civilization.

The second common thread is a turn to human community as an, or even the, alternative to what the West had to offer. In particular, all these writers deemphasize the Enlightenment notion that the individual is the center of moral concern, in favor of community and communal survival. Curiously, this reaction to Western Enlightenment sensibility bears some parallels to the Nazis' own rejection of prevailing norms. They, we recall, demanded that each individual subordinate his or her own welfare to the needs of the community—in their terms, the race—at large. It was communal survival that had the highest moral value, not what might happen to individuals in pursuit of that good. The emergent Jewish reaction takes a similar angle of attack on Western individualism, although in different terms. For these writers, communal solidarity and survival are of paramount importance, not to serve the interests of a race or nation but for their own sake. Human community is a value in its own right and is to be pursued everywhere for its own sake. This seems to me to be a second theme developing out of all of the Jewish theologians reacting to the Holocaust.

This represents a sea change for Jewish attitudes in the West as they have existed since the late eighteenth century. As Europe in the last part of the eighteenth century moved into the Enlightenment, Jews were offered a full and equal place in Western civilization. With the rise of scientific thinking, rationalist philosophy, and then the Industrial Revolution, it was self-evident to everyone that Europe represented the most advanced state of human civilization. The Jews by and large were swept up in this same perception. The Jewish Reform movement, for example, gained the following of the vast majority of Western European Jewry on the simple premise that Western civilization and moral culture were perfectly compatible with the highest ideals of Judaism. Jews could be fully loyal to the moral teachings of torah while still fully participating in Western culture. Some radical thinkers in the Jewish Reform movement even began to talk of Western civilization in terms of the moral and intellectual perfectibility constitutive of the "messianic age."

Obviously, such optimism fell apart under the impact of the Holocaust. That is not to say that all Jews have abandoned the ideals of the Enlightenment: this is far from the case. But the balance of weight has shifted away from trust in Western civilization to a more cautious appraisal and evaluation. The reevaluation of the relationship between Judaism and the West is one factor in the increasing conservatism of Judaism. The push away from a too-close association with Western liberal culture, combined with the pull toward Jewish survival, has moved the center of contemporary Judaic life away from accommodation with the West and toward a reexamination of traditional Judaic values. These perceptions frame the context for the various Jewish theological evaluations of the Holocaust that we are about to review.

It is important to note that for traditional Jewish thinkers the Holocaust presents no particular theological challenge at all. They see in the Holocaust nothing more than one more repetition of a pattern that began with Pharaoh and threads its way through the destruction of the first temple, the evil plot of Haman (as described in the Book of Esther), the Roman wars, the crusades, the Inquisition, the massive Chmielnicki pogroms in seventeenth-century Poland, and so forth. On this view, the Jews have always been subject to persecutions by "heathen" who were outraged at Jewish loyalty to God and God's torah. The Holocaust is but another example of that, albeit much more brutal and pervasive than was formerly possible. The Holocaust, in short, is perfectly understandable on this view as part of the three-thousand-year-old battle of evil against good in our unredeemed world. Those who hold to this view certainly concede that the Holocaust.

is different in degree from what went before, but they are not ready to concede that it is truly different in kind. For these people, no special post-Auschwitz theology is necessary. The old, traditional patterns of thought still operate and can account adequately for the Holocaust.

All the thinkers we are considering here, however, are united by the conviction that the Holocaust is substantially different from other persecutions in Jewish history and that it accordingly does present new theological problems. For each of the theologians, there is a problem in the Nazi persecution of the Jews that is not explained by the tradition. This implies that none of these writers are speaking fully out of traditional patterns of Jewish thought. Each by the simple fact of seeing a new problem and thinking of it theologically has moved somewhat beyond the boundaries of traditional Judaic thinking. This underscores a curious correlation. The Holocaust provokes the need for explanation only within the context of Western culture. Jewish thinkers who have never made their peace with Western Enlightened thinking tend to see no new problem. It is for this reason that I want to claim that the American Jewish theological response to the Holocaust is a type of Western critique on its own inherited ethic.

RICHARD RUBENSTEIN

Richard Rubenstein's *After Auschwitz* can be taken as a bench mark for the emergence of Jewish post-Holocaust theological thinking.[1] To be sure, there were writings and theological speculations about the Holocaust before the appearance of Rubenstein's book. Rubenstein's collection of previously published essays was, however, the first theological treatment of the Holocaust that received broad and sustained public attention. There are a number of reasons for this. For one, the Holocaust was by then twenty years past, and people were willing, for the first time, openly to think and talk about it. For another, there was the Arab-Israeli war of 1967, when the existence of the state of Israel suddenly seemed to be on the line. The perception of silence once again on the part of the West confronted a new generation of American Jews with their own vulnerability. Facing the existential threat of communal extinction, the Jewish community in America found the Holocaust to be a powerful mythic paradigm. Finally, we cannot dismiss the fact that Rubenstein's thesis was so radical that it was simply impossible to ignore. Whatever the reason, Rubenstein is the logical starting point for our inquiry. Not only was he chronologically the first to bring theological or philosophical speculation about the Holocaust to the public but his views were so startling that they established the agenda of discussion for years to come.

Because Rubenstein was the first to take the Holocaust in full seriousness as a new phenomenon that required new explanations, he virtually had to invent the field from scratch. The kind of thinking he felt compelled to do would go well beyond what was possible in the traditional fields of history, sociology, and political science. These could account for specific aspects of the Holocaust but could not give the grand, overall picture that Rubenstein sought. To evaluate the Holocaust as a phenomenon of human behavior, Rubenstein stretched beyond these methodologies to the discipline that he considered prepared to deal with the vicissitudes of human behavior on the grandest scale, namely, psychology. It was psychology then, especially Freudian psychology, that provided Rubenstein with his basic framework for understanding the forces behind the Holocaust.

The Holocaust, he notes, did not invent a new relationship between Europe's Christian population and the Jews. Jews had been the object of European hatred for centuries. One of the roots of the hatred was, of course, the church's claim to be the New Israel, supplanting the old Israel, which was now to be left to wither and die. Yet the old Israel continued to survive and even flourish. This angered the church. The developing relationship might conveniently be described in psychological terms as one of sibling rivalry: two sister religions claiming the love and blessing of a single parent—God the Father. Deep inside, Rubenstein claimed, the church knew, or at least feared, that the old Israel was still the chosen of God, thus fueling the church's jealousy even more. The instinct of the church, again following the psychological model, was to kill the rival sibling and thus win the Father for herself. Yet this was a moral impossibility. Individual Jews were tortured and killed, at times even whole communities were devastated, but the instant gratification of totally eliminating the rival could not be achieved.

This then was the situation when Hitler appeared. Hitler established himself as the spokesman of the race and so, in effect, a kind of superego. As a superego, Hitler could change moral standards simply by fiat. Under his rule, the innate striving of Germans to eliminate its sibling rival, Judaism, became possible: the rival for God's love was killed. Yet, Rubenstein continues, the psychological drive was still not fully satisfied. The sibling rivalry between the church and Judaism was based, after all, on the yearning for the Father's undivided love. Yet on a deeper level, even the Father was an object of resentment because he was the rule-giving superego. It was, of course, impossible to contemplate killing God, just as a child cannot bear to admit wishing to commit parricide. But if the Father could not be attacked directly, he could be harmed through the killing of his daughter Israel. This added a further impetus to the German orgy of killing. When this was accomplished, however, the weakness of the Father was revealed, and so the Father himself became vulnerable to displacement: the Father himself could now be replaced. That is precisely what happened when Hitler usurped the role of superego. Hitler now became the new God, or rather the deeply buried German id now operating as superego. The displacement of the father/superego of course meant that the fantasies of the German id could now seek fulfillment without restraint. This is why, Rubenstein asserts, the death camps reveal such fascination with feces and filth. By killing the rival sibling and then displacing the Father, the long-repressed infantile wishes of the Germans achieved the power of instant gratification. Thus the return to infantile fascinations within the camps.

The Holocaust, for Rubenstein, was thus a mythic struggle. It was structured by deep psychological drives that operate not only on an individual level but also on a cultural, historical level. That is, the conflicts that animate individual struggles for identity can be detected as well in the German Volk's relations with other people. Human psychological tensions came to be played out in the very real arena of politics and physical warfare. The dangers of this are now manifestly visible. But how can such a psychological mythologization be avoided? The only way, Rubenstein suggests, is by becoming aware of our mythic ways of thinking and counteracting them. If the Holocaust was a result of the tensions of sibling rivalry read onto the relation between church and Judaism, then the way to defuse that myth must be by rediscursivizing the relationship between the two religious communities. A new definition of the relationship between Jews and Christians has to be found. In this, Judaism too has its role to play. It was, Rubenstein claims, Judaism's continued insistence that it was the chosen people that helped solidify the mythic definitions that structured the Holocaust. If future Holocausts are to be avoided, Rubenstein concludes, both the church and Judaism will have to recast the terms of their interrelationship.

The first step, Rubenstein suggests, is for both to recognize that the very claim that they are the daughters of a single Father is a psychological myth. What the Holocaust reveals to Rubenstein is that all of our encounters are ruled by psychological imperatives. The claim that there is a God who protects us or who has especially chosen our community is itself a result of making over psychological structures into mythic projections. Since it is precisely this myth that created the possibility of the Holocaust, our most important task now is to debunk that entire scheme. It is for this reason that Rubenstein became associated with the "God is dead" theology of the late sixties. For him, the image of a God, or at least the image thrown up by traditional Judaism and Christianity, is no longer viable. Auschwitz, as it were, has killed the received notion of God.

What, then, is left? For Rubenstein the answer is community. It is in community that our personality takes shape and is nurtured. It is there, then, that we find a transcendent entity worth supporting. Rubenstein decides to remain associated with Judaism, because the Jewish community is his heritage. It offers him companionship in what is otherwise a silent and uncaring universe. But he also retains this affiliation as a means of combating the pseudo-Christian myth that gave birth to the Holocaust. Jewish communal survival becomes important not because Judaism is chosen by God but because Judaism rejects the Christian description of reality and so is a platform for dismantling the entire theological perspective of the West.

Whatever we may think of Rubenstein's use of Freud, we must acknowledge that he has cast the problem in a fresh light. He has in essence said that what the Nazis did was a new ethic, proclaimed by a new superego. Nazi evil was not random or malicious per se but reflected deeply inherent motives in human behavior. The Holocaust in the end has an understandable ethical and psychological form. Rubenstein also makes it clear that the ethic that comes to control a society takes shape within a particular social and religious matrix. There are, then, formal parameters that are the conditions within which Holocausts take shape. These can be isolated and described. We need not accept Rubenstein's use of Freud to appreciate the intellectual leap he has made. The Holocaust is no longer a matter of this atrocity and that atrocity but a coherent system of thought and action.

Rubenstein's analysis contains within itself two features that seem to ensure its rejection by many readers. One is his heavy reliance on Freud. Rubenstein's own use of Freud to launch a critique of mythic systems seems contradictory. One might sympathize with Rubenstein's attempt to demythologize Jewish-Christian relations, but it hardly seems an advance to remythologize this relationship by casting it in Freudian terms. Rubenstein has shown the awful power of dealing with myth instead of reality, and then has turned around and applied a new myth. This is his first apparent weakness. The other is his rejection of God. For succeeding Jewish thinkers, this would be obviously unacceptable. On both grounds, then, Rubenstein's first foray demanded a response. But the responses, as we shall see, had to be on his level, at the level of mythic systems.

ELIEZER BERKOVITS

Eliezer Berkovits, an Orthodox rabbi and thinker, was even in his earliest writings in the late fifties and early sixties struggling to combine philosophical thinking with what he saw as the demands of traditional Orthodoxy. He felt, on the one hand—as expressed in his *God, Man, and History*—that religion and reason should not be made to inhabit different spheres of human cognition. Religion and reason are compatible and can be made mutually supportive. At the same time he rejected attempts to turn Judaism into nothing more than a philosophical system such that traditional religious feelings and values were no longer possible. He thus severely criticized Martin Buber, for example, because the existential Judaic philosophy he fashioned could not allow a divine revelation of torah to have objective status. Berkovits, in short, wanted a philosophy that supported traditional Jewish Orthodoxy. Obviously, Rubenstein's claim that God is dead, that torah is simply a community's expression of its need to survive, and that Judaism reduces to identity with a community is entirely incompatible with Berkovits's interests. In *Faith after the Holocaust*, Berkovits set out, one might say, to reintroduce God into speculations on the meaning of the Holocaust. He was forced to play out his argument on the field prepared by Rubenstein, that is, on the level of myth. Yet Berkovits would not stretch beyond Judaism for his myth, as Rubenstein did, but went back into the Jewish tradition itself.

Berkovits's systematic construction of a post-Holocaust theology proceeds in four steps.[2] The first step is to affirm that faith in God is indeed possible and, in fact, demanded after the Holocaust. His argument here is emotional rather than academic or rational. Millions of victims, he argues, went to their death in Auschwitz still believing in the ultimate triumph of good. If they, in direct confrontation with the fires of Auschwitz, could still have faith, who are we to abandon it?[3] If *they* could believe, *we* surely can and indeed must do no less. But if we continue to believe in a God even after the Holocaust, then how can we account for what happened there? This question leads to Berkovits's second step: the assertion that the blame for the Holocaust falls not on God but on human civilization, in particular on Western Christian culture. What we witness in the Holocaust is not the absence of God, he claims, but the collapse of Western morality and Western religion. For Berkovits the unmistakable token of this is the brutal murder of one and a half million innocent children accomplished in the very presence of a silent church, the institutional representative of Western morality. The central problem for him is thus not the *presumed* absence of God but the *actual* silence of the Christian population in the midst of which the Holocaust occurred. Moral opposition failed to coalesce during the twelve years of the Holocaust because the religious and moral culture of the West had disintegrated. That is what really died at Auschwitz. It is clear now why Berkovits will not draw on Western or Enlightenment motifs, as Rubenstein did, to explain the Holocaust.

Having said this much, Berkovits moves to his third step. Even if we concede that the Holocaust is really a problem of human morality and the collapse of Western religion, we must still account for the failure of God to intervene. This brings him face to face with Rubenstein's central challenge. To respond, Berkovits turns to medieval Jewish mystical conceptions, specifically that of *El HaMistater* (the hiding God). This is the conception in the Jewish theological tradition that there are times in history when God's presence is not felt: during the destruction of the Jerusalem temple, for example, or the crusades. In fact, this doctrine holds, God is not really absent but has temporarily chosen to hide the divine presence. The withdrawal of the divine presence is not a punishment or a sign of rejection but a loving attempt on the part of God to allow people to experience true autonomy and freedom. That is, God voluntarily restricts divine power so that people may exercise their own initiative. There is, of course, a negative side to this withdrawal, namely, that people must also be prepared to suffer the consequences of their freedom. The Holocaust, Berkovits says, occurred during an episode of divine withdrawal. The real failure was that people, given the freedom to do what they wanted, chose to perpetrate a Holocaust. We cannot blame God for what resulted but must blame the religion and culture of the perpetrators.

A corollary of this thesis, and the fourth step in Berkovits's response, is that God's presence always returns and manifests itself again in history. We must then ask if such a return of God's presence is evident in the post-Holocaust world. To this, Berkovits answers with a clear yes: God's presence was felt, even in Auschwitz. We know, first of all, that among inmates in the camps there were frequent acts of caring and human kindness. The prisoners, brutalized and tortured to the point of death, still cared for others. In tender moments in the midst of hell, Berkovits tells us, we can see God's presence reasserting itself. Further, there is the overall outcome. The people of Israel, despite unspeakable sufferings and a concerted attempt to annihilate them, survived after all. God's grace ultimately did protect the community of Israel despite the most sustained human effort ever launched to exterminate it. The rise of the state of Israel out of the ashes of the Holocaust is for Berkovits the most powerful single image of the continued working of God's power in history, of the reappearance and blessing of the hiding God.

Whether Berkovits has really dealt with the depth of Rubenstein's critique is open to question. What he has done is to take Rubenstein's claim of the moral bankruptcy of the West and construe it in such a way that faith in a benevolent and omnipotent God is still possible. Further, he has done so through the use of traditional Jewish theological images. His contention that the rise of the state of Israel out of the ashes of the Holocaust is a sure sign that God is in ultimate control has become a virtual commonplace in contemporary Western Jewish thinking. The historical accuracy of this claim is not important. Its value lies in the opportunity it grants people to situate the Holocaust within traditional patterns of accounting for disaster and recovery, and thus for continuing to believe in the traditional God. In the end, what he has done is formulate a way in which the traditional patterns of thought can continue to apply.

His formulation, however, bears some striking similarities to the analysis we have been pursuing here. Berkovits clearly wants to place blame for the Holocaust not merely on the individuals who perpetrated and witnessed it but especially on their religion and civilization. It is not always clear that he considers the perpetrators themselves to be evil. He does, however, certainly consider the culture in which they operated to be the major factor in what occurred. This is very close to the conclusion reached earlier regarding the activities of Martin Luther in the German foreign office (see pp. 182–86)—the conclusion that Luther was not himself a wicked person but simply an aggressive bureaucrat who saw a way of advancing his career within the structure in which he worked. I think Berkovits would have no trouble with this characterization. Normal people ended up doing wicked things because their society and culture failed to define their acts as evil. The problem of evil is one of human culture, one that occurs when people are left to construct their own societies in the absence of God.

Of course, if we are to place the blame for the Holocaust on Western culture and civilization, we must direct the praise for those acts of goodness that occurred in the camps toward the culture or civilization of those who acted honorably. That is why, it seems to me, Berkovits ascribes their acts of goodness not to individual choice but to God. They, like the perpetrators, were acting not as individuals but as exemplars of an ethic. His attempt to sketch out the boundaries of that ethic occurs in his third step, his invocation of the mythic notion of *El HaMistater*. The acts of human kindness performed in the camps, the continuation of faith after Auschwitz, the foundation of the state of Israel are not individual achievements but the result of an ethic flowing out of the appearance of the hiding God. Just as the various agents in the Holocaust acted out of a particular ethic, so too did the victims, and it follows, so too must we, the generations of the survivors. Our frame of reference, however, cannot be that of the civilization that nurtured the Holocaust. Our frame must be that of the victims, that of the disappearing but yet reappearing God. While this response to Auschwitz does manage to make faith in God possible, and even mandatory, it has turned out to have limited appeal. The reason, I think, is that it relies on a presentation of God that is foreign to most modern, Western Jews. It is cast in a form that is unable to attract assent from most of Berkovits's readers.

EMIL FACKENHEIM

Emil Fackenheim also wishes to create a new mythic structure for understanding the Holocaust, but the form of discourse he chooses is quite different from Berkovits's. Fackenheim is a philosopher and an academic and so approaches the Holocaust primarily as a philosopher, albeit one who has a deep faith in God. For Fackenheim, the challenge the Holocaust presents can be depicted as a series of logical dialectics. The first dialectic occurs in traditional Judaic theological speculation, especially as reflected in the Midrash. In this literature we find that the foundational verities and rituals of Judaism—what he calls "root experiences"—contain within themselves deep contradictions. They try to bridge the unbridgeable gap between the divine and the human, and they try to hold both the past and the future together in the present. Jewish thinking has always dealt with these tensions through the midrashic method, that is, by creating stories and myths that allow the individual to find meaning within the tensions. This solution has been challenged in the modern age by a new opposition, that between religion and secular science. For the preponderance of contemporary Jews, modern secular science and culture have proved to be so attractive that the older midrashic (religious) myths for explaining reality are no longer persuasive. The tension between the secular and the religious has been resolved in favor of the secular. That is why, Fackenheim claims, we have talk of the eclipse of God (Buber, Berkovits) and even the death of God (Rubenstein).

The Holocaust throws all of this into a new dialectic. The Holocaust represents the ultimate meaning of modern secularism, namely, the desacralization of human life, the turning of people into commodities. In the light of Auschwitz, we obviously no longer can hold to the foundational tenets of modern secularism. On the other hand, a return to the ancient midrashic world is also impossible. A new synthesis has to be found, says Fackenheim. That synthesis, will, of course, take the form of a new myth. For Fackenheim the new myth will be modeled on the original foundation myth of Judaism, the giving of the torah at Sinai. Auschwitz, he claims, is so overwhelming that it must be understood in terms of the experience of the Mosaic revelation. At Sinai, according to Jewish tradition, God gave 613 commandments. These became the basis of Jewish identity and continuity. At Auschwitz, a six hundred fourteenth was proclaimed: the cosmic importance of Jewish survival.[4] The divinely revealed truth at Auschwitz is that Jews must continue to believe in the life-giving God of Israel and must look upon the continued survival of Judaism as a divine imperative. To do less is to concede final victory to Hitler. The continued existence of mankind, we can read out of Fackenheim, depends on the acceptance of the Judaic God and the concomitant commitment to the sacredness of all human life. The opposed myth, the secular myth that makes human beings into desacralized commodities, must not be allowed to prevail.

Because he is a modern philosopher, Fackenheim presents his case in the form of a direct existential challenge. The experience of utter evil such as occurred in Auschwitz presents a challenge to all our thinking. On the one hand, its evil cannot simply be ignored. On the other, each of us needs to have faith in a transcendent deity. But now that deity must be one that is reconcilable with Auschwitz. Since it is impossible for the authentic Jew to deny God entirely and since seeing God as a refuge of safety is impossible, we are faced with a dilemma. The solution, the called-for synthesis, says Fackenheim, is simply to accept the reality of God on faith with all the complex ambiguity that that involves. Since the Holocaust represents utter evil and death, the called-for response must be for the individual to dedicate himself or herself to the opposite, to survival and life. That is simply a psychological need, a strategy for making sense of the world after Auschwitz.

The symbol of Jewish faithfulness to this command to survive, for Fackenheim, is the state of Israel. To make this point, Fackenheim points to a number of evocative images. He refers, for example, to Mordecai Anielewicz, one of the leaders of the uprising in the Warsaw ghetto. Anielewicz represents the spirit of life that struggled to the end against the Holocaust forces of death and destruction. In the end, the real Mordecai Anielewicz died in Warsaw, a victim of uncontrollable evil. But his memory remains alive, and receives a new life as it were, in the Israeli border kibbutz Yad Mordecai (Remembrance of Mordecai). This kibbutz was founded along the Israel border with Gaza to serve as a defensive position against invading Egyptian tanks in 1948. When the invasion came, the communal incarnation of Mordecai Anielewicz fought back against the forces bent on destroying the Jewish people. This time Mordecai was victorious: the Egyptian advance was stopped within the kibbutz. The state of Israel emerged, ensuring the corporate survival of the Jewish people and vindicating Anielewicz.[5] This is but one image of the Jewish commitment to life and survival.

The point is that the Holocaust represents cruelty and death for their own sakes, phenomena made possible only by the complete mythic and scientific desacralization of human life. The commanding voice at Auschwitz points in the opposite direction: to the need for a remythologization and resacralization of life. To struggle for this resacralization during and in the wake of the Holocaust is an act of ultimate faith, hope, and affirmation. On the other hand, to remain committed to secularism is to hand Hitler a posthumous victory, to be an accomplice in the victory of evil. If Judaism finally disappears, the forces of evil will finally have triumphed after all. The struggle for Jewish survival thus is a struggle between mythic conceptions of the world. In the struggle, one of the most powerful weapons in the Judaic arsenal is memory: if we forget Judaism, the victims will have died in vain; if we forget the martyrs and what they stood for, their pain will be for nought; if we despair and give up the fight, then Auschwitz will have the last word. Our memory of the Holocaust must be kept alive to demonstrate to all that life and survival, love and faith must prevail despite everything.

The real point of the Holocaust, Fackenheim seems to be saying, is that all people act out of mythic constructs of the world. We now have before us two possibilities, that of secularism, culminating in Auschwitz, and that of an existential Judaism, pointing to a faith in God simply for the sake of survival. The mythic construct we choose will determine the future course of events. This seems to be congruent once again with the thesis of this book. Individuals do not act as independent moral agents. They make decisions within a given framework of meaning. The failure of the Holocaust rests ultimately not in its individual actors but in the mythic cosmos they inhabited. Our response should take the form not of this or that act but of choosing a countermyth. As long as we frame future discourse in these terms, we can effectively and authentically defeat what Auschwitz represents.

ELIE WIESEL

Berkovits and Fackenheim both create a basis for a remythologization of ethical discourse, one drawing on the traditional Judaic concept of *El HaMistater* and one on modern existentialism. Both have enjoyed somewhat limited appeal. Elie Wiesel is quite different. Wiesel has become a tremendously influential figure both among Jews and for the Western world at large. What is curious is that he has achieved his influence despite presenting his material in an unusual form for ethical or theological discourse. He is strictly speaking neither a theologian nor a philosopher. He is a storyteller and a writer of fiction. Yet he has been able through his forms to work a revolution in ethical thinking. An examination of how this is so is crucial for the purposes of this study.

Part of Wiesel's power lies precisely in the fact that he does not use traditional philosophical or theologica! forms. In fact, Wiesel is an outsider in comparison with the other thinkers reviewed here, in more ways than one. First of all, he is a survivor of Auschwitz, the largest of the death camps. He saw the Holocaust in its full immediacy, which is not true of the other writers. (The closest is Fackenheim, who fled Germany as a young rabbi in 1940.) Further, unlike the other writers, Wiesel was not raised in western Europe. Rather, he was raised in a small Jewish town in Hungary, in a culture heavily influenced by eastern European religiosity. Although Wiesel is not, strictly speaking, Hasidic, he is deeply marked by that somewhat mystical tradition and keeps its images, patterns, and concepts close at hand. It is largely through his eastern European, Hasidically influenced eyes that he perceived and assimilated his experiences at Auschwitz. Wiesel thus brings to his task entirely different intellectual tools from those of the other thinkers. He is not really in radical discontinuity with Berkovits and Fackenheim. After all, he writes for, and is read by, the same general audience. He needs to hold on to some image of God, as does Berkovits, and he relies heavily on the power of memory, as does Fackenheim. But Wiesel has fused these elements into a new form of discourse that has proved surprisingly powerful.

Wiesel's early novellas—*Night, Dawn, The Accident, The Town beyond the Wall,* and *Beggar in Jerusalem*—can be seen as systematic attempts to investigate in a literary way a series of possible responses to the Holocaust.[6] *Night,* a description of Wiesel's experience in Auschwitz, is the intellectual center. It raises in a powerful and unforgettable way the question of what could possibly be an appropriate response. The succeeding books explore various possibilities. *Dawn* tries and rejects political activism; *The Accident* renounces suicide; *The Town beyond the Wall* takes seriously the option of madness; *Beggar in Jerusalem* investigates the power of historical memory. What emerges for Wiesel through these various exercises is the recognition that true comfort and reconciliation come only when the victim is able to share the pain with others. Only in sharing and dialogue with fellow human beings is there any foundation for hope and reconstruction.

Wiesel's exploration does not take place in a vacuum. Rather, it occurs within a framework that draws heavily on certain forms of Jewish mystical thought, a way of thinking that was much a part of his background. At the center of that tradition stands the notion that creation is not perfect but deeply flawed. The flaw can be understood, in some ways, as a consequence of the necessary separation between God and creation. Whatever the cause of such discontinuity, its effect is the occurrence of evil, randomness, and injustice. By the same token, such disjuncture by its very nature means that God has only limited control over the evil that occurs. The view described here bears some similarity to the tradition that Berkovits cites, that of *El HaMistater*. For Berkovits, however, the withdrawal of God is voluntary, a gift of freedom by a loving deity. For the tradition upon which Wiesel draws, the absence of the divine is not voluntary but a necessary consequence of the flawed character of creation. God's power to prevent evil is for this theological tradition indeed limited. It is within such a cosmos that we have to understand the creation of humankind. People are unique in creation in that, because they contain elements of both the earthly and the divine, they can bridge the cosmic disjuncture by performing divine deeds as described by torah. In this way, people create holiness. If enough human goodness—with its divine character—is released into creation, the gap producing evil can be overcome. According to Wiesel, the most significant and powerful tool available for the release of human acts of goodness are words with their power to produce memory, and so, intention. For Wiesel, memory and especially the articulation of memory in words unleash a mystic power transcending the individual and possessing the ability to affect both creation and God. Death, suicide, madness, and silence are tools of compliance. They allow the development of evil to take place unnamed and unchallenged. These options must be rejected. The only option that holds hope open is remembering and thereby directing human intentions and acts toward what God requires.

For Wiesel, then, it is not merely the act of telling stories that is important but the content of the stories. The truly desperate situation of creation must be revealed by those who have seen it so that occurrences of evil can be transformed into occasions for the production of holiness. In the *Trial of God,* Wiesel tells a story about a hideous pogrom—an anti-Jewish riot. After these events, three rabbis form a rabbinical court in order to place God on trial for murder, and by extension, for being an accomplice to all the murders and atrocities that have taken place on earth. Wiesel introduces into the story one character who consistently defends God's actions. In the end, the defense is to no avail: God is condemned. Nonetheless, the judges are still willing to worship God with prayers. Only later does Wiesel reveal the identity of the one spokesperson for God: it is Satan. The point, of course, is that to abdicate our own moral response and so to accept the atrocities committed on earth is to align ourselves with evil. Only when people recognize their moral duty and do it no matter what, even despite God, is there hope for a universal redemption. Acquiescence, says Wiesel, is the greatest danger, the silent onlooker the most troubling character. In this context, the point of storytelling becomes clear. Stories are meant not to glorify God or celebrate God's power. Rather, stories are meant to reveal our true condition and to urge human actions so that the tragic condition of creation can finally be overcome.

By building on the tradition of an imperfect creation and a constrained God, Wiesel has addressed directly the tension that the Holocaust creates between the conviction that God has chosen Israel, on the one hand, and the unqualified evil that people must face, on the other. In his retelling of the tradition, these realities must not stand in contradiction; they must be held in tension, good and evil, blessings and curses together, with human-kind caught in the middle.

The popular appeal of Wiesel indicates that his message has struck a responsive chord in America in general, and in the American Jewish community in particular. This observation raises its own interesting questions. Why, of all people, should Wiesel become the paramount American Jewish spokesperson of the Holocaust? On the surface, Rubenstein or Fackenheim have better credentials. Both have earned doctorates and are university professors (although Wiesel, too, is a university teacher). Further, both Rubenstein and Fackenheim publish their reflections in academic books and journals, a genre with which the highly educated American Jewish community is comfortable. Wiesel's major form of expression is the novel, and his thinking is not along Western philosophic or theological lines but along the lines of eastern European Hasidic culture. He is an odd candidate for popularity in America. The fact that he has nonetheless become a central voice in America on the Holocaust tells us something of the American Jewish psyche. If we can identify the characteristics that make him so attractive, we shall have gained insight into the thinking of American Jews in the wake of the Holocaust.

There seem to be a number of influences at work. One is that Wiesel is a survivor of the death camps (Fackenheim left Germany in 1940). That allows him to speak with an authority that others cannot claim (although many other survivors have written on the Holocaust without achieving the fame of Wiesel). Related to this is the fact that Wiesel talks so much of his own experiences and questions. That is, he makes the issues not abstract or academic but intensely personal. For Wiesel, the Holocaust is not a historical problem, it is an existential one, much as it is also for Fackenheim. Finally, and by no means least, Wiesel has gained popularity, possibly precisely, because of his mysticism. Over the last generation liberal American Jews have moved away from their once easy association with the Western Enlightenment. They no longer assume that truth and morality flow automatically from the scientific rationalists of Western culture. This is seen, for example, in the gradual return among American Jews to traditional Judaic forms of culture and worship. Thus the public imagination has been caught not by Rubenstein, a former university chaplain and a current professor of religion, nor by Fackenheim, a philosopher with special interest in German idealist philosophy, but by a Hungarian Jewish survivor who tells Hasidic stories and writes in French. Wiesel struggles with the Holocaust not in Western academic terms but in intensely eastern European Jewish ones. The fact that his formulation has resonance may indicate that the centuries-long attempt to find an accommodation between Judaism and the Enlightenment has come to an end. Instead, the remnants of western European Jewry find that the mystical, traditional discourse of eastern European Yiddish piety is more compelling. The older, "mythic" view of a wounded God bound up with the exile of Israel curiously speaks to modern Westernized Jews much more powerfully now than the abstract God of the Western intellectual tradition. This may be because the contemporary Jewish community can identify so easily after Auschwitz with such a wounded and constrained deity. Curiously, this same shift in the kind of discourse that proves persuasive to modern American Jews has its counterpart in the Nazis' successful invocation of the mythic Teutonic past as the source of true understanding and authentic identity. This is not to say that the two discourses are morally on a level. It is to say, however, that each in its own way rejects the Enlightenment universe of discourse for some alternative.

In terms of the overall thesis of this volume, Wiesel's emphasis on words and stories is of great interest. In his writing, he consciously constructs new myths that instruct us how we are to live. His deeper theory, drawn from the generations of Hasidic thinkers before him, is that people do have a hand in determining the character of creation. Power is exercised through the day-to-day activities of each person. Through proper intention and understanding, our every act can be turned into a ritual of sanctification. Our divine power, then, is projected through consciousness, and consciousness is formed through words and images, and hence stories. The stories we tell, or the myths we relate, construct our world of meaning. We then act out our lives in that world and either sanctify it or bring it to ruin. Wiesel, through his stories, means to bring reconciliation, healing, and holiness. The stories that created the Holocaust brought, and will bring again, agony and death. In this ultimate message, Wiesel is very much in line with what this study has tried to show.

THE HOLOCAUST AND US

The investigation pursued here has gone well beyond the limits both of the twentieth century and of Germany. The woof of the Holocaust stretches back into Roman times. Its warp extends over the entire Western world. The loom has turned out to be the human mind. As people contemplated the past in light of the present, they wove the universe of meaning in which the Holocaust flourished. Study of the Holocaust, if it is to serve any ongoing end, must move beyond itself to the human capacities that made it possible. There is, of course, no denying that the actual events were designed, implemented, and administered by Germans. This volume means in no way to deny that. Its purpose, rather, is to shift the focus away from Germany exclusively and to address broader issues of human culture. If we truly wish to comprehend what happened and draw the lessons the Holocaust holds, we must look further. To conceive of the Holocaust as only a series of responses to unique events in Germany is to ignore its most powerful lesson.

It is to adduce some of those lessons that this volume was written. The hope is to make Holocaust studies part of a wider academic discourse. Over the past forty years, Holocaust studies have taken two approaches, each potentially limited.[1] The first is, in effect, to trivialize the Holocaust. This has become, unfortunately, the most common stance. Students of modern literature, history, sociology, and psychology acknowledge the impact of the Holocaust on certain areas of their disciplines. Textbooks of psychology will have the requisite paragraph about human behavior in the concentration camps or about the psychology of guards at Auschwitz, for example. The result, however, is that the Holocaust becomes a series of isolated facts and vignettes that are interesting in themselves but point to no intellectual frontiers. The systematic and coherent character of the whole remains lost to sight. Fresh lessons are not learned, because none are seen.

A second type of trivialization is to acknowledge the utter horror of the Holocaust but then to treat such horror as nothing unusual, as just another example of people's inhumanity. On this view, the Holocaust can be set alongside the Armenian massacres of the early twentieth century, the American treatment of the native American Indians, the war in Vietnam, the Soviet invasion of Afghanistan, Stalin's purges, and so on. There is a surface logic to such comparisons: all the examples represent the human capacity to commit genocide when the political climate seems favorable. But the result is that the Holocaust becomes a commonplace: everybody does it all the time. We become numbed to the implications. We again are not able to learn lessons—now because the Holocaust is nothing special. It occasions no surprise, and so, no reflection.

The alternative approach has often been to stress both the enormity and the specific character of the Holocaust. The danger here is that attention becomes so focused on detail that the wider implications cannot emerge. The Holocaust becomes as it were a singular constellation of events from which it is impossible to adduce lessons applicable elsewhere. One form of this approach portrays the German of the Nazi period as an utterly unique type of human being. The implication, of course, is that they therefore cannot teach us about others. We end up with a wealth of insight into the myriad inner workings of the Holocaust, yet precious little insight into what this all means for us. The end result is the same as that of the first approach we mentioned: the Holocaust fails to address a broader academic agenda.

But there is a third possibility, one that recognizes the specific historical, intellectual, and social background of the Holocaust and yet tries to find in this congeries of events a larger pattern that is relevant beyond those events' time and place. Although the Holocaust is unique in its awfulness, it is a firm part of normal human history, the manifestation of consistent and ongoing characteristics of human thought. In studying the Holocaust, we study not only a particular society of the past but ourselves as well. The methodological problem, then, has been to frame an inquiry that takes seriously the particular events of the Holocaust in all their singularity and yet yields insight that illuminates more universal truths.

The strategy here has been to focus on the frame of thought that made the Holocaust possible, in the process trying to account for the actions not only of the grand designers but also of the tens of thousands of more or less common people who carried out the everyday tasks of modern genocide. The claim has been that if we can understand in detail how the people came in good conscience to espouse a Nazi-like ethic, we will have gained insight into an important and relevant dynamic of human culture in general.

This volume, then, has taken its task to be to trace the trajectory of a new widely held ethic as it was conceived, given birth, and allowed to reach maturity so as to control the reality of an entire modern civilization. To be sure, there were always dissenters, but they never constituted a critical mass and thus never were able materially to affect the course of events. The Holocaust was not the result of the machinations of a few people at the top but required over its twelve-year history the active participation and toleration of hundreds of thousands of people in every walk of life. These people were not unintelligent, amoral, or insensitive. They acted consciously, conscientiously, and in good faith in pursuit of what they understood to be the good. What is unique about the Holocaust is not that its ethic operated with such force but that it allows us to achieve an insight into just how greatly an ethic does condition what we see as we relate to other people. It is just this power of an ethic to shape conceptions that the preceding pages have, I hope, begun to define.

One of the more frightening aspects of the Holocaust is that it became what it did not start out to be. I have argued that few people who supported the Nazi program in 1933 or 1934, let alone in the late twenties, conceived of places like Dachau, Chelmno, and Auschwitz. Yet the first acts of acquiescence by the broad population to a new way of characterizing good and evil left the door open for future development of the Nazi way of thinking, until by 1941 or so the possibility of Chelmno came into view. It is this dynamic, the receptivity of common folks to a new ethical discourse as early as 1933, that made the Holocaust inevitable eight years later. This is the really compelling lesson of the Holocaust. And in this, I claim, the Germans—or French, or whoever—are no different from anyone else. Our own ethic is shaped by the social, economic, and political grid from within which we make sense of the world. To ignore this fact seems to me, in Fackenheim's words, to allow the Nazis' victims finally to have died in vain.

I end with a comment by Albert Speer, one of the few perpetrators who managed to break out of the Nazi ethic and look back on it with some distance. He speaks not only for himself but for all of us who know that something like the Holocaust happened and are faced with the possibility of learning its lessons:

> I no longer give any of these answers. For they are efforts at legalistic exculpation. It is true that as a favorite and later as one of Hitler's most influential ministers I was isolated. It is also true that the habit of thinking within the limits of my own field provided me, both as architect and as Armaments Minister, with many opportunities for evasion. It is true that I did not know what was really beginning on November 9, 1938, and what ended in Auschwitz and Maidenak. But in the final analysis I myself determined the degree of my isolation, the extremity of my evasions, and the extent of my ignorance.[2]

Notes

1. CONCEPTUALIZING EVIL:
THE JEW AS SYMBOL

1. See Leon Poliakov, *The History of Anti-Semitism,* vol. 1, *From the Time of Christ to the Court Jews* (New York: Vanguard Press, 1965). See also Vamberto Morais, *A Short History of Anti-Semitism* (New York: W. W. Norton & Co., 1976). A shorter account of anti-Semitism through modern times is Edward H. Flannery's *The Anguish of the Jews* (New York: Macmillan Co., 1964).

2. For this period, see esp. Ernest Abel, *The Roots of Anti-Semitism* (Rutherford, N.J.: Fairleigh Dickinson Univ. Press, 1975). See also David Winston, "Pagan and Early Christian Anti-Semitism," in *The Holocaust: Ideology, Bureaucracy, and Genocide,* ed. Henry Friedlander and Sybil Milton (New York: Kraus Intl., 1980), 15–26.

3. Tacitus *Hist.* 5.11–13. Quoted by Poliakov in *History of Anti-Semitism* 1:9–10.

4. Mary Smallwood, *The Jews under Roman Rule* (Leiden: E. J. Brill, 1976), 205ff.

5. This fear among Roman patricians was heightened by the political power displayed by Judaism. By the first century, the Roman imperial government had agreed to grant Judaism the status of a *religio licta,* which gave Jews certain legal privileges not extended to other Romans. See ibid., 135, 135n. This special status continued even after the revolt of 66–70 C.E. See ibid., 344–45.

6. Poliakov, *History of Anti-Semitism* 1:25.

7. David A. Rausch, *A Legacy of Hatred: Why Christians Must Not Forget the Holocaust* (Chicago: Moody Press, 1984). An especially good study of the theological roots of anti-Semitism is Rosemary Radford Ruether's *Faith and Fratricide: The Theological Roots of Anti-Semitism* (New York: Seabury Press, 1974). For a discussion of church attitudes toward the Jews, see Edward Synan, *The Popes and the Jews in the Middle Ages* (New York: Macmillan Co., 1965).

8. For a general characterization of this period, see Abram L. Sachar, *A History of the Jews* (New York: Alfred A. Knopf, 1938), 184–203; Max Margolis and Alexander Marx, *A History of the Jewish People* (Philadelphia: Jewish Pub. Soc., 1980); and Robert Seltzer, *Jewish People, Jewish Thought* (New York: Macmillan Co., 1980), 350–73. For more detailed information, refer to Salo Baron, *A Social and Religious History of the Jews* (Philadelphia: Jewish Pub. Soc., 1952–), esp. vols. 9–11. For a

brief review of anti-Semitism in the medieval period, see Gavin Langmuir, "Medieval Anti-Semitism," in *Holocaust,* ed. Friedlander, 27–36.

9. Solomon Grayzel, *The Church and the Jews in the Thirteenth Century* (New York: Hermon Press, 1966).

10. See Robert Chazan, *Medieval Jewry in Northern France: A Political and Social History* (Baltimore: Johns Hopkins Press, 1973).

11. Israel Abrahams argues that popular attitudes toward the Jews remained relatively friendly until the thirteenth century. See his *Jewish Life in the Middle Ages* (New York: Macmillan Co., 1896), 399–400. Many churchmen, including local bishops, also refused to condone attacks on Jews and even attempted to shield them. See, e.g., Margolis and Marx, *History,* 360.

12. *Encyclopedia Judaica* (New York: Macmillan Co., 1971), 3:106. The full text is in *Luther's Works,* vol. 47, *The Christian in Society IV,* ed. Franklin Sherman (Philadelphia: Fortress Press, 1955), 268–72 (see also pp. 285ff.).

2. THE DYNAMICS OF EVIL: NINETEENTH-CENTURY THEORIES OF RACIAL CONFLICT

1. Rosemary Radford Ruether, *Faith and Fratricide: The Theological Roots of Anti-Semitism* (New York: Seabury Press, 1974).

2. Charles Frankel, *The Faith of Reason* (New York: Octagon Books, 1969), esp. 1–5. The French philosophes' reliance on reason gave their writings an at times utopian optimism. They felt that social and moral problems could indeed be solved by the proper application of reason. See, e.g., Peter Gay, *The Party of Humanity* (New York: Alfred A. Knopf, 1964), 114–32, 269–77.

3. Hannah Arendt, *The Origins of Totalitarianism* (New York: Harcourt, Brace & Co., 1951).

4. For a review and critique of racial theories, see Ruth Benedict, *Race and Racism* (London: Routledge & Kegan Paul, 1983). A detailed discussion along these lines is C. Loring Brace's "A Nonracial Approach towards the Understanding of Human Diversity," in *Man in Evolutionary Perspective,* ed. C. Loring Brace and James Metress (New York: John Wiley & Sons, 1973), 341–63.

5. Jean Hiernaux, "The Concept of Race and the Taxonomy of Mankind," in *The Origins and Evolution of Man,* ed. Ashley Montagu (New York: Thomas Y. Crowell Co., 1973), 486–95; and Ashley Montagu, *The Idea of Race* (Lincoln: Univ. of Nebraska Press, 1965), 81ff.

6. An excellent discussion of nineteenth-century theories of race as these provide part of the intellectual background to the Holocaust is George L. Mosse's *Toward the Final Solution: A History of Racism* (New York: Howard Fertig, 1978). See also Hannah Arendt's provocative study, *Origins of Totalitarianism,* esp. 158–266.

7. Michael D. Biddis, *Father of Racist Ideology: The Social and Political Thought of Count Gobineau* (New York: Weybright & Talley, 1970).

8. Count A. de Gobineau, *The Moral and Intellectual Diversity of Races* (Philadelphia: J. B. Lippincott, 1856), 438.

9. Georg Friedrich Hegel (1770–1831) was one of the most influential of German idealist philosophers of the nineteenth century. He developed the theory that the state was but the political and cultural expression of the intellectual capacity of

the underlying Volk or nation. This theory led some of his followers to reject revolution and democracy as political events that interrupted the free expression of the national idea. His theory also provided some with a basis for claiming that the level of culture achieved by a state was an objective standard by which to measure a nation's intellectual and civil capacities. See Frederick Hertz, *The German Public Mind in the Nineteenth Century* (Totowa, N.J.: Rowman & Littlefield, 1975), 190ff.

10. Roderick Stackelberg, *Idealism Debased* (Kent, Ohio: Kent State Univ. Press, 1981), 105–31. See also Geoffrey G. Field, *Evangelist of Race: The Germanic Vision of Houston Stewart Chamberlain* (New York: Columbia Univ. Press, 1981).

3. THE ARENA FOR FIGHTING EVIL:
THE POLITY OF FASCISM

1. The review of fascism presented in this chapter is drawn largely from Paul Hayes's *Fascism* (New York: Free Press, 1973). My discussion of the two perspectives on German fascism—one, that it is an internal development; the other, that it is part of a synchronic pattern across Europe—benefited greatly from Renzo De Felice's *Interpretations of Fascism,* trans. Brenda Everett (Cambridge: Harvard Univ. Press, 1977), esp. chap. 3.

2. See Hayes, *Fascism,* 63–64.

3. Although the concept of the bourgeoisie, and the notion that the bourgeoisie is to be blamed for social inequality, gained particular prominence after Karl Marx, earlier thinkers also directed criticism to this propertied class. These themes can be seen already in Jean-Jacques Rousseau and Francois Noel Babeuf. See Alfred S. Lindemann, *A History of European Socialism* (New Haven: Yale Univ. Press, 1983), 8–25.

4. Cited in Zeev Sternhall's "Fascist Ideology," in *Fascism: A Reader's Guide,* ed. Walter Laqueur (Berkeley and Los Angeles: Univ. of California Press, 1976), 344.

5. Since the fascist parties drew considerable support from the powerless and the dispossessed, this militarism gave their followers the sense that they could indeed gain political power for themselves. This, of course, fitted in nicely with the fascists' claim to be champions of the interests of the common people. See Franz Neumann's analysis in his *Behemoth: The Structure and Practice of National Socialism, 1933–1944* (New York: Octagon Books, 1972), 62–68.

4. DISSOLUTION OF THE OLD ETHIC:
THE GERMANY HITLER INHERITED

1. A good exposition of the content and major literary expressions of this myth is George L. Mosse's *The Crisis of German Ideology* (New York: Grosset & Dunlap, 1964), esp. 67–87.

2. See John L. Snell, *The Democratic Movement in Germany, 1789–1914* (Chapel Hill: Univ. of North Carolina Press, 1976), 3–21. For Snell, the intellectual awakening of the *Aufklärung* was the major impetus behind German reunification (p. 7). This would account for the deeply ideological character that subsequent reactions to German unification—and dismemberment—would have.

3. For Napoleon's general policy for Germany, see Snell, *Democratic Movement.* See also Koppel S. Pinson, *Modern Germany: Its History and Civilization* (New

York: Macmillan Co., 1954), 1–11, 23ff. Along these lines, a good summary of Napoleon's overall purpose is given by Owen Connelly in *Napoleon's Satellite Kingdoms* (New York: Free Press, 1965), 184: "Initially, at least, Napoleon hoped to create a model state for the edification of the other *Rheinbund* states—a liberal, progressive, constitutional monarchy that would demonstrate the value of 'French principles.'"

4. For our purposes, the reaction in Prussia is most relevant. On this, see Frederick Hertz, *The German Public Mind in the Nineteenth Century* (Totowa, N.J.: Rowman & Littlefield, 1975), 3–27, 119–20.

5. Pinson, *Modern Germany,* 50–51. In some sense, the political history of the German states from Napoleon through the revolutions of 1848 and even beyond can be viewed as a long struggle between antireform conservatives and proreform liberal elements. For a good accounting of these struggles see Theodore S. Hamerow, *Restoration, Revolution, Reaction* (Princeton: Princeton Univ. Press, 1958). See also Ernst Nolte, "Germany," in *The European Right: A Historical Profile,* ed. Hans Rogger and Eugen Weber (Berkeley and Los Angeles: Univ. of California Press, 1965).

6. This sketch of Bismarck and his policies depends heavily on Edward Crankshaw's *Bismarck* (New York: Viking Press, 1961).

7. See Arthur Rosenberg's profound analysis of these developments in his *Imperial Germany: The Birth of the German Republic, 1871–1918* (Boston: Beacon Press, 1964). For a more general view, see Peter Stearns, *European Society in Upheaval* (New York: Macmillan Co., 1967).

8. For a detailed analysis of the relationship between Bismarck's domestic policy and his foreign policy, see Wolfgang Mommsen, "Domestic Factors in German Foreign Policy before 1914," *Central European History 6* (1973): 3–43.

9. For a discussion of the effects of the *Burgfrieden,* see Rosenberg, *Imperial Germany.*

10. Ibid., esp. chaps. 5–7. See also Warren B. Morris's detailed account in *The Weimar Republic and Nazi Germany* (Chicago: Nelson-Hall, 1982), chap. 4.

11. See Morris, *Weimar Republic,* 73ff. An analysis of the failures of Weimar democracy and the opportunity this failure opened up for Hitler can be found in Karl Dietrich Bracher's "Democracy and the Power Vacuum: The Problem of the Party State during the Disintegration of the Weimar Republic," in *Germany in the Age of Total War* (Totowa, N.J.: Barnes & Noble, 1981), 189–202. In addition to having a politically weak beginning, the republic was never able to fashion an image of itself and the Germany culture over which it presided that earned public loyalty. That is, the government was unable to fashion a civil religion that could draw on symbols of Germany's cultural past to establish its own legitimacy. For a general discussion of Weimar culture, see Walter Laqueur, *Weimar: A Cultural History* (New York: G. P. Putnam's Sons, 1974).

12. For the social background of Weimar's political fragmentation, see Mosse, *Crisis of German Ideology.*

5. THE SOCIAL CONTEXT OF THE
NEW ETHIC: JEWS AND JUDAISM
IN THE SECOND REICH

1. One of the first, and still one of the most outstanding, expressions of this sentiment is Wilhelm Friedrich Dohm's "On the Civic Betterment of the Jews," an

essay that has been translated into English by Helen Lederer (Cincinnati: Hebrew Union College Press, 1957); a condensation appears in *Modern Jewish History: A Source Reader,* ed. Robert Chazan and Marc Lee Raphael (New York: Schocken Books, 1969), 2–13. A good example of the medieval restrictions that this revoked is supplied by the charter decreed for Prussian Jews by Frederick II in 1750; an English translation is printed in *The Jew in the Medieval World: A Source Book, 315–1791,* ed. Jacob R. Marcus (New York: Atheneum, 1972), 84–97.

2. Simon Schwarzfuchs, *Napoleon, the Jews, and the Sanhedrin* (London: Routledge & Kegan Paul, 1979). See also *Modern Jewish History,* ed. Chazan and Raphael, 14–31.

3. An excellent study of this response to modernist pressure is Michael A. Meyer's *The Origins of the Modern Jew* (Detroit: Wayne State Univ. Press, 1967).

4. A good survey of this movement is in Marc Lee Raphael's *Profiles in American Judaism* (San Francisco: Harper & Row, 1984), 3–19.

5. See, e.g., Sanford Ragins, *Jewish Responses to Anti-Semitism in Germany, 1870–1914* (Cincinnati: Hebrew Union College Press, 1980).

6. See also Heinrich von Treitschke's essay in *Modern Jewish History,* ed. Chazan and Raphael, 80–84. Cited in Ragins's *Jewish Responses,* 15–16.

7. *Encyclopedia Judaica* (New York: Macmillan Co., 1971), 6:224–29. This, of course, did not occur in a vacuum. For the background of anti-Semitism in France, see Robert Byrnes, "Anti-Semitism in France before the Dreyfus Affair," *Journal of Semitic Studies II* (1949): 49–68 (reprinted in *Emancipation and Counter Emancipation,* ed. Abraham Drucker and Meir Ben-Horin [New York: Ktav, 1974], 262–82).

8. For some of these effects, esp. in France, see Michael R. Marrus, *The Politics of Assimilation: The French Jewish Community at the Time of the Dreyfus Affair* (Oxford: Clarendon Press, 1971). The nonacceptance of Jews was, of course, not limited to the French. There is a similar pattern evident in imperial Germany. I concentrate on France here because the Napoleonic Sanhedrin and the Dreyfus Affair are arresting examples of the struggle Europe was undergoing in its attempts to come to terms with Judaism. The struggle in Germany was much more decorous. That struggle is studied in exhaustive detail by Alfred D. Low in *Jews in the Eyes of the Germans: From the Enlightenment to Imperial Germany* (Philadelphia: Institute for the Study of Human Issues, 1979).

9. Norman Cohen, *Warrant for Genocide* (New York: Harper & Row, 1966), 65.

10. Ibid., 156–64.

6. THE SMALLEST CIRCLE:
GERMANY, 1933–1939

1. There is a detailed discussion and critique of the Nazi attempt to find a definition of "Jew" and "Aryan" in Raul Hilberg's *The Destruction of the European Jews* (Chicago: Quadrangle Books, 1961), 43–53.

2. I discuss this concept of race in chap. 11.

3. The economic drive behind the entire Holocaust process has not yet been fully investigated. Some aspects are taken up in chap. 16. A full discussion of the conception and implementation of various Nazi economic policies is found in Hilberg's *Destruction,* 60–90.

4. For a brief discussion of the political background of this pogrom, see Lucy Dawidowicz, *The War against the Jews* (New York: Holt, Rinehart & Winston,

1975), 132ff. See also William L. Shirer, *The Rise and Fall of the Third Reich: A History of Nazi Germany* (New York: Simon & Schuster, 1960), 580–87.

5. Cited from Dawidowicz's *War,* 136.

6. Hilberg (*Destruction,* 112–13) gives an account of the development of these restrictions, including a transcript of Goebbels's request.

7. The shopping restrictions are discussed in ibid., 102.

8. See ibid., 90ff.

9. See, e.g., the remarks of Count Schwerin von Krosigk, minister of finance, after the *Krystallnacht* pogrom: "We will have to do everything to shove the Jews into foreign countries" (cited from Shirer's *Rise and Fall,* 585).

10. There was even an arrangement in effect for a while with the Jewish Agency to encourage German Jews to migrate to Palestine. In general, money left behind in Germany by departing Jews was to be used by the state to reimburse the Jewish Agency, which made grants of roughly equivalent value to emigrants. This cushioned the economic impact of migrating. The arrangement, called the *Haavarah* Agreement (*haavarah* is a modern Hebrew word for "transfer"), has been the subject of considerable controversy in that it appears to have brought the Jewish Agency into collaboration with the Nazis in the dismantlement of German Jewry. The basic mechanism is described in Hilberg's *Destruction,* 95.

11. Documented in ibid., 267–300.

12. These procedures are described in detail in ibid., 300ff.

7. EXPORTING THE ETHIC: AUSTRIA, CZECHOSLOVAKIA, AND POLAND

1. For the politics leading up to the annexation, including the plebiscite on April 10, 1939, which, according to government figures, ratified the annexation by just over ninety-nine percent, see H. Stuart Hughes, *Contemporary Europe: A History,* 4th ed. (Englewood Cliffs, N.J.: Prentice-Hall, 1976), 311ff.

2. Cited from William L. Shirer's *The Rise and Fall of the Third Reich: A History of Nazi Germany* (New York: Simon & Schuster, 1960), 477.

3. In fact, the German government had been carefully laying the groundwork for this takeover for years. As early as 1935, the Sudeten German party, which enjoyed financial backing from Berlin, was the largest single party in Czechoslovakia. Thus the successful takeover in 1938 was the end result of a dynamic set in motion, undetected by the West, years earlier. See Vojtech Mastny, *The Czechs under Nazi Rule* (New York: Columbia Univ. Press, 1971), esp. 12–20. A more detailed study of the organization and implementation of this dynamic is Hans Umbreit's *Deutsche Militaerverwaltungen 1938/39: Die militaerische Besetzung der Tschechoslovakei und Polens* (Stuttgart: Deutsche Verlags-Anstalt, 1977), 34ff.

4. The political and military intrigues that allowed for the "peaceful" occupation of what was left of Czechoslovakia is treated by Mastny in *Czechs,* chaps. 2 and 3.

5. Some historians maintain that Hitler in fact hoped his demands would not be met, thus creating a pretext for a full military invasion. Hitler, like Bismarck before him, saw war as the mechanism for advancing Germany's "cause." He, of course, eventually did provoke war with his invasion of Poland a few months later. See ibid., 25.

6. This invasion, too, was carefully orchestrated with diplomatic moves. See, e.g., Lucy Dawidowicz, *The War against the Jews* (New York: Holt, Rinehart & Winston, 1975), 269–72.

7. See Umbreit, *Deutsche Militaerverwaltungen,* 85–272.

8. On the originally temporary nature of these ghettos, see Yehuda Bauer and Nili Keren, *A History of the Holocaust* (New York: Franklin Watts, 1982), 155.

9. The following figures are from Raul Hilberg's *The Destruction of the European Jews* (Chicago: Quadrangle Books, 1961), 139–40. This topic is covered by Hilberg in detail on pp. 107–74.

10. Ibid., 152.

11. Ibid., 140.

12. Ibid., 168ff.

8. THE INVASION OF RUSSIA

1. See Raul Hilberg, *The Destruction of the European Jews* (Chicago: Quadrangle Books, 1961), 177–256; and Nora Levin, *The Holocaust* (New York: Thomas Y. Crowell Co., 1968), 234–35. See also Lucy Dawidowicz, *The War against the Jews* (New York: Holt, Rinehart & Winston, 1975), 167–71. The eagerness of these units is documented by Levin (p. 259) and Hilberg (pp. 191–92).

2. From Shirer's *The Rise and Fall of the Third Reich: A History of Nazi Germany* (New York: Simon & Schuster, 1960), 1252–53.

3. Hilberg, *Destruction,* 192. A complete report of this type may be found in Raul Hilberg's *Documents of Destruction* (Chicago: Quadrangle Books, 1971), 47–57.

4. Joel Dimsdale, ed., *Survivors, Victims, and Perpetrators: Essays on the Nazi Holocaust* (Washington, D.C.: Hemisphere, 1980), 301–2.

5. On this see Hilberg, *Destruction,* 215ff.

6. Cited from ibid., 218.

7. Drawn from ibid., 183–84.

8. Dimsdale, ed., *Survivors,* 331.

9. The following account of Franz Stangl, including the quotations, is from Gitta Sereny's *Into That Darkness* (New York: Random House, 1983), 111–14.

10. Herbert Kelman, "Violence without Moral Restraint," *Journal of Social Issues* 29 (1973): 29–61. Lest we think that what was now happening in the Nazi universe is somehow unique to it, let me refer briefly to a rather famous experiment conducted several years ago by Stanley Milgram (see his *Obedience to Authority* [New York: Harper & Row, 1974]). The experiment consisted of two "volunteers," one chosen to be a teacher and one a learner. In fact, the one always chosen to be a learner was part of the experimental staff. This learner was supposedly strapped to a chair in another room with electrodes attached to his skin. The teacher was to read the learner a series of words that the learner was then to repeat correctly. If the learner made a mistake, he or she was to be given a shock. In front of the teacher was a mock electrical shock generator that had switches numbered from fifteen volts to 450 volts in twenty-five-volt increments. Each successive wrong answer received a shock of the next higher voltage. The experiment was set up so that the learner would give a certain set of wrong answers. At specific intervals, the learner would scream in pain at the shocks, then demand to be set free, and finally fall silent. The experimenters wanted to see how far people

randomly chosen from the population would be willing to go in administering what they took to be extremely painful electric shocks. If the "teacher" expressed hesitation he was simply told by the experimenter that he must continue. The results of the experiment were unsettling. Fully two-thirds of the randomly selected teachers continued to administer shocks up to the 450-volt maximum. The experimenters recorded numerous symptoms of nervousness and moral resistance among the teachers. Yet the fact remains that two out of three, with only the slightest amount of coercion, were persuaded to continue. The experiment underwent a number of changes in variables, but the outcome was always distressingly the same. High proportions of subjects obeyed the requirements of the situation and continued to torture their "victim." Even when the teacher and the learner were seated next to each other and the teacher physically had to hold the electrode to the learner, fully thirty percent of the teachers worked their way to the 450-volt shock. In this completely safe, voluntary, and temporary environment, moral inhibitions proved to be extraordinarily weak. The ethic of scientific inquiry took over. The formal presentation of the "requirement" to administer torturous shocks for the sake of scientific advance, despite its clearly negative content, proved overwhelmingly persuasive. Like the Nazi commanders, people struggled with their moral feelings while continuing to act as they were told they had to in order to serve a higher good.

9. THE EXPANSION INTO WESTERN EUROPE

1. The observation is made that the Nazi genocide was carried out to different degrees in the different countries of Europe, and some of the methodological possibilities for further study that this suggests are worked out, in the excellent study by Helen Fein, *Accounting for Genocide* (New York: Free Press, 1979). Her book is a model for understanding the character of the Holocaust as an extension of each area's own political, social, and religious history.

2. Lucy Dawidowicz, *The War against the Jews* (New York: Holt, Rinehart & Winston, 1975), 502–3; Fein, *Accounting for Genocide,* 116 (see esp. p. 77); and Raul Hilberg, *The Destruction of the European Jews* (Chicago: Quadrangle Books, 1961), 235.

3. Fein, *Accounting for Genocide,* 70, 77; Dawidowicz, *War,* 503; and Hilberg, *Destruction,* 357.

4. Fein, *Accounting for Genocide,* 141–52, 51.

5. The unusual case of Denmark's rescue of Jews is told in Leni Yahil's *The Rescue of Danish Jewry* (Philadelphia: Jewish Pub. Soc., 1969). See also Dawidowicz, *War,* 504–5; and Yehuda Bauer and Nili Keren, *A History of the Holocaust* (New York: Franklin Watts, 1982), 293–94.

6. Fein, *Accounting for Genocide,* 265–68. See also Dawidowicz, *War,* 495–96; Nora Levin, *The Holocaust* (New York: Thomas Y. Crowell Co., 1968), 402–19; and Hilberg, *Destruction,* 365–81.

7. Hilberg, *Destruction,* 365. See also Fein, *Accounting for Genocide,* 287–88; and Levin, *Holocaust,* 404.

8. Levin, *Holocaust,* 419.

9. Dawidowicz, *War,* 494–95; and Hilberg, *Destruction,* 381–82.

10. See Levin's comparison (*Holocaust*, 402–22); Dawidowicz, *War*, 491–94.

11. Figures are from Levin's *Holocaust*, 419; and Hilberg's *Destruction*, 383. See also Bauer and Keren, *History*, 238; and Fein, *Accounting for Genocide*, 153.

12. The complexity of the French Holocaust makes it difficult to summarize. See Hilberg, *Destruction*, 393. For the information here, see Levin, *Holocaust*, 423ff.; and Dawidowicz, *War*, 487ff. The account of the rescue of Jews from France is from Bauer and Keren's *History*, 291–92. See also Michael Marrus and Robert O. Paxton, *Vichy France and the Jews* (New York: Basic Books, 1981).

13. Bauer and Keren, *History*, 236–38.

14. Hilberg, *Destruction*, 416.

15. Dawidowicz, *War*, 498–501; and Levin, *Holocaust*, 459–68.

16. Hilberg, *Destruction*, 421–22. See also Fein, *Accounting for Genocide*, 57; and Levin, *Holocaust*, 459ff.

17. These conclusions are documented in Fein's *Accounting for Genocide*.

10. THE FINAL STAGE: INCLUDING THE BALKANS

1. Although the camps are now associated in particular with the Nazis, they have a considerable history prior to the Nazi period. The first modern use of such camps to control internal enemies was apparently in South Africa during the Boer War. Internment camps of this type are thus a British development. Reports of conditions in these camps show that they were no better than the later Nazi counterparts. It should also be noted that the Russians under Stalin developed a system of prison and labor camps as extensive as the Nazi system. The United States resorted to the use of such camps during World War II for the imprisonment of Japanese-Americans. It is one of the ironies of the war that the major Allied countries, who so self-righteously combated the Nazis, did not hesitate to use similar tactics against their own populations when they felt it necessary to do so.

2. Raul Hilberg, *The Destruction of the European Jews* (New York: Holmes & Meier, 1985), 2:687–88.

3. Yehuda Bauer and Nili Keren, *A History of the Holocaust* (New York: Franklin Watts, 1982), 208–9.

4. On this, see Raul Hilberg, *The Destruction of the European Jews* (Chicago: Quadrangle Books, 1961), 629.

5. See Bauer and Keren, *History*, 215–16.

6. From Saul Friedlander's *Kurt Gerstein: The Ambiguity of Good*, trans. Charles Fullman (New York: Alfred A. Knopf, 1969), 106–8. Cited also by Bauer and Keren in *History*, 210–11.

7. See Hilberg, *Destruction* (Chicago), 645–46. In fact, as late as June 1943, we have cases of the Supreme S.S. and Police Court convicting an S.S. officer of murder for killing a Jew! As the court took care to note, the crime consisted not in the death of the Jew but in the officer's conducting the killing as a personal matter. On this, see Helmut Krausnick et al., *The Anatomy of the SS State*, trans. Richard Barry et al. (London: William Collins Sons, 1968), 351ff.

8. For more detail, see the relevant chapters in Helen Fein's *Accounting for Genocide* (New York: Free Press, 1979), Hilberg's *Destruction*, or Lucy Dawidowicz's *The War against the Jews* (New York: Holt, Rinehart & Winston, 1975).

11. ETHICS AS PARTISAN IDEOLOGY

1. Alan Bullock, *Hitler: A Study in Tyranny* (New York: Harper Torchbooks, 1962), 63–68.
2. Ibid., 65.
3. Ibid., 67–68.
4. See Yehuda Bauer and Nili Keren, *A History of the Holocaust* (New York: Franklin Watts, 1982), 82. See also Dietrich Orlow, *The History of the Nazi Party, 1919–1933* (Pittsburgh: Univ. of Pittsburgh Press, 1969), 41.
5. Orlow, *History,* 21–37.
6. Bullock, *Hitler,* 85ff.
7. William L. Shirer, *The Rise and Fall of the Third Reich: A History of Nazi Germany* (New York: Simon & Schuster, 1960), 104–14; and Bullock, *Hitler,* 99–113.
8. Shirer, *Rise and Fall,* 114–15.
9. Bullock, *Hitler,* 127; and Orlow, *History,* 51ff.
10. Shirer, *Rise and Fall,* 170ff. See also Bullock, *Hitler,* 141.
11. Bullock, *Hitler,* 140.
12. Bauer and Keren, *History,* 85–87.
13. Shirer, *Rise and Fall,* 246ff; and Bullock, *Hitler,* 255.
14. Bullock, *Hitler,* 256; and Shirer, *Rise and Fall,* 258.
15. See Hans Mommsen, "The Reichstag Fire and Its Political Consequence," in *Republic to Reich: The Making of the Nazi Revolution,* ed. Hajo Holborn (New York: Pantheon Books, 1972), 129–222.
16. Cited from Alan Bullock's *Hitler,* 263.
17. Karl Dietrich Bracher, "Stages of Totalitarian 'Integration' (*Gleichschaltung*): The Consolidation of National Socialist Rule in 1933 and 1934," in *Republic to Reich,* ed. Holborn, 109–28.
18. For details on this, see Raul Hilberg, *The Destruction of the European Jews* (Chicago: Quadrangle Books, 1961), 56–57.
19. Shirer, *Rise and Fall,* 305ff. See also Bullock, *Hitler,* 283–96. A good analysis is found in Hermann Mau's "The 'Second Revolution'—June 30, 1934," in *Republic to Reich,* ed. Holborn, 223–47.
20. Shirer, *Rise and Fall,* 310.

12. THE BUREAUCRATIZATION OF THE ETHIC: THE S.S.

1. The material in this chapter is based largely on Eugen Kogon's *The Theory and Practice of Hell,* trans. Heinz Norden (New York: Farrar, Straus & Co., 1950).
2. See Hans Mommsen's study of the development of Nazi ideology in his "National Socialism: Continuity and Change," in *Fascism: A Reader's Guide,* ed. Walter Laqueur (Berkeley and Los Angeles: Univ. of California Press, 1976), 196–201.
3. On the co-opting of the bureaucracy, see Christopher Browning, "The Government Experts," in *The Holocaust: Ideology, Bureaucracy, and Genocide,* ed. Henry Friedlander and Sybil Milton (New York: Kraus Intl., 1980), 188ff.
4. For a study of this phenomenon, see Joseph Nyomarkay, *Charisma and Factionalism in the Nazi Party* (Minneapolis: Univ. of Minnesota Press, 1967).
5. See Konnilyn Feig, *Hitler's Death Camps: The Sanity of Madness* (New York: Holmes & Meier, 1981), 43–64.

6. Helmut Krausnick et al., *The Anatomy of the SS State,* trans. Richard Barry et al. (London: William Collins Sons, 1968), 367.

7. See Gerald Fleming, *Hitler and the Final Solution* (Berkeley and Los Angeles: Univ. of California Press, 1984), esp. Saul Friedlander's intro., xix–xxviii. For an excellent discussion of the argument, see Hugh Trevor-Roper, "The Will to Exterminate," *Times Literary Supplement* (January 28, 1983): 74–76.

8. Krausnick et al., *Anatomy,* 357.

9. Ibid., 352.

10. Ibid., 363.

13. THE POLITICIZATION OF THE ETHIC: THE GERMAN GOVERNMENT

1. The details of the process described here, and the underlying legal and organizational institutions, are amply documented by Raul Hilberg in *The Destruction of the European Jews* (Chicago: Quadrangle Books, 1961), esp. chap. 8, part 1, pp. 257–307. For my account here, I rely heavily on this pioneering work.

2. From Eric H. Boehm's *We Survived* (New Haven: Yale Univ. Press, 1949), 288. For a general discussion of Leo Baeck's involvement on the *Reichsvertretung* and the *Reichsvereinigung,* see Leonard Baker, *Days of Sorrow and Pain: Leo Baeck and the Berlin Jews* (New York: Oxford Univ. Press, 1978).

3. Hilberg, *Destruction,* 299.

14. THE IDEAL INSTITUTION OF THE ETHIC: AUSCHWITZ

1. Heinrich Himmler was formally appointed chief of the German police in June 1936. On the rise of the S.S., see Edward Crankshaw, *Gestapo: Instrument of Tyranny* (New York: Viking Press, 1957), esp. chap. 9.

2. Eugen Kogon, *The Theory and Practice of Hell,* trans. Heinz Norden (New York: Farrar, Straus & Co., 1950), 23.

3. For a general introduction to the camp system, see Konnilyn Feig, *Hitler's Death Camps: The Sanity of Madness* (New York: Holmes & Meier, 1981). Her chapter on Dachau (pp. 43ff.) shows that the camp there served as both Himmler's model for other camps and his training ground for the new camp cadres.

4. This periodization depends on Raul Hilberg (*The Destruction of the European Jews* [Chicago: Quadrangle Books, 1961], 555–56).

5. Ibid.

6. Kogon, *Theory and Practice,* 30–38.

7. Ibid., 44–46.

8. Ibid., chap. 4.

9. Hilberg, *Destruction,* 572–73.

10. Alexander Donat, *Death Camp Treblinka* (New York: Schocken Books, 1979), 78–83.

11. Kogon, *Theory and Practice,* 77.

12. These extracts, among others, are collected by Terrence Des Pres in *The Survivor* (New York: Pocket Books, 1976), 58–69.

13. Gisela Pearl, *I Was a Doctor in Auschwitz* (New York: International Univs. Press, 1948), 33.

14. Halina Birenbaum, *Hope Is the Last to Die,* trans. David Welsh (New York: Twayne Pubs., 1971), 134.

15. Olga Lengyel, *Five Chimneys: The Story of Auschwitz,* trans. Paul P. Weiss (Chicago: Ziff-Davis, 1947; London: Mayflower, 1972), 26.

16. Pelagia Lewinska, *Twenty Months at Auschwitz,* trans. Albert Teichner (New York: Lyle Stuart, 1968), 41–42.

17. Raul Hilberg, *The Destruction of the European Jews* (New York: Holmes & Meier, 1985), 3:971–72, 975–76.

18. Azriel Eisenberg, "The Lost Generation," *Aleph-Tav: Tel Aviv University Review* (1975): 41–42.

19. See Hilberg, *Destruction* (Chicago), 628ff.; Kogon, *Theory and Practice,* 246.

15. SCRIPTING THE VICTIM:
JEWISH COUNCILS

1. There is now general agreement among scholars that the Jewish councils had no power to change the course of events. Within that general agreement, however, different conclusions are drawn by American and Israeli scholars. The Americans tend to view the councils as part of the Nazi machinery, with no autonomy whatever. Israeli scholarship, which has tended to focus on the functioning of specific councils, raises more questions about the personal choices council members made. On this, see Yehuda Bauer, "Conclusions," in *Patterns of Jewish Leadership in Nazi Europe, 1933–1945,* ed. Yisrael Gutman et al. (Jerusalem: Yad Vashem, 1979), 343–405.

2. The nature of the authority these councils could draw on is discussed by Raul Hilberg in "The Judenrat: Conscious or Unconscious 'Tool,'" in *Patterns,* ed. Gutman et al., 34–38.

3. The most comprehensive story of these councils is Isaiah Trunk's *Judenrat: The Jewish Councils in Eastern Europe under Nazi Occupation* (New York: Macmillan Co., 1972). Valuable data on these councils are also found in Raul Hilberg's *The Destruction of the European Jews* (Chicago: Quadrangle Books, 1961).

4. Trunk, *Judenrat,* 2–4.

5. Raul Hilberg, ed., *The Warsaw Diary of Adam Czerniakow* (New York: Stein & Day, 1979), entries for November 4 and 5, 1940.

6. Lucjan Dobroszycki, *The Chronicle of the Lodz Ghetto, 1941–1944,* trans. Richard Louries et al. (New Haven: Yale Univ. Press, 1984). On Rumkowski, see Yehuda Bauer and Nili Keren, *A History of the Holocaust* (New York: Franklin Watts, 1982), 157–61. An account concerning Rumkowski survives in *Notes from the Warsaw Ghetto: The Journal of Emmanuel Ringelbaum,* ed. and trans. Jakob Sloan (New York: Schocken Books, 1974), 33–34.

16. REWARDING THE PERPETRATORS:
THE ECONOMICS OF THE HOLOCAUST

1. These periods are characterized by Irvin Agus in his introduction to *The Heroic Age of Franco-German Jewry* (New York: Yeshiva Univ., 1969), 1–22. He

argues that a significant portion of the early Roman settlers were agriculturists but that many of these were killed or driven from the land by the invading Goths during the fourth through eighth centuries. It was the traders and merchants who had the mobility and intellectual acumen to survive. They provided the demographic base for the flourishing of Jewish urban culture in the ninth and tenth centuries. See also the relevant chapters in *The Dark Ages,* ed. Cecil Roth, World History of the Jewish People 11 (New Brunswick, N.J.: Rutgers Univ. Press, 1966). Israel Abrahams (*Jewish Life in the Middle Ages* [New York: Atheneum, 1969]) describes this period as it was portrayed by the Jewish traveler Benjamin of Tudela.

2. See, e.g., *Dark Ages,* ed. Roth, 115–16 (Italy), 150–54 (France), 172–74 (Germany). See also Abrahams, *Jewish Life,* 225–26.

3. See Cecil Roth's general introduction (*Dark Ages,* ed. Roth, 302–4). The rise to prominence of Jewry in the general area of Poland is described in Simon Dubnow's *History of the Jews in Russia and Poland,* trans. I. Friedlander (Philadelphia: Jewish Pub. Soc., 1916; New York: Ktav, 1975). See also Bernard Weintryb, *The Jews of Poland: A Social and Economic History of the Jewish Community from 1100–1800* (Philadelphia: Jewish Pub. Soc., 1976).

4. Raphael Mahler, *Hasidism and the Jewish Enlightenment* (Philadelphia: Jewish Pub. Soc., 1985), 4–5.

5. This is due to the largely economic links between Jews and Gentiles in Russia and Poland. For the rioters—as opposed to government officials, who had their own political agenda—anger was directed at Jewish property more than at Jewish lives. For the background in Poland, see Weintryb, *Jews of Poland,* 185ff. The economics of gentile-Jewish relations in Russia in the nineteenth century is detailed by Hans Rogger in *Jewish Policies and Right-Wing Politics in Imperial Russia* (Berkeley and Los Angeles: Univ. of California Press, 1986), 113–75. That plunder and destruction of property were more a factor than killing is seen in Steven Zipperstein's account of the pogroms in Odessa (*The Jews of Odessa* [Stanford: Stanford Univ. Press, 1985], 121ff.).

6. It must also be said that full control of economic resources of any kind is also bound up with fascist ideology. See, e.g., Alan Milward, "Fascism and the Economy," in *Fascism: A Reader's Guide,* ed. Walter Laqueur (Berkeley and Los Angeles: Univ. of California Press, 1976), 379–412. See also S. J. Woolf, *The Nature of Fascism* (New York: Random House, 1968), 119–51. A contemporary view with remarkable insight can be found in David Guerin's *Fascism and Big Business* (Paris, 1936; New York: Pathfinder Press, 1973), esp. 208ff. The point here is from Lucy Dawidowicz's *The War against the Jews* (New York: Holt, Rinehart & Winston, 1975), 134–39.

7. Raul Hilberg, *The Destruction of the European Jews* (Chicago: Quadrangle Books, 1961), 615.

8. Ibid., 616.

9. Ibid., 613.

10. Ibid., 615n.

11. Ibid., 64–65.

12. For people with connections in the Nazi hierarchy all of this had the potential for immense profit. There is an excellent example of economic empire building in the story of Friedrich Flick and the emergence of the industrial giant known as the Flick combine. For details, see ibid., 76–81. The story of Hermann Goering provides another good example.

13. Ibid., 158.

14. For details of I. G. Farben's collaboration in the economic plunder of Europe and its use of slave labor, see Joseph Borkin, *The Crime and Punishment of L. G. Farben* (New York: Free Press, 1978).

15. William Manchester, *The Arms of Krupp, 1587–1968* (Boston: Little, Brown & Co., 1968), 482ff.

16. Albert Speer, *Inside the Third Reich* (New York: Bonanza, 1982), 370.

17. Hilberg, *Destruction,* 588–90.

18. Borkin, *Crime and Punishment,* 111–27.

19. This is documented in detail in Hilberg's *Destruction,* 567–71.

20. Ibid., 586–87.

21. On this, see ibid., 723–24; and Monty Noam Penkower, *The Jews Were Expendable* (Chicago: Univ. of Chicago Press, 1983), 185–88. A more detailed account is in Nora Levin's *The Holocaust* (New York: Thomas Y. Crowell Co., 1968), 619–30.

22. Richard Rubenstein, *The Cunning of History* (New York: Harper & Row, 1975).

17. THE PERSPECTIVE OF INSIDERS

1. The possibility of choosing not only among alternatives within an ethic but among ethical systems themselves seems to be a characteristic of the modern world. On this, see Peter Berger's brief discussion in his *Invitation to Sociology* (Garden City, N.Y.: Doubleday Anchor Books, 1963), 49–52.

2. The illustrations in this chapter are drawn from two excellent studies. The first is Philip Hallie's *Lest Innocent Blood Be Shed* (New York: Harper & Row, 1979). The second is Christopher Browning's *The Final Solution and the German Foreign Office* (New York: Holmes & Meier, 1978). The willingness to become part of the Nazi endeavor was hardly limited to government bureaucrats. It marked doctors, lawyers, professors, and virtually every other segment of German society, including theologians. A general overview of this phenomenon can be found in *The Holocaust: Ideology, Bureaucracy, and Genocide,* ed. Henry Friedlander and Sybil Milton (New York: Kraus Intl., 1980).

3. Browning, *Final Solution,* 35–43.

4. Ibid., 64.

5. Ibid., 59–67.

6. Ibid., 83, 86.

7. Ibid., 81–86.

8. Ibid., 94ff., esp. 102.

9. Ibid., 141–42.

10. Ibid., 149.

11. Hallie, *Lest Innocent Blood,* 77–78.

12. Ibid., 81–91.

13. Ibid., 94–98.

14. Ibid., 99–100.

15. Ibid., 119–25.

16. Ibid., 127.

17. Ibid., 107ff.
18. Ibid., 134–35, 167–68.

18. THE REACTION OF OUTSIDERS

1. Walter Laqueur, *The Terrible Secret* (London: Weidenfeld & Nicolson, 1980), 3.
2. Laqueur, *Terrible Secret*. For a full presentation of what was published in the religious press in this country, see Robert Ross, *So It Was True: The American Protestant Press and the Nazi Persecution of the Jews, 1933–1945* (Minneapolis: Univ. of Minnesota Press, 1980).
3. Ross, *So It Was True,* 266–67. Italics his.
4. Laqueur, *Terrible Secret,* 17–18; and Raul Hilberg, *The Destruction of the European Jews* (Chicago: Quadrangle Books, 1961), 216, 652ff.
5. Laqueur, *Terrible Secret,* 135.
6. His story is in Alexander Donat's *Death Camp Treblinka* (New York: Schocken Books, 1979), 77–145.
7. Hilberg, *Destruction,* 210–15.
8. Konnilyn Feig, *Hitler's Death Camps: The Sanity of Madness* (New York: Holmes & Meier, 1981), 279–82; an excerpt from his eyewitness account is in *Witness to the Holocaust,* ed. A. Eisenberg (New York: Pilgrim Press, 1981), 250–52. There are numerous studies of Gerstein. General accounts of his actions, both as regards Baron von Otter and as regards the Vatican, are in Laqueur's *Terrible Secret,* 48–50; and in Nora Levin's *The Holocaust* (New York: Thomas Y. Crowell Co., 1968), 307–13. There are also several book-length studies, including Saul Friedlander's *Kurt Gerstein: The Ambiguity of Good,* trans. Charles Fullman (New York: Alfred A. Knopf, 1969), and Pierre Joffroy's *A Spy for God: The Ordeal of Kurt Gerstein,* trans. Norman Denny (New York: Harcourt Brace Jovanovich, 1970). Gerstein is, of course, the subject of Rolf Hochhuth's controversial play *The Deputy.*
9. Laqueur, *Terrible Secret,* 104–5.
10. Ross, *So It Was True.*
11. For an account of British policy considerations, see Nathaniel Katzberg, "British Policy on Immigration to Palestine during World War II," in *Rescue Attempts during the Holocaust,* ed. Yisrael Gutman et al. (Jerusalem: Yad Vashem, 1977), 183–203.
12. The British attempt to keep refugees out of Palestine created some unpleasant situations for them. In a number of cases, the British apprehension of illegal refugee ships, and the subsequent internment by the British of Jewish refugees, made international news and, of course, lent credibility to Hitler's propaganda. Two incidents in particular, the sinking of the *Patria* in Haifa harbor in 1939 and the torpedoing of a ship loaded with refugees—the *Struma*—in 1941, were especially notorious. See Monty Noam Penkower, *The Jews Were Expendable* (Chicago: Univ. of Chicago Press, 1983), 30–58.
13. For the American government's attempt to ignore the Holocaust, see Arthur D. Morse, *While Six Million Died: A Chronicle of American Apathy* (New York: Random House, 1967). See also David Wyman's devastating account in his *The American Abandonment of the Jews, 1941–1945* (New York: Pantheon Books, 1984), and his earlier study *Paper Walls: America and the Refugee Crisis* (Amherst: Univ. of Massachusetts Press, 1968). A similar indictment of Canada is found in Irving Abella's *None*

Is Too Many: Canada and the Jews of Europe, 1933–1948 (Toronto: Lester & Orpen Denny, 1982). See also Henry L. Feingold, *The Politics of Rescue* (New Brunswick, N.J.: Rutgers Univ. Press, 1970). This theme is also present in Levin's *Holocaust,* 619–37.

14. Thomas Gordon, *Voyage of the Damned* (New York: Stein & Day, 1974). See also Morse, *While Six Million Died,* chap. 15.

15. On rescue attempts in Hungary, see Penkower, *The Jews Were Expendable,* 183–222; and Levin, *Holocaust,* 638ff.

16. There is a description of these rescue attempts, and the political barriers put in their way by the Germans, by the Allies, and by the World Zionist Organization, in Yitzhaq Ben-Ami's *Years of Wrath, Days of Glory* (New York: Robert Speller & Sons, 1982), 199–348.

19. NUREMBERG: THE FAILURE OF LAW

1. See Werner Maser, *Nuremberg: A Nation on Trial,* trans. Richard Barry (New York: Charles Scribner's Sons, 1979), 259ff.

2. James F. Willis, *Prologue to Nuremberg* (Westport, Conn.: Greenwood Press, 1982), 173ff.

3. Bradley F. Smith, *Reaching Judgment at Nuremberg* (New York: Basic Books, 1977), 20ff. See also Robert E. Conot, *Justice at Nuremberg* (New York: Harper & Row, 1983), 9–26.

4. Smith, *Reaching Judgment,* 23.

5. Ibid., 26–27.

6. Ibid., 46–73. See also Maser's discussion on the indictments (*Nuremberg,* 27–39).

7. Maser, *Nuremberg,* 27–39; and Smith, *Reaching Judgment,* 46–73.

8. Conot, *Justice,* 15–26; and Smith, *Reaching Judgment,* 50–52.

9. Smith, *Reaching Judgment.*

10. Ibid., 4–5.

11. Conot, *Justice,* 36–38; and Maser, *Nuremberg,* 93–98.

12. See Smith's discussion (*Reaching Judgment,* 127–39).

13. A fairly comprehensive accounting of the various defendants and their sentences can be found in Raul Hilberg's *The Destruction of the European Jews* (Chicago: Quadrangle Books, 1961), 704–15. See also Maser, *Nuremberg,* 239ff.

20. EPILOGUE: JEWISH THEOLOGY
AND THE RETHINKING OF ETHICS

1. Richard Rubenstein, *After Auschwitz* (Indianapolis: Bobbs-Merrill, 1966). For a further development of his thought, casting the Holocaust as the result of purely secular, historical forces, see his *The Cunning of History* (New York: Harper & Row, 1975).

2. See esp. Eliezer Berkovits, *Faith after the Holocaust* (New York: Ktav, 1973), and idem, *With God in Hell* (New York: Sanhedrin, 1979).

3. For a study of the actual effect the Holocaust experience had on the faith of the victims, see Reeve R. Brenner, *The Faith and Doubt of Holocaust Survivors*

(New York: Free Press, 1980). The study indicates that many once-Orthodox Jews lost faith but that others did not.

4. Emil Fackenheim, *God's Presence in History* (New York: New York Univ. Press., 1970), and idem, *The Jewish Return into History* (New York: Schocken Books, 1978). For an examination of Fackenheim's reaction against Orthodoxy, see Michael Meyer, "Judaism after Auschwitz: The Religious Thought of Emil Fackenheim," *Commentary* 53/6 (January 1972): 55–62.

5. The correlation between the destruction of the Holocaust and the revival of a Jewish state in Israel has become a fixture in American Jewish thinking. For a discussion of this phenomenon, see Jacob Neusner, *Strangers at Home: "The Holocaust," Zionism, and American Judaism* (Chicago: Univ. of Chicago Press, 1981).

6. Eli Wiesel, *Night* (New York: Avon Books, 1969); idem, *Dawn* (New York: Avon Books, 1970); idem, *The Accident* (New York: Avon Books, 1970); idem, *The Town beyond the Wall* (New York: Avon Books, 1969); and idem, *A Beggar in Jerusalem* (New York: Avon Books, 1971). For an excellent study of Elie Wiesel's thought, see Robert McAfee Brown, *Elie Wiesel: Messenger to All Humanity* (Notre Dame, Ind.: Univ. of Notre Dame Press, 1983).

AFTERWARDS: THE HOLOCAUST
AND US

1. There are also attempts to deny that the Holocaust happened at all, the most notorious being *The Myth of the Six Million* (Torrance, Calif.: Noontide Press, 1973), written anonymously, and Arthur Butz's *The Hoax of the Twentieth Century* (Torrance, Calif.: Noontide Press, 1977). For a review of these books and of the movement to deny the Holocaust in general, see Lucy Dawidowicz's "Lies about the Holocaust," *Commentary* 70/6 (December 1980): 31–37.

2. Albert Speer, *Inside the Third Reich* (New York: Bonanza, 1982), 113.

Index

Acknowledgments

Excerpts from Joel Dimsdale, ed., *Survivors, Victims, and Perpetrators: Essays on the Nazi Holocaust* (Washington, D.C.: Hemisphere, 1980), reprinted by permission of Hemisphere Publishing Corp.

Excerpt from Alexander Donat, *The Death Camp Treblinka* (New York: Schocken Books, 1979), reprinted by permission of the Holocaust Library.

Excerpt from *Kurt Gerstein: The Ambiguity of Good* by Saul Friedlander, translated by Charles Fullman, copyright © 1969 by Alfred A. Knopf, Inc. Reprinted by permission of Alfred A. Knopf, Inc.

Excerpts from William L. Shirer, *The Rise and Fall of the Third Reich,* copyright © 1959, 1960 by William L. Shirer. Reprinted by permission of Simon and Schuster, Inc.

Excerpt from the *Encyclopedia Judaica* (New York: Macmillan, 1971) reprinted by permission of Keter, Inc.

Excerpt from Azriel Eisenberg, *The Lost Generation: Children in the Holocaust* (New York: Pilgrim Press, 1982), reprinted by permission of Pilgrim Press and Rose L. Eisenberg.

Excerpt from Raul Hilberg, ed., *The Warsaw Diary of Adam Czerniakow* copyright © 1979 by Raul Hilberg. Reprinted by permission of Stein and Day Publishers.

Excerpts from Raul Hilberg, *The Destruction of the European Jews,* Revised and Definitive Edition, volumes 2 and 3 (New York: Holmes & Meier, 1985). All rights reserved. Reprinted by permission of Holmes & Meier Publishers Inc.